You Are Legend

The Welsh Volunteers
in the Spanish Civil War

GRAHAM DAVIES

welsh academic press

Cardiff

Published in Wales by Welsh Academic Press, an imprint of

Ashley Drake Publishing Ltd
PO Box 733
Cardiff
CF14 7ZY

www.welsh-academic-press.wales

First Impression – 2018

ISBN
978-1-86057-130-5

British Library Cataloguing-in-Publication Data.
A CIP catalogue for this book is available from the British Library.

Typeset by Prepress Plus, India (www.prepressplus.in)

Cover design by Siôn Ilar, Cyngor Llyfrau Cymru, Aberystwyth.

CONTENTS

For Ellen, my endlessly patient wife, and for James, my inspirational son.

In memory of those from Wales who, in their fight against fascism in Spain, were heroes ahead of their time.

ACKNOWLEDGEMENTS

I am indebted to many who have helped me to gather the information for this book and guided my thinking.

In the UK Richard Baxell, Hywel Francis and Rob Stradling have offered valuable advice. Staff at the South Wales Miners' Library and at the Richard Burton Archives in Swansea University have been particularly helpful. Others in the UK who have provided information and resources are Terry Norman of Ammanford; Mary Greening of Cardiff; Betty Strangward of Onllwyn; David Williams of Rhondda; Keith Jones of Cardiff; Judith Langdon of Aberdare; Anthony Richards of Pembrokeshire; Peter Qualters of Burry Port; Kevin Buyers of Aberdeen; Robert Havard of Aberystwyth; Julie Norton of Cwmllynfell; Ruth Muller of Johannesburg; Jim Carmody and Jim Jump of the International Brigade Memorial Trust; Meirian Jump and Rose Brown at the Marx Memorial Library; Don Watson of North East Labour History Society; John Mehta of Yorkshire, and Richard Felstead of Maesycwmmer.

In Spain, local historian, guide and book publisher Alan Warren of Barcelona has taken me to places in Catalonia and Aragon I would never have found without his help. In addition, the following people have provided valuable information and guidance: Gregorio Salcedo Diaz in Morata de Tajuna; Dani Moren of *Brigada Internacional* in Barcelona; Joan Sambro of *Associacio Lo Riu de la Fatarella*; Caridad Serrano and Alfredo Alcahut Utiel of Madrigueras; M. Lourdes Prades Artigas at the *Crai Biblioteca, Universitat de Barcelona*; Ernesto Viñas of Brunete; Angel Luis Arjona Marquez of Albacete; and Juan Carlos Talavera, Mayor of Madrigueras.

Cover image © Richard Burton Archives, Swansea Univ.

Back row – Alwyn Skinner, Alfred Morris, Ben Davies, Charles Palmer.
Middle row – Archie Cook, Hector Manning, Harry Dobson, Arthur Williams.
Front row – Jack Roberts, Ted Edwards, Morris Davies.

GLOSSARY

Africanista: Spanish officers who served in the Moroccan colonial war.

Alfonsist: monarchist followers of Alfonso XIII, who left Spain in 1931. Rivals of the Carlists.

Aviazione Legionaria (Legionary Air Force): a corps from the Italian Royal Air Force, established in 1936.

Carlists: monarchist followers of Alfonso Carlos who supported Catholic traditionalism. Rivals of the Alfonsists.

CEDA (*Confederacion Espanola de Derechas Autonomas*): the large, right-wing, Catholic conservative party.

Comintern: the international communist organisation.

CNT (*Confederación Nacional del Trabajo*): a confederation of anarcho-syndicalist trade unions.

Condor Legion: a German *Luftwaffe* unit sent to support Franco.

Cortes: the Spanish Parliament.

FAI (*Federación Anarquista Ibérica*): militant anarchists within the CNT.

Falange Espanola: *the* Spanish fascist party founded by José Antonio Primo de Rivera.

Fifth Column: Nationalist supporters engaged in anti-Republican activities in Republican areas.

Generalitat: *the* government of Catalonia.

Guardia Civil: Spanish national police force founded in 1844.

ILP (Independent Labour Party): formed in 1893 under the leadership of Keir Hardie.

MacPaps (The Mackenzie–Papineau Battalion): Canadians who fought as part of the 15th International Brigade.

Nationalists: individuals, groups and armed forces that supported the military coup in 1936 against the Second Spanish Republic.

Non-Intervention Agreement: signed by 27 countries in 1936 – including Germany and Italy –banning the sale of armaments to the Republican Government and Nationalist forces, but flouted by Hitler and Mussolini who openly supported Franco.

NKVD (People's Commissariat of Internal Affairs): the Russian secret police.

NUWM (National Unemployed Workers' Movement): established in Britain in 1921 to raise the plight of unemployed workers.

PAC (Public Assistance Committee): a local authority based body responsible for poor relief.

PCE (*Partido Comunista de España*): the Communist Party of Spain.

Popular Front: the Leftist electoral alliance in the Spanish parliament.

POUM (*Partido Obrero de Unificación Marxista*): anti-Stalinist Marxists and Trotskyists.

PSOE (*Partido Socialista Obrero Español*): the Spanish socialist party.

PSUC (*Partit Socialista Unificat de Catalunya*): an alliance of Catalonian socialist parties.

Republican: supporters of the Spanish Republican government or members of one of the many republican groups.

RGASPI: Russian centre for the study of modern history, located in Moscow, containing the Archives of the International Brigades.

SIM (*Servicio de Información Militar*): the Republican Government's intelligence service.

Trotskyist: a supporter of Leon Trotsky's theory of Marxism, and critical of Stalinism.

TUC (Trades Union Congress): the federation of trade unions in Britain.

UGT (*Unión General de Trabajadores*): a socialist trade union.

Unión Militar Española: the pro-fascist society of Spanish military officers.

FOREWORD

T he writing of this book resulted from a confluence of emotive experiences. They began with a mesmerising assault on the senses from the masterpiece, *Guernica*, by Pablo Picasso, and were nurtured by the discovery, in the Burry Port Institute in Carmarthenshire, of a plaque commemorating the men from south Wales who were killed fighting against fascism in Spain. The outcome is a book which examines the phenomenon of Welsh volunteering in response to the fascist coup against Spain's democratically elected Republican Government in 1936.

The bombing of Guernica

With its own pre-Indo European language, *Euskal Herria* (the land of the Basque language) has a colourful history, including a struggle for independence. On Monday 26th April 1937 people from surrounding villages flocked into Guernica, the spiritual capital of the Basque people, for the weekly farmer's market, the largest in the region. Many will have felt fearful following recent bombing of the area, in particular of nearby Durango, where shrapnel holes can still be seen on many buildings.

On that day in April, General Francisco Franco, military leader of the uprising, supported by the *Luftwaffe*'s Condor Legion and the Italian *Aviazione Legionaria*, unleashed a devastating aerial attack on Guernica. Although the town was in Republican territory and had a munitions plant, this was terror bombing with the aim of destroying the morale of the Basque people. Strategic sites such as the Renteria Bridge, an easy target on the edge of the town, and the Astra weapons factory, a stone's throw from the railway station, were untouched. One of the first aerial bombings of defenceless citizens, it was a rehearsal of the bloody terror unleashed by the *Luftwaffe*'s *blitzkrieg* of World War II. Memories of the day and of the subsequent reconstruction of the town have been collected since 1985 by *Gernikazarra History Taldea*.[1]

Two journalists, Noel Monks and George Steer, who had seen the flames reflected in the sky from more than 10 miles away, reached Guernica soon after the bombing. A line had been crossed by what appeared to be a technical

The Astra weapons factory in Guernica – untouched by the bombing. (© Author)

experiment. A firestorm in the centre of a populated town, an attempt to demoralise the civil population and a strike at the heart of the Basque people, added up to what historian Paul Preston has called a raid unparalleled in military history.[2]

Picasso's Guernica

Exhibited first in Paris, *Guernica* portrays the atrocity committed by Franco on the citizens of the town and epitomises the outrage widely felt in Europe at the time. It was Picasso's powerful response to the horror of the bombing and the obscenity of war. There is despair in the woman grieving with her dead child in her arms, but hope in the dove holding an olive branch and the flower growing out of a shattered sword. Picasso's *Guernica* is a testament to the horrors of fascism, a potent statement against the brutality of war and the violation of the vulnerable and innocent, and a glimpse of the possibility of hope and peace.[3]

The reproduction of Picasso's masterpiece in the town of Guernica. (© Author)

Spanish Civil War Memorial

Around the same time as the visit to Madrid where I saw *Guernica* for the first time, I came across the memorial plaque on the wall of the foyer of the offices of the Burry Port Institute, which hangs awkwardly opposite a memorial to those killed in World Wars I and II, since volunteers went to Spain without the blessing of the British government.

Most were politically active as trade unionists, members of the Communist or Labour parties, hunger marchers; many were unemployed miners and most were working class, with the fighting spirit of the coalfield and the impoverished. Unprepared and sometimes incredulous, these volunteers became immersed in a civil war that created a cruel rupture in the heart of Spain which has never fully healed.

Today, many people in Spain are reluctant to discuss the Civil War, reflecting *el pacto del olvido* (the pact of forgetting). Others want to know about the conflict in which many of their family perished, including popular Spanish singer Dani Moren, whose great uncle died in the fighting. I met him in the ruined church at Corbera, where he led a group of musicians keeping alive memories through song.[4]

When the Welsh volunteers returned home they were greeted in their communities as heroes, but many felt betrayed by the British government and were at first unwilling to share their experiences. However, as time went on, plaques were erected, memoirs and biographies were written and historians began to carefully curate the individual pieces of this fascinating jigsaw,[5] which this book attempts to assemble into one remarkable story.

As much as possible, I trace the experiences of the Welsh volunteers in the Spanish Civil War through their eyes. I have taken the interviews, biographies and autobiographies – where available – into account, along with information gathered from family members and the material contained in files in the Moscow Archives of the International Brigades. The latter are referenced as RGASPI, the Russian centre for the study of modern history, Moscow. In addition I have used information from local historians in Spain and insights from visits to all the battlefield sites including: the Casa de Campo, Madrid; Morata de Tajuna and the Jarama valley; Brunete and Villanueve de la Cañada;

Singer Dani Moren (Dani Caracola) – fourth from the left – with musicians of Brigada Intergeneracional *in concert at Corbera d'Ebre. (© Author)*

Teruel, Quinto, Belchite, Caspe and other towns in Aragon; Corbera d'Ebre, Gandesa and other towns around the river Ebro; Albacete, Madrigueras and Tarazona de la Mancha; Catalonia and especially Barcelona; Guernica and Durango in the Basque country.

The Wales national memorial to the volunteers of the International Brigades, Cardiff. (© Welsh Academic Press)

Notes

1.   See especially Iturriarte et al, *The Bombing of Gernika*, Gernika-Lumo, 2010.
2.   See Nicholas Rankin's *Telegram from Guernica*, London, Faber and Faber, 2003. It was Erich Ludendorff, in his 1935 book *Der Totale Krieg*, who developed the theory of 'Total War' which suggested that in war all available resources and people are mobilised and the distinction between combatants and civilians is blurred. See also Paul Preston, *The Destruction of Guernica*, London, Harper Press, 2012.
3.   Picasso's *Guernica* was preceded by a series of etchings satirising Franco.
4.   *Brigada Intergeneracional* is an open collective of musicians who wish to build knowledge of the past conflicts. *Asociación de la Recuperación de Memoria Histórica* (Association of Recuperation of Historical Memory) and Memorial Democratic now work to recognise the victims, and recover and commemorate those memories.
5.   *In the Footsteps of the Spanish Civil War*, compiled by Wendy Lewis and Ray Davies, IBMT, 2005, is a guide to the monuments in south Wales commemorating the International Brigades.

I was ever a fighter, so – one fight more,
the best and the last!
I would hate that death bandaged my eyes, and forbore,
and bade me creep past.

Robert Browning

1

Spain – The Struggle for Reform

The Background to the Civil War

The immediate cause of the Spanish Civil War was a military coup, in July 1936, against the democratically elected Republican government. However, there was a multifaceted and complex lead-up to that traumatic event. As Paul Preston lucidly points out, the dualisms of regionalists and centralists, anti-clericals and Catholics, landless peasants and estate owners, workers and industrialists are essentially 'the struggles of a society in the throes of modernisation'.[1]

The political kaleidoscope

Books such as George Orwell's *Homage to Catalonia* and Laurie Lee's *A Moment of War* provide many people's introduction to the Spanish Civil War. Orwell admitted that when he joined the POUM (*Partido Obrero de Unificación Marxista*) militia in Spain, he was not sufficiently politically aware to recognise the complexity of the situation, especially in Catalonia. He wanted to fight against fascism and for common decency, but was plunged into what he called the kaleidoscope of political parties with tiresome names and a plague of initials.[2]

An Independent Labour Party publication from 1937 expresses a powerful and propagandist, but not unrealistic, view doubtless held by many who were spurred to action: 'On the one hand we have the Spanish workers – defending the pitiful conditions of existence…and fighting to endeavour to obtain the full fruits of their labour and complete emancipation. On the other hand we have, not only all the reactionary and fascist forces of Spain, but of Europe also. The military class almost in its entirety, most of the regular army, the banks, all the high dignitaries of the Church…countless arms and airplanes from fascist Italy, Germany and Portugal, the Moors brought over in foreign airplanes from Morocco, and generally all the conservative and reactionary forces of a brutal feudalism and a rampant capitalism'.[3]

The Popular Front, the electoral alliance in the Spanish parliament (*Cortes*), at the outbreak of the war included, among others, the POUM, mainly anti-Stalinist Marxists and alleged Trotskyists; the PSOE (*Partido Socialista Obrero Español*) a centre-left socialist party linked to the UGT (*Unión General de Trabajadores*), the socialist trade union; the PSUC (*Partit Socialista Unificat de Catalunya)*, an alliance of various socialist parties in Catalonia; and the PCE (*Partido Comunista de España*), the Communist Party of Spain. Another key supporter of the Popular Front government was the CNT (*Confederación Nacional del Trabajo*), a confederation of anarcho-syndicalist trade unions within which was the militant anarchist grouping, the FAI (*Federación Anarquista Ibérica*).

This broad popular front had been consolidated by the decision of the Seventh Congress of the Comintern, the Communist International, to allow cooperation between communists and socialists. However, there were fissiparous tendencies in most of the groupings, particularly the PSOE, which threatened to weaken the alliance.

Supporting the rising, which General Franco was to eventually lead, were the *Unión Militar Española*, military officers who opposed the Republic and joined in the fascist coup; Alfonsist and Carlist monarchists, the followers of Alfonso XIII and Alfonso Carlos I; the *Falange Espanola*, right-wing, fascists and anti-communists; and the CEDA (*Confederacion Espanola de Derechas Autonomas*) which was Catholic, conservative and defensive of religion, family and property.

Orwell soon realised that Spain offered more than the simplistic mantra of a battle between democracy and fascism, or good and evil. It was a clash of political ideologies involving many shades of opinion, but with anarchists, socialists, communists and fascists as the main players. The mix included the class struggle between peasants and landlords, between workers and factory owners, the desire for revolution and the end of feudalism, the aspirations of national and regional minorities, such as the Basques and Catalans, and the Roman Catholic Church.

It was, in the words of Spanish historian Julian Casanova, a 'melting pot of universal battles between bosses and workers, Church and State, obscurantism and modernisation' in the context of democratic crisis.[4] The two sides expressed Spain's long-term polarisation of Left and Right. The Nationalists were mainly representative of the military, the Roman Catholic Church and the majority of landowners and businessmen, while the Republicans tended to be the landless peasants, industrial and agricultural workers supported by the unions and many of the educated middle class.

The Catholic Church

Most places in Spain still have reminders of the terrors of the Civil War. For example, on a walk along Alicante's Calle Mayor in the heart of the old city one finds the Basilica de Santa Maria d'Alacant. Overlooking the Rococo high altar and the Bautismo chapels is the large image of the priest murdered at the outbreak of hostilities in 1936. Across Alicante, 46 priests suffered the same fate. Historians now suggest that a fifth of all clergy in Spain were murdered during the Civil War: 13 bishops, more than 4,000 priests, more than 2,000 monks and friars, and almost 300 nuns and sisters. Conversely, the plaque on the wall of the town's market marks the site of a devastating, savage Nationalist air attack. It reminds the citizens of Alicante that on May 25th, 1938, Italian SM.79 and SM.81 bombers of the *Aviazione Legionaria* bombed the city, killing over 400 civilians.

Violence against the Church had flared up dramatically in a simmering Madrid on May 11th, 1936, with a spate of church burnings. Arson and vandalism then spread to other cities in Andalucia, particularly Malaga. Over 100 churches were attacked during the violence in what came to be referred to as the *'quema de conventos'* (the burning of the convents). The government appeared slow to respond, anti-clerical fever was allowed to escalate and the Church began to feel insecure. What was the reason for the violence towards the Church? Spanish historian Julian Casanova shows how the constant power and presence of the Church produced a counter-tradition of criticism and hostility. Historical anti-clericalism entered a new, radical phase as it challenged the Church's inextricable links with public power, the monarchy and right-wing politics. The Church, unable to sensibly self-analyse, dug in. Indeed, Casanova argues that the Church was delighted that arms would eliminate the unfaithful and restore the 'material order'; that it needed to give constant reminders of the martyrdom suffered by the clergy; that it idealised the figure of Franco and acknowledged his authority as dictator.[5]

D.R. Davies, a radical former Congregationalist minister from Pontycymmer, visited Bilbao in the spring of 1937 as part of a second delegation of largely Anglican and non-conformist church representatives. He found a substantial bond and accord between the people of the Basque country and the Catholic clergy, unlike anything in the rest of Spain. Experiencing the horrors of a Nationalist attack on Durango, he reminded his readers that 'it was Franco who burnt the churches in Northern Spain'.[6]

Indeed, both delegations to Spain concluded that the Catholic church had invited the violence against it by its neglect of social justice and lack of support for the poor. In the rest of Spain the Catholic clergy were largely seen as pillars of the establishment and supporters of the agrarian system. Many believe that the Church helped to polarise the political situation as it allied itself to the landowners and the political Right, enjoying privilege, power and wealth. Yet the Catholic priest and religious historian Hilari Raguer's fascinating study of the Catholic Church and the Civil War contests the view of religion as a catalyst in the conflict between Church and State.

Raguer argues that there was no political programme against the Catholic faith, and that Azaña's claim that Spain had ceased to be Catholic was a sociological observation and not an inflammatory statement. This view of the country's spiritual impoverishment and changing patterns of belief was also shared by some Catholic bishops. Raguer also points out that the Nationalist coup was not declared in defence of religion.

Nevertheless several measures in the new Republican constitution, while not necessarily an attack on religion, were certainly intended to rein in the power and privilege of the Church. The popular perception was that the Church was historically monarchical, overtly supportive of, and subordinate to, the Nationalist cause, and sympathetic to the rich and powerful. The bishops had become instruments of capitalist ownership and exploitation. The sentiment was not anti-religious but anti-clerical.[7]

The perception of the Church was that the Republic had declared its intention in the phrase: '*El Estado español no tiene religión official*' ('The Spanish state has no official religion'). While the Vatican initially fell short of describing the conflict as a holy war or crusade, Church leaders in Spain denounced the Republic as its enemy and espoused Franco and the Nationalists as their saviour.[8] Sermons were often political tirades ending with '*Viva Espana*', and fuelled by the news of persecution and the killing of priests. From the start, Archbishop Segura had denounced the new government and urged Catholics to vote against a regime which he suggested wanted to destroy religion.[9]

The conflict certainly became, in part, a spiritual battle, and was portrayed in the Catholic press as a crusade against a Jewish-Masonic-Bolshevik plot.[10] Cardinal Gomá, primate of the Catholic Church, denounced the Republicans as "the bastard sons of Moscow" alongside Jews and Freemasons. Franco, a practising Catholic, was viewed as the Church's champion. The strongest indication of the Church's support for Franco came after Guernica when Cardinal Goma arranged for a letter to be sent to every bishop in the world claiming the right to defence against the 'anti-divine' forces which aimed at revolution.

Today, the Catholic Church still refers to its time of persecution, and continues to beatify its 'martyrs'. Any representation of the conflict as a spiritual one between Christianity and communism is facile and one-dimensional, but the perennial marriage of sword and cross is amply represented in the allegory of the war by the Spanish poet José María Pemán, published in 1938: 'The smoke of incense and the smoke of cannons…constitute a single affirmation of our faith.'

Sammy Morris, an International Brigades volunteer from Ammanford, reflected in a letter home much of the popular feeling among both the Spanish people and the Brigades towards the Church: '…the Roman Catholic priests used their power before the revolution to keep the people in ignorance and as the biggest landlords in Spain they were in a position to tax the people even to the point of poverty and semi-starvation, but they continued to pray and pose as the saviour and guardian of the people'.[11] In Franco's new order, Catholicism, militarism and fascism became the pillars of his dictatorship, and for Cardinal Goma there was to be no forgiveness for, or negotiated peace with, the enemies of God.

The military

Toledo has an old walled city, built on a rocky mound, steeped with Jewish, Christian and Muslim culture and architecture, city gates and bridges. The city is crowned by the majestic Alcazar, a huge fortress rebuilt by Franco as a monument to the Nationalist defenders who, under the leadership of Colonel José Moscardó, were besieged for two months at the beginning of the Civil War. Despite an ultimatum that his son would be shot if he did not surrender, Moscardó is believed to have replied to his son: "If it be true, commend your soul to God, shout *'Viva Espana'*, and die like a hero." Franco diverted his army from its advance towards Madrid in order to relieve the fortress. General José Varela succeeded in the attack and took no prisoners. The Alcazar was used for many years as a military academy where – even after the restoration of democracy in the 1970s – each class would dedicate a plaque to the memory of its Civil War defenders, and remains today, with its extensive military museum, as a reminder of the status and role of the Spanish military.

At the end of the 19th century, after its empire had dwindled to a few African possessions, Spain's army had little to do. Often badly equipped and generally incompetent, the army was led by a large number of officers, sometimes one officer for every 12 conscripts. The army in Morocco saw the only real action and the mystique of the *'Africanista'* led to a heady mixture of nostalgia, elitism and arrogance.

Despite their humiliating defeat at Annual in Morocco in 1921, the officers were proud of a role perceived as bringing progress and civilisation to North Africa and now turned to the mainland which they believed needed a strong hand. The army began to see itself as the guardian of the unity and cultural integrity of Spain and, by definition, the enemy of the Left and the national

The Alcazar in Toledo, a fortress and military academy rebuilt by Franco after the Civil War. (© Author)

minorities who threatened to splinter the country. They saw in their own traditions 'a timeless, supremely Castilian Spain, without politics, creating order and banishing all things non-Spanish', i.e. a vehement hostility to separatism, socialism, freemasonry, communism and anarchism.[12]

Military grievances grew when the Republican government questioned military salaries and reversed what they regarded as unwarranted privileges and promotions awarded for colonial ventures. As Helen Graham comments: 'this did not bode well for despised civilian politicians – Republicans to boot – who were bidding to reform the army head on'.[13]

Azaña's reforms as minister of war in the first government of the Second Republic did little to endear him to senior army officers. His efforts to make the army more efficient threatened careers and salaries, and were interpreted by the Right as an attempt to reduce its power and even crush it.

The reforms included closing the military academy in Zaragoza, where Franco was director of a staff largely composed of *'Africanista'* officers, and restricting the jurisdiction of the military over civilians. The academy was regarded as a focus for military unrest, and a breeding ground for imperialistic and nationalist politics. The conservative newspapers read by army officers presented the Republic as 'responsible for the economic depression, for the breakdown of law and order, and disrespect for the army and anti-clericalism'.[14]

The Welsh writer and broadcaster Gwyn Thomas had a foretaste of Spanish military values as a student in the new University of Madrid in 1934, when hearing a captain in the army say of the young and hopeful Republic: "Of course it will have to be destroyed...the system of ideas will have to be destroyed...the guns that won South America will regain Spain for the faith and traditional values."[15] Yet the army was at the same time fairly poorly organised and equipped and top-heavy with officers who had no experience of modern warfare.

Regionalism

The perennial challenge for Spain has been the relationship between the centre of Castilian power in Madrid, and the political and cultural aspirations of its diverse collection of national minorities such as the Basques, Catalans and Galicians. This balance of maintaining the integrity of the Spanish 'motherland', and addressing the calls for increased 'regional' autonomy is as intriguing now as it was in the 1930s. Post-Franco Spain was decentralised and divided territorially into municipalities, provinces and autonomous communities but, with the state retaining full sovereignty, calls for increased powers and independence remain central in Spanish politics.

These separatist movements still flourish, with Catalonia normally getting most publicity and, at the time of writing, in conflict with the central government after another move towards independence. It has a long history of separatist desires, radicalism and anarchism. Catalonia's national day is, especially in Barcelona, a lively day-long festival in which people raise and dress in the flag and political groups promote their views. Even in sport, old rivalries flourish with *El Clásico*, the footballing clash between FC Barcelona and Real Madrid the prime example. The latter, *Los Blancos*, favoured by Franco, is often still regarded as a symbol of the former state's dictatorial regime; while the former represents the language and culture of Catalonia and flies the flag of aspirational Catalan nationhood.

By the beginning of the 1930s both Catalonia and the Basque country mixed an inclination towards autonomy with support the Republican cause. Asturias (mining), Catalonia (textiles) and the Basque country (iron and steel) were undergoing industrial development which sat uncomfortably in an essentially agrarian economy. When Spain remained neutral in World War I, these industrial areas prospered by making their products available to the warring nations, but achieved little recognition from the Madrid government, which still favoured an agrarian economy.

However, Basque nationalism was built around opposition to rapid industrialisation and immigration, which were perceived as a threat to traditional social life. Nevertheless, the Republic offered more hope of independence and economic growth than the right-wing nationalist parties. During the dictatorship of Primo de Rivera, Catalans became disillusioned with his methods and his hostility towards their national aspirations, language and culture. Catalan republicans joined the Republican pact in 1930 on the understanding that there would be a statute of autonomy.

Placa de Sant Jaume in Barcelona has always been the focus of Barcelona's civic life. It now houses, opposite each other, the *Palau de la Generalitat* (Catalan Parliament) and the *Ajuntament* (Barcelona Town Hall). It was on a balcony in this square after the elections of 1931 that Colonel Macia appeared with Manuel Azaña, not to announce a 'Catalan State and Republic', but a *Generalitat* with no real powers beyond public order, education, communications and public works.

Palau de la Generalitat de Catalunya – *in* Plaça de Sant Jaume *in Barcelona - the seat of the Government of Catalonia and the Presidency of the Generalitat. (© Author)*

Centralist fears about the unity of Spain were given priority over Catalan autonomy, a policy continued by the Lerroux government after the right-wing victory in the 1933 elections. Alejandro Lerroux had confrontations with Catalan leader Lluís Companys over agrarian reform, and with the Basques over tax issues. Amid strikes, threats of violence and political confusion, Companys, who had legislated to provide protection for tenants against landowners, declared Catalonia an independent state within the Federal Republic of Spain. This was regarded by the Right as an attack upon Spanish unity but serious bloodshed was averted by moderate behaviour on all sides.

Exiled to France in 1939, Companys was arrested and brought back to Spain where, refusing to wear a blindfold, he was executed by a firing squad at Montjuïc Castle which towers over the city of Barcelona. His iconic tomb stands on the edge of Montjuïc cemetery in the *Fossar de la Pedrera* (Cemetery of the Quarry), which also contains the mass grave of 4,000 victims of Franco's regime of terror. Other memorials share the space, including one to the memory of the International Brigades.

The Agrarian economy

The two decades before the outbreak of the Civil War were marked by conflict between landowners and workers. They were characterised by anarchist risings, strikes and land seizures, against the background of a rise in communist influence. This was a country sharply divided between the upper and middle classes on the one hand, and peasants and workers on the other. The latter were often illiterate, maintained their traditional ways of life, and kept and were left to themselves. Between the upper class and the workers and peasants were the small shopkeepers and artisans.[16] Half of the population lived off the land – of which 25% was totally unproductive – that had little rainfall, was often arid and sterile, and on which farmers might be toiling their whole life for a pitiful yield. The Basque provinces fared a little better, with more regular rainfall and better relations between landowner and tenant. There, priest and community worked well together in a brand of more enlightened Catholicism.

In other northern territories, including Navarre, Aragon and Catalonia, tenant farmers managed a fairly regular existence, although the lease agreements in old Castile were probably the least secure. However, in much of the central and southern areas the plight of landless labourers (*los braceros*) working on the large estates (*latifundia*) was desperate. Owned by the Church in the 19th century, the *latifundia* were bought cheaply by middle class families, and were now in the possession of a land-owning oligarchy with little interest in putting money back into the land by improving conditions, using fertilizers, using irrigation or investing in new crops. This was crucial where land could offer a greater variety of crops but was often poor in quality and needed time to recover between growing seasons.

The owners, usually absentee landlords who used stewards to organise the estates, exploited day labourers to the brink of starvation. Many were only employed at sowing and harvesting. The owners brutalised the workers, who had no recourse to welfare provision and faced the repression of the *Guardia Civil* to keep them in line. Unemployment was high and those who were employed were paid a pittance – about three *pesetas* a day for four or five months of the year. During the periods of ploughing and harvest, the workers would be forced to move away from their families and live perhaps 20 miles away from their villages. In such conditions class hatred inevitably thrived, and workers became more open to revolutionary ideas and anarchist influence.

In the rest of the country there were small farms (*minifundia*). Owners struggled to make any kind of a living on small plots, and few tenant farmers had satisfactory fixed tenures. Even so, agriculture provided about two-fifths of the country's income. Journalist Henry Buckley painted a vivid picture of his stay in a cold and damp peasant home in a tiny village, perched draughtily and waterless on a hilltop. From here, after a breakfast of thin greasy soup made of flour and olive oil, the family would trudge off to a strip of land where they scratch the surface of the soil with a wooden plough.[17] The crops were invariably wheat and barley, with perhaps some garden vegetables. With short and insecure leases, and needing sometimes to resort to moneylenders, they were a ready audience for anarchists who were calling for the seizure of estates and the setting-up of collectives.

There were many strikes and demonstrations, and more serious bloodshed inflicted by the *Guardia Civil*. Buckley described the example of the village of Casa Viejas near Cadiz in 1933 where, following a call for direct action by the anarchists, peasants staged their own revolution. The government came down hard on the village, where a shoot-out between locals and the Civil Guard – and the burning of houses – led to the brutal deaths of 18 villagers, as they were dragged out of their houses and shot. Three of the assault guards were also killed in the fighting.

It was clear that the new Republic was struggling to exert its political authority in the face of the opponents of reform. Things did not improve when the Right gained power later in 1933. The poor and marginalised remained so, and became disillusioned with the promises and aspirations. Reforms to introduce arbitration committees, redistribute land, institute an eight-hour day, ban the hiring of outside blackleg labour, and give security of tenure raised the hopes of the workers. However, they did not make the desired impact. It was clear not only that politicians did not give the reforms high priority, but also that wealthy and important landowners and local officials were largely ignoring the demands of central government. Unemployment rose in the cities and among unskilled labourers. So there was no change to the common pattern in Spain in which the wealthy, privileged and noble opposed any attempts to reform the agricultural system and raise the standard of living of the poorest in their country.

The slide to Civil War

What we earlier called a multifaceted and complex story leading to the traumatic event of the military *coup* in July 1936, and the ensuing Civil War, is

General Miguel Primo de Rivera, military dictator and prime minister of Spain from 1923-1930. (© Wikimedia Commons)

likened by Helen Graham to the other European fascist takeovers in Italy and Germany: 'All these…had their origins in the cumulative political, social and cultural anxieties provoked by a process of rapid, uneven and accelerating modernisation…a fear of where change was leading.'[18]

In 1923, Spain became a military dictatorship after a coup in which General Miguel Primo de Rivera came to power, supported by King Alfonso XIII. Some saw de Rivera as a moderate or benevolent dictator, bringing the UGT into his government, but he also proscribed the CNT and attacked the Catalan language and culture, including outlawing the iconic *sardana* dance.

Initially, de Rivera won public support by seeking to grow the economy through improved transport links, the generation of hydroelectric power, increased wages for town workers and by nationalising the oil industry. The economic boom was welcomed by the industrialists, intellectuals and the middle classes, but they soon tired of his political inexperience and were critical of the state's growing interference in their business affairs. In January 1930, as the global economic collapse hit Spain and having already alienated the business classes, he lost the support of the king and the army, and was forced to resign.

The political regime continued, however, with the king turning to other military leaders to follow Rivera, firstly General Dámaso Berenguer and then Admiral Juan Batista Aznar Cabañas. With the exception of the Church, enthusiasm for the monarchy was now waning and, in August 1930 with the Republican movement gaining strength, an alliance of socialist politicians and intellectuals led by the lawyer Niceto Alcalá Zamora – a former minister of works, and of war, first elected to the *Cortes* in 1905 – met in the Basque coastal resort of San Sebastian and signed an anti-monarchist electoral pact.

The following April, and preceded by a general strike led by the UGT, unrest in the universities as well as a failed coup, the socialist alliance won a resounding victory in municipal elections called by the king, winning 46 out of 50 provincial capitals. On April 14th, 1931, the Second Spanish Republic was proclaimed with Zamora as prime minister. Regarded as a clear vote against the monarchy, King Alfonso XIII was told that he and his family should leave Spain immediately and promptly departed on the battleship *Jaime I.*

A provisional government, drawn from supporters of the San Sebastian pact, was formed leading to former prime minister Admiral Aznar reputedly telling the press: "A nation which went to bed Monarchist wakes up Republican."

Perhaps embodying the optimism of a liberated nation, the Republic was often caricatured with the bold female allegory of *la niña bonita* (the beautiful girl), as the new government quickly replaced the red and gold royal flag with the red, yellow and purple tricolour, and changed the royalist national anthem to the *Hymn of Riego*. Many streets were given Republican names and compulsory religious instruction was abandoned in state schools.

Opponents of the Republic did not disappear, however, and still lurked menacingly, agitating against the transformation of Spain and growing increasingly determined to regain power. Moreover, the perennial social and political divisions remained: Catalan leaders wanted to see some progress on the San Sebastian pact which promised autonomy within a federal state; the planned military reorganisation produced a disgruntled officer corps; the Church believed that its very existence was in danger; and the CNT continued its revolutionary rhetoric and activities.

The remarks of Manuel Azaña, the Republic's new minister for war, that Spain had ceased to be Catholic and he "preferred that every church should burn rather than a single Republican be harmed" certainly – even if his comments were taken somewhat out of context – did nothing to lessen political tensions. As Antony Beevor notes: 'leaders of the Republic faced immense problems deeply rooted in Spanish society: agrarian reform, the intransigence of the armed forces, the Catalan and Basque questions, and the issue of relations between the Catholic Church and the state'.[19]

The new Republic also suffered a number of setbacks as the June elections to the *Cortes* approached. Cardinal Segura, the fundamentalist Archbishop of Toledo, was expelled from the country after writing a pastoral letter denouncing the plans of the Republic to separate Church and State, and for calling for a mass mobilisation of the faithful. In Madrid, an incident involving a Republican taxi driver outside a Monarchist club frequented by army officers, aristocrats and Alfonso loyalists escalated until about a hundred churches and convents throughout Spain were burned down (acts usually attributed to the anarchists), leading to the introduction of martial law. Yet the June elections confirmed popular support for the Republic. The Socialists were the largest party, with the non-Republican Right now a weak opposition.

The new constitution drafted by the Republican Government, and adopted in December, clearly stated the intent of the new regime by proclaiming: 'Spain is a democratic republic of workers of all classes, organised in a regime of liberty and justice.' Hugh Thomas notes that it was a grave mistake to make the constitution of the Republic such a controversial political document, full of emotive phraseology.[20] The legislative programme was no less controversial, including: measures for agrarian reform; Catalan autonomy; giving women the vote; the legalisation of civil marriage and divorce; and free, compulsory secular education. In addition, the state funding of the Church was to end, its property to be nationalised, processions on feast days banned; and the Jesuit order outlawed.

If the established order was under threat, the Republic also faced major challenges. It was very inexperienced and patently misguided in adopting a 'top-down' political strategy which distanced and alienated itself from its supporters. The publication of a new 121-clause constitution did not bring about the immediate change in fortunes that the poorest sections of society expected, and the increasingly impatient far Left soon regarded Azaña's government as a betrayal of the people.

A strike of telephone workers, called by the CNT in July 1931, was followed by many other strikes and uprisings, often involving violence. In Seville, a general strike called by the CNT led to ugly clashes with the *Guardia Civil* in which four anarchists and three civil guards died. The CNT's increasingly militant FAI activists had, by now, effectively split the organisation and initiated further strikes and industrial unrest that became known as *la gymnasia revolucionaria* (revolutionary gymnastics), with the intention of extracting further concessions from the weakening Republican government.

Faced by these huge challenges, the government's unity began to falter. Zamora resigned as prime minister in October, in protest at the

Manuel Azaña, second prime minister of the Second Spanish Republic and later to serve as president. (© Wikimedia Commons)

anti-clerical measures in the new constitution, and was succeeded by Manuel Azaña, a lawyer, writer, intellectual and reluctant politician who later became known as the 'father of the Republic'.[21] In December, when the new constitution came into effect, Zamora returned as president of the Republic with Azaña continuing as prime minister, but this did nothing to abate the worsening *la gymnasia revolucionaria* as the same month saw more violent incidents in the village of Castilblanco in the Rioja, and in the province of Cadiz.

The inability of the government to end the industrial and social unrest emboldened the increasingly agitated right-wing factions and, in August 1932, General José Sanjurjo and other right-wing sympathisers including José Antonia Primo de Rivera – future leader of the *Falange* and son of the former military dictator – launched an attempted *coup d'état*. It failed and the conspirators were arrested, but Azaña's government was now in deep trouble. Born at the beginning of the Great Depression, it faced declining exports and rising unemployment, while its attempts at agrarian reform left peasants scarcely better off. It now faced elections in November 1933 dangerously weakened.

This time it was the right-wing elements which organised themselves into a coalition, led by the conservative and Catholic CEDA, including monarchists, the red-bereted Carlists and the Radicals. Leftist in-fighting – the CNT opted out of the election and the Socialists refused to form a united front – and the newly enfranchised women of Spain each played a part in a victory for the Rightist coalition. However, although the CEDA 'won' the election with the largest number of seats in the *Cortes*, because it refused to commit itself to the Republic's constitution, the president named the leader of the Radicals, Alexandro Lerroux, as prime minister.

The period following the election became known as *el bienio negro* – two black years – during which much of the Republican government's legislation, particularly in agrarian reform, was reversed. There was also change at both ends of the political spectrum. On the Right, the fascist *Falange* emerged as a powerful force, while on the Left the rise of the Spanish Communist Party (PCE) coincided with a dramatic shift to the revolutionary Left by the Socialists (PSOE), led by Largo Caballero. Increased fear and hostility led to sporadic strikes and hundreds of violent incidents.

The ugly face of fascism was reflected not only in Falangist José Antonio Primo de Rivera and his violent blue-shirted militia, but the hailing of José Maria Gil-Robles, leader of CEDA, with cries of *Jefe! Jefe*! (*Duce*! *Duce*!) by thousands of young people at a rally reminiscent of those occurring at Hitler Youth events

José Antonio Primo de Rivera, son of Miguel Primo de Rivera and leader of the Falange Española. *(© Wikimedia Commons)*

in Germany. Although these attempts to promote Spanish fascism had limited success, the Falangists were a destabilising force and Primo de Rivera, who'd cultivated contacts with Mussolini, Hitler and other fascist movements, was transformed into a saintly martyr by the Right following his execution by a Republican firing squad in November 1936. The *Falange* lived on after de Rivera's death, however, and was maintained as a useful political device by Franco after the Civil War.[22]

1934 was a year of growing political division and hostility between Left and Right, with an increasing spiral of violence. The inclusion of three CEDA members in the cabinet was denounced by leading Republicans and the calling of a general strike by the UGT in October 1934, forced the government to declare martial law. They also moved quickly to challenge Lluís Companys, leader of the Republican Esquerra party, who had declared an independent Catalan state within a federal Spanish republic from the balcony of the *Generalitat* in Barcelona.

The declaration of independence was driven by the right-wing government's reneging on the agreed statute of autonomy for Catalonia, and their challenging of measures to protect tenants from eviction by landowners. However, faced with the threat of a violent military intervention from Madrid, Companys refused to arm the Catalan people, surrendered to the central government authorities and was given a 30-year prison sentence. Despite inflamed emotions on both sides, a bloodbath was avoided. That was not the case in Asturias, where working conditions remained appalling in spite of the government's measures, and an uprising led to serious disorder, with clashes between armed workers and Civil Guards spreading to Gijon, Aviles, Oviedo, Santander and Bilbao.

After seven days in which communists and revolutionaries engaged in street fighting, set up communes, requisitioned buildings and transport and abolished money, the government sent in the Spanish Foreign Legion and Moroccan mercenaries to regain control. Led by General Francisco Franco they stormed the mining villages, looting and executing prisoners on the spot. Franco's tactics of artillery and bombing raids, plus shelling from the battleship *Libertad* were a chilling foretaste of things to come a couple of years later. It also immediately raised the status of Franco and the Army of Africa, and perhaps reignited the military's zeal to protect what they regarded as the true values of the motherland.

In just two weeks a thousand lives were lost and damage was widespread. Thousands more lost their jobs for taking part in the uprising, and up to 30,000 were jailed including ex-prime minister Azaña – wrongfully implicated by the Lerroux-CEDA coalition – and Largo Caballero. It is said that prison was where Caballero read Marx for the first time, preparing himself for the revolution he believed he would lead. Some have seen this as the first battle of the Civil War, with miners brandishing packets of dynamite against the military's rifles and machine-guns, and the bizarre occurrence of Muslim Moors entering Spain, to bring order, at the invitation of the Catholic Right. Others have called it the 'most substantial revolutionary episode in 20th century Europe after the Russian Revolution'.[23]

Against the background of constant unrest, the continuing impoverished state of the peasants, and the threat of plots by junior army officers, the Left attempted to re-establish itself as a more solid and united force. What became known, in the spirit of working class co-operation, as the Popular Front was ranged against the National Front, which linked a spectrum from conservative republicans to fascists. At the same time as the communists and socialists were moving closer together, the scandal-prone Lerroux government collapsed, yet instead of replacing Lerroux with Gil-Robles, leader of CEDA, President Zamora announced elections for February 16th, 1936. Despite a huge financial and propagandist effort by the National Front, the Popular Front won the election, and Spain held its breath. The Left feared a move by the army, and the Right feared nothing less than revolution. Moscow saw the Popular Front's electoral triumph as a great victory in the struggle for the unity of the proletariat against fascism, and the PCE proposed further cooperation with the PSOE.

Azaña, prime minister until May when he became president and was succeeded by Galician Casares Quiroga, moved quickly to reintroduce the reforms of the 1931-3 government, such as reviving Catalan autonomy

Calvo Sotelo, a leading anti-Republican politician, who had been minister of finance under Miguel Primo de Rivera. His killing triggered the plan for the military coup. (© Wikimedia Commons)

and dispersing generals, including Franco, to garrisons in distant parts of the country. Yet the Left remained fragmented and the new government was plagued by problems, from dissension within its ranks – in particular the obduracy of the PSOE's Caballero – to attacks by a rapidly growing *Falange*, and action against landowners by workers in revenge for the oppression of the past.

While Spanish society began to break down into chaos, disorder and violence, Largo Caballero raved about revolution (*Pravda* had called him the 'Spanish Lenin') and Calvo Sotelo, leader of the right-wing opposition gained popular support with inflammatory speeches. Army generals concluded that their intervention to save Spain from the politicians was now inevitable.

Co-ordinated by General Mola, previously posted to the Carlist heartland of Pamplona, the *coup* was to begin with an uprising in Spanish Morocco and depended on gaining swift control of the Spanish provinces with the military garrisons rebelling in support. The partial failure of this plan, with the Republic retaining large parts of the country, led to the long and bitter struggle that was to come.

The last acts of the drama that led to Civil War unfolded in Madrid. José del Castillo, a member of the Republican Assault Guards, was murdered by Falangists at 10pm on July 12th. As revenge, in the early hours of July 13th, a group of Assault Guards and other Leftist militiamen took Calvo Sotelo from his house and killed him with a bullet to the back of his neck, dumping his body at the entrance to one of the city's cemeteries. The generals saw the murder of such a prominent and experienced politician as further proof that they should act.

While this was happening in Madrid, a cryptic telegram from General Mola signalled the uprising in Morocco and, at 7.15am on July 11th, 1936, Captain Cecil Bebb, a commercial pilot, took off from Croydon Airport, London, in a Dragon Rapide aircraft, bound for the Canary Islands. His mission was to make contact with General Franco and fly him to Tetuan in Morocco, where he would meet up with the Spanish Army of Africa. Cecil Bebb was from Church Village, near Pontypridd and had attended Pontypridd Grammar School. So, it seems the first action of a Welshman in the Spanish Civil War was to assist Franco. The extent of MI6 complicity in this secret journey remains a matter of conjecture, but it has been alleged that Franco was accompanied by MI6 agent Major Hugh Pollard, and that the plot was hatched over lunch at Simpson's in the Strand.[24]

The generals' eventual success could not have been foreseen. The Republican government held the gold reserves, air power, legality and the major cities of Madrid and Barcelona. The Republicans also assumed that the British and French would come to their aid as a democratically elected government and that Germany was hardly in a position to intervene in support of the *coup* leaders. Order would be restored, it was believed, within a few months and Spain's democratic civil liberties would be saved.[25]

Many of the volunteers who went to fight in Spain were outraged by the non-intervention policy of the European countries, which included a Non-Intervention Agreement, arranged mainly by the British and French governments and signed by 27 countries including Germany and Italy, that essentially banned the sale of armaments to the Spanish government.[26]

Yet, even as the agreement was being discussed, German Junkers and Heinkel bombers, pilots and technicians were already in action in the south of Spain, with the German consul in Seville at pains to ensure that such personnel were not to be seen on the streets in German uniforms. In Madrid, the Germans even requested that one of their Junkers 52s, which had come down in Republican territory, be returned! By September, Majorca was full of Italian military personnel, with the main street, *La Rambla*, renamed *Via Roma*, while the bay of Pollensa was converted into an Italian naval base.

British Prime Minister Stanley Baldwin and France's Léon Blum no doubt believed that their countries, along with Spanish stability and European peace, would be best served by the prevention of military assistance, and they did their best to keep to the agreement. They hoped that a potential European conflagration would be avoided if there were no arms with which to fight.

However, that sentiment made little sense to those pounded by the latest German

Will Paynter, the miners' leader who volunteered for Spain. In 1959 he was appointed general secretary of the National Union of Mineworkers. (© NUM)

military equipment in rehearsals for later bombardments in World War II. Undoubtedly the Non-Intervention Agreement, blatantly breached by the Germans and Italians, contributed to the defeat of the Spanish government, and the policy of appeasement towards Nazism and fascism was more about the fear of communism and revolution following the depression years.[27]

Despite the Labour peer Lord Strabolgi's claim that the government's policy was of 'malevolent neutrality', influential voices within the British government, often patronising and ideologically driven – including the more conciliatory foreign secretary, Anthony Eden – made it quite clear that it favoured a victory for the National Front. The desired outcomes were the avoidance of a European conflict, the defence of Britain's strategic interests, the containment of communism and a stable, independent Spain with a more liberal Franco dictatorship.

Most of the labour and trade union leadership also favoured non-intervention, although positions were later modified. It took the veteran Liberal, and former-prime minister, David Lloyd George to make a passionate speech in the House of Commons, claiming that "if fascism is triumphant in this battle, His Majesty's Government can claim that victory for themselves."

The combination of an overwhelmingly Conservative National Government with commercial interests in Spain, and concern to protect the Straits of Gibraltar, made non-intervention predictable. Both President Azaña and Prime Minister Juan Negrin would describe Britain's hypocrisy and deceitful pretence of neutrality stance as the Republic's worst enemy.[28]

Claims by pro-Franco revisionists of an even balance of aid from the Soviet Union and Germany/Italy have been demolished by Spanish historians.[29] Britain had been easily persuaded that Spain was fighting against a communist enemy, and that Franco was heading a nationalist and counter-revolutionary battle to save Western civilisation, prompting Orwell's description of the 'deep, deep sleep of England'.[30]

Men like miners' leader Will Paynter believed that the British government was putting pressure on other countries to maintain the Non-Intervention Agreement. He recalled claims about the danger of inciting the fascist powers to attack other European countries, or that the fighting in Spain was a war between communism and fascism – so let them destroy each other.[31]

Paynter tells the bizarre story of how, in the summer of 1936, he led a deputation of communist councillors, miners and officials, driven by taxi driver Harry Stratton of Swansea – who later volunteered for Spain – to the palatial residence of Lord Davies of Llandinam, near Newtown.[32] Prime Minister Stanley Baldwin was staying there, and the group were intent on making clear their demand of a recall of parliament to address the situation in Spain. The Welsh maid who answered the door was as surprised as the delegation, but Mr Baldwin was not at home. The following day the delegation returned to find the grounds guarded by plainclothes police who were not as hospitable as the maid had been.

These perceptions only fuelled the passion of the volunteers, and contributed to the surge of recruitment at the end of 1936. In January 1937, the British government amended the Foreign Enlistment Act of 1870 to curb the flow of volunteers to Spain by threatening heavy fines and imprisonment for offenders, but it was very difficult to enforce.

Notes

1. Paul Preston, *The Spanish Civil War*, London, Harper Perennial, 2006.
2. George Orwell, *Homage to Catalonia*, London, Penguin Books, 1986, p.197.
3. Found in the collection of C. Stanfield, South Wales Miners' Library.
4. Julian Casanova, *A Short History of the Spanish Civil War*, London, I.B.Tauris, 2013, p.95.
5. Ibid., pp.44-80.
6. D.R. Davies, *In Search of Myself*, London, Geoffrey Bles, 1961, p.178.
7. Hilari Raguer, *Gunpowder and Incense*, Abingdon, Routledge, 2007.
8. See the ILP pamphlet 'Why Bishops back Franco' by John McGovern MP, a report of a visit of investigation to Spain. South Wales Miners' Library.
9. See especially, Antony Beevor, *The Battle for Spain*, London, Phoenix, 2006, p.25.
10. In an unpublished lecture, *La Guerra Civil Española vista por los mineros galeses y la revista católica The Tablet: dos versiones contrarias*, Professor David George of the University of Swansea considered two contrasting views of the Spanish Civil War through the eyes of south Wales miners and the Catholic weekly *The Tablet*. The paper consistently supported the Franco cause, due largely to the perceived threat to the Catholic Church from Spanish Republicanism.
11. Provided by local historian Terry Norman.
12. Hugh Thomas, *The Spanish Civil War*, London, Penguin Books, 2006, p.23.
13. Helen Graham, *The Spanish Civil War: A Very Short Introduction*, Oxford, Oxford University Press, 2005.
14. Paul Preston, The Spanish Civil War, op. cit., p.48.
15. BBC Cymru television documentary 1980.
16. See especially Gerald Brenan, *The Spanish Labyrinth*, Cambridge, Cambridge University Press, 1960, pp.87ff – a book written during and immediately after the Civil War.
17. Henry Buckley, *Life and Death of the Spanish Republic*, London, I.B.Tauris, 2014, p.93.
18. Helen Graham, *The Spanish Republic at War 1936-1939*, Cambridge, Cambridge University Press, 2002, p.1.
19. Antony Beevor, *The Battle for Spain*, op. cit., p.23.
20. Hugh Thomas, *The Spanish Civil War*, Harmondsworth, Penguin Books, 1977, p.74.
21. For a fascinating insight into the mind of Azaña, 'The prisoner in the guilded cage', see Paul Preston, *Comrades*, London, Harper Collins, 2000, pp.195-223.
22. For a short account of the contribution of Primo de Rivera see Paul Preston in *Comrades*, pp75-108. A translation of the 'Guidelines of the Falange' can be found in Alun Kenwood (Ed), *The Spanish Civil War: A Cultural and Historical Reader*, Oxford/USA, Berg Publishers, p.42-46. Also, in his fascinating book of oral histories, Ronald Frazer gives an insight into the political and economic thinking of a farmer convert to Falangism and a Falangist leader – *The Blood of Spain*, New York, Pantheon Books, 1979, pp.86-94 and 313-320.

23. George Esenwein and Adrian Shubert, *Spain at War*, Harlow, Longman, 1995, p.82.

24. For the story told by journalist Peter Day, see *Franco's Friends,* London, Biteback Publishing Ltd., 2011.

25. See especially the response of Henry Buckley, the *Daily Telegraph*'s correspondent in Spain in *Life and Death of the Spanish Republic,* op. cit., p.208.

26. Hugh Thomas, *The Spanish Civil War*, op. cit., pp.387-399, provides a detailed account of the deliberations of the Non-Intervention Committee and he describes how it was to 'graduate from equivocation to hypocrisy'.

27. For a longer discussion of governmental and political party views of the conflict see Tom Buchanan, *Britain and the Spanish Civil War,* Cambridge, Cambridge University Press, 1997, pp.37-92.

28. Francisco J. Romero Salvado ends a lecture with a damning indictment of the British and French governments shielding their duplicity, cowardice and hypocrisy behind the safe cover of non-intervention and thereby delivering forty years of 'enlightened and benign dictatorship' to Spain and, as a result of their appeasement, about to experience themselves aggression and tyranny. See 'Killing the Dream' in *Looking Back at the Spanish Civil War,* Ed. Jim Jump, London, Lawrence & Wishart, 2010.

29. See Julian Casanova, *A Short History of the Spanish Civil War*, op. cit., p.93.

30. George Orwell, *Homage to Catalonia*, op. cit., p.196.

31. Will Paynter, *My Generation*, London, George Allen and Unwin Ltd., 1972, p.64.

32. Ibid., p.59.

2

Working Class Activism

The Wales of the Volunteers

For some, the 1930s were a time of prosperity. Sitting in the living room of your new semi-detached residence, your 'wireless' radio would keep you up to date with the latest news and current affairs courtesy of the BBC, and your new gramophone would provide musical entertainment. The evening might be rounded off with a relaxing read of a Penguin paperback, while you tucked into one of the range of new chocolate bars that had appeared in the shops. If you went out, there was almost always a good 'talkie' film worth seeing, sometimes in colour. Throughout much of the country the standard of living was rising with electricity, petrol engines and various kinds of light industry replacing the heavy industry of the previous century – and mass-producing new consumer goods as well. More council houses were being built, and almost one in three homes were owned by the occupants. For your holidays you may well have tried the extremely popular Butlins camps, whose founder Billy Butlin had been spurred into offering more satisfying family holidays by a poor experience in a Barry Island bed and breakfast establishment.

Yet the picture in Wales in the 1920s and 1930s was quite different. While the worst of the interwar depression – unemployment across Britain reached more than 20% in the early 1930s – was over by 1938, with the rate declining to about 10%, the slump hit longer and harder in south Wales, which suffered in common with other heavy industrial areas like northern England and Scotland. In the south Wales valleys, which provided most of the Welsh volunteers for Spain, mass unemployment and extreme deprivation remained commonplace into 1938, with 25% out of work in many towns.

Juliet Gardiner, in her seminal book on the 1930s,[1] identifies the major features which led to the despair and frustration of so many. In the first place, the Great War not only deprived the country of a generation but disabled over two million men, many of whom were unable to work again. In the 1920s an unbalanced economy was exacerbated by the transition from the heavy industrial requirements of war to the quite different needs of a peacetime workforce. Secondly, London was no longer the financial capital of the world, and the return to the Gold Standard in 1925 led to rising unemployment with British exports unable to compete in world markets. The New York Stock Market Crash in 1929 had caused shockwaves throughout the world and triggered a global depression. Thirdly, the traditional industries of coal, iron, steel, textiles and shipbuilding – the foundation of Britain's earlier prosperity – had been challenged by other industrialised nations, and newer chemical, electrical and engineering industries were being developed. Shipbuilding had suffered a sharp decline and the textile industry in the north west of England was severely affected by the loss of foreign markets. Britain had lost its claim to be the 'workshop of the world'.

This was the background to a south Wales in which unemployment was rife, families destitute and long queues at soup kitchens became a way of life. Edwin Greening, a Welsh volunteer in the Spanish Civil War, recalled Aberdare in the 1930s as a society of poverty, misery and frustration.[2] Thousands of men were unemployed, and many had no option but leave home and look for work in the English Midlands and London. Many shops had closed, the streets were dirty and in a state of disrepair, as were the houses. This atmosphere of decay further depressed the unemployed miners, who felt inferior and neglected compared to the postal workers, policemen or civil servants who were now regarded as eligible young men.

For out-of-work colliers the day was long and often spent wandering the streets seeking any way to earn a few pennies, or sitting for hours in the reading rooms of the libraries or miners' halls. Some enrolled in night school classes and, in contrast to the passivity – borne of hopelessness – of others, were proactive in furthering their education or enhancing their skills. Many also organised and agitated against the unemployment and poverty that had blighted their

Edwin Greening, the miner and coalfield activist who wrote a book about his time in Spain. (© Mary Greening, Edwin's daughter)

communities. Edwin Greening had started work at the pit at the age of 14. He remembered descending the shaft, with bells clanging loudly, that led to the vast network of tunnels at the bottom and the mile-long walk into the darkness of the pit, with its pungent smell of sweat, dust and timber. There were many times when the family was without coal, so Greening and his father would take a sack and shovel to collect waste coal from the tips, selling any surplus bags if they were lucky. The family was burdened with debt in the late 1920s and faced a pitiful future of poverty and despair.

When, in 1926, coal owners demanded an extra hour's work each day and cuts in their wages, the miners' slogan, 'Not an hour on the day. Not a penny off the pay', reflected their indignant response. In April 1926, miners who refused to accept these new terms were locked out and coalfields came to a stop. The TUC called on all trade unionists to strike, and the country was paralysed. However, after only nine days the other unions returned to work, leaving the miners to battle on to the end of the year by when many were close to starving. The outcome was twofold: a decade of decay, unemployment and poverty for many; but also a growth in activism and 'extra-parliamentary' activity. As well as hunger marches there were numerous local meetings and demonstrations, often involving future Brigaders.[3]

In Tonypandy, 50,000 colliers and their families crowded De Winton Field, while in Merthyr, Ceridwen Brown of Aberdare led a large group of women, some carrying babies, who wrought havoc at the Merthyr Tydfil Unemployed Assistance Board (UAB) offices. Future International Brigaders were heavily involved in this action – Ceridwen's son was to serve in Spain, and two other leaders, J.S. Williams of Dowlais and Griff Jones of Merthyr, also fought there. In one demonstration in Abertillery, three future volunteers – Clarence and Harold Lloyd, and Bert Vranch – were arrested, but not charged, for singing anti-royalist songs. Clarence Lloyd, from the nearby village of Cwmtillery, was also at the centre of disorder in Blaina – spending the night in Nantyglo Hospital after being kicked by police – after the Public Assistance Committee (PAC) refused to receive a delegation led by the communist councillor Phil Abraham. A march to the offices, negotiated with police (who later denied their agreement), caused confusion and resentment. There were ugly scenes with baton charges by police, stone throwing by the marchers, many injuries and the arrest and trial of 18 men.

In 1932 almost a third of all coalminers were unemployed, and those who did find a job struggled not only with conditions at the coalface and the gruelling lifestyle but also the increasingly harsh terms imposed by mine owners. Life in the pits began early, and a miner in his mid-thirties might have already been working underground for 20 years. Health and safety at some pits was derisory and industrial disease was rife. Jack Roberts, another volunteer to Spain, was

14 when he went to work in the mine in Abertridwr. After the colliery lock-out in 1921, Jack joined the Communist Party and witnessed the grinding poverty and incredible hardship force striking miners back to work for longer hours and lower wages in 1926. His ardent political activities brought him numerous fines, a prison sentence and the nickname 'Jack Russia'.[4]

His memories of the pit lockouts included men wandering the streets bereft of hope, families dependent on soup kitchens and the police marching through the coalfield escorting the despised blacklegs to work. It was hard to feed families, and clothes were threadbare and patched. There was no coal to heat homes, yet millions of tons of the black gold lay under their feet. Roberts exemplified the man of action won over to communism, yet still retaining Christian views: a nonconformist foundation common to many Brigaders. Like many volunteers, Roberts became disillusioned with the Labour Party. He believed that it was the Communist Party that had stood solidly by the workers, that had represented the miners in 1926, and had been unwilling to compromise. His was a continuous battle with the authorities, joining the ranks of rebels and activists across south Wales as he became critical of the mine owners and their officials, and clashed with the police and courts on numerous occasions.

The young Jack Roberts, a miner and Welsh volunteer, who was wounded at Quinto. His biography was written by his grandson, Richard Felstead. (© Richard Felstead)

Will Paynter had a similar experience in the Rhondda Valleys, his 12-hour day from dressing in the morning to bathing at night, starting with a two-and-a-half mile walk to arrive at the pit before 6am. Conditions in Coedely Colliery were difficult with the constant and terrifying dangers of roof collapses and gas explosions caused by sparks or overturned oil-filled lamps. It was not long before he was aware of the industrial strife that dominated the coalfields, recognising its significance as he observed incessant attacks by owners on wages and conditions.

It was the 1926 lockout which politicised Will Paynter, on his own account turning him from a spectator on the sidelines to a militant activist. He saw the rise of fascism in Italy and Germany as a political force to preserve capitalism by eliminating democratic government and suppressing freedom and liberty, calling it a 'product of capitalism in dire crisis'.[5] His activism led to skirmishes with police and finally a spell in jail in Cardiff. Described by the police as a violent agitator, he had – like many others – graduated from passivity, through participation and confrontation, to leadership at his colliery. Paynter called himself 'a working class militant dedicated to the working-class movement, a revolutionary socialist and an active member of the Communist Party'.[6] Clearly impressed with him, the Communist Party sent Paynter to the Lenin School in Moscow where he was used by the Comintern as a 'courier for financial and other assistance' to help the anti-fascists in Berlin who had been driven underground by the Nazi regime.

Leo Price was similarly politicised through his experiences of the coalfield communities. His reading of Robert Tressell's *The Ragged Trousered Philanthropists* confirmed first-hand experience of the exploitation of the working class dating back to his first days at Aberbeeg as a 14-year-old miner, lying in water and crawling on hands and knees through tunnels scarcely a foot higher than he was. At Bedwas colliery his pay was £1 3s a week, of which a pound went on board and lodgings. His activism began in 1926, after bailiffs took a striker's furniture to auction.[7]

Leo Price, a miner, who was later wounded at Brunete. (© Richard Felstead)

This working-class consciousness and revolutionary enthusiasm, which led to such social activism in Welsh mining communities, forms much of the backdrop for volunteering for the Spanish Civil War. Many volunteers had joined hunger marches. The first, in 1927, was a protest against the new Unemployment Bill and Ministry of Health requirements that local Boards of Guardians refuse or limit relief notes for unemployed miners and their families. Two hundred and seventy men from Rhondda, Caerau, Aberdare, Merthyr, Pontypridd, Tonyrefail, Ogmore, Gilfach Goch, Nanyglo and Blaina marched to London. Organised in military style with detachments and companies, the marchers were harassed along the way by fascist elements.

Men were forced to look for work across Britain, walking from town to town in desperation, with many heading for London only to end up sleeping on park benches. Where they did find work, it was for a pittance. At home, relief arrangements were in chaos, and campaigning and agitation were co-ordinated largely by the Communist-led National Unemployed Workers' Movement (NUWM). The 10% cut in employment benefit in September 1931 met a vigorous response. Councils of Action were set up, and another hunger march with the theme 'Struggle or Starve' headed for Bristol, where the TUC was meeting. The TUC shamefully refused an audience to the marchers, which was broken up by mounted police.

As unemployment reached 2,500,000 in October 1932, it was the NUWM – with its communist leadership – that led protests against mass unemployment and, after a number of localised hunger marches, organised the first Britain-wide hunger march to London, when 375 marchers from south Wales were among the 2,500 who descended on Britain's capital after passing through 188 towns *en route*. They carried a petition for the reversal of the 10% unemployment benefit cuts and the abolition of the unemployment means test, an assessment which covered all forms of household income including pensions or savings, money coming into the house from a working son or daughter, and household possessions. The means test had led to much anger, and in some cases family break-ups, when working children left home to live with a relative or in lodgings so that their parents would not lose benefits. The march provoked an intense police response including, according to documents unearthed in the Public Record Office by Hywel Francis and Dai Smith, an attempt by the Assistant Commissioner of the Metropolitan Police to frame Will Paynter by linking him to a van allegedly containing weapons such as sticks and iron bars.[8]

The marchers, their numbers swelled by tens of thousands of Londoners, were met at Hyde Park on October 27th, by thousands of police, some on horseback, and special constables who lacked the training or discipline of their regular colleagues. The outcome was predictable yet shocking, with baton charges and the imprisonment of the marchers' leaders. Fleet Street had a field day, concocting spurious yet widely believed connections with Moscow, a view that complemented the Labour Party's view of the NUWM as an instrument of the British Communist Party.

The second hunger march in 1934 was triggered by the new Unemployment Insurance Bill, which retained both the previous benefit cuts and the means test while transferring the administration of relief from local Public Assistance Committees (PACs) – which had taken over the administrative functions of the Poor Law, and had some local discretion about payments – to a UK-wide body, the Unemployed Assistance Board. Organised once more by the NUWM, the hunger marchers represented a wide range of bodies from all over Britain with the support of some more radically-minded Labour MPs and local union branches. Police hostility continued, with Tom Mann and Harry Pollitt served summonses on the day of the march for earlier 'seditious' speeches.

Mann, a veteran communist activist with strong religious beliefs, had been a leader of the London Docks strike in 1889, a founding member of the Independent Labour Party in 1893, and had helped create the International Transport Workers' Federation. Pollitt, a revolutionary socialist instrumental in the foundation in 1920 of the British Communist Party and its general secretary from August 1929, was to play such a central role in the recruitment of volunteers to fight in the Spanish Civil War that a unit of the International Brigade, the Tom Mann Centuria, would be named after him.

Edwin Greening joined up with the west Wales contingent – that had started in Neath – having waited, shivering, in the foggy Aberdare night. When he heard the sound of their bugle he rushed to join the marchers as they made their way down the valley to Mountain Ash, where they slept the night on a floor. That weekend was a momentous one in his life, which saw him classified as a 'dangerous person' by the local police, and join the Communist Party.

Upon reaching London, a couple of hundred marchers went into Parliament still singing, and interrupted the debate, only to be ejected before they could present their petition. However, their opposition to the means test and the centralisation of relief payments was beginning to motivate mining communities to unite against the government. They had the growing support of Aneurin Bevan (the Labour MP for Ebbw Vale since 1929), other MPs and local councillors, while the South Wales Miners Federation was coming increasingly to the fore.

In north Wales, another young miner destined to volunteer for Spain soon found that his work supporting the shot firer, who used detonators to bring down rock, was dangerous, poorly paid and made him vulnerable to dust diseases.[9]

Following the 1921 lockout, which saw the miners isolated in their dispute with the coal owners, Tom Jones of Rhosllanerchrugog, near Wrexham, became

Tom Jones, who was captured by the Nationalists and imprisoned at San Pedro Concentration Camp. (© Marx Memorial Library)

much more aware of the plight of his fellow-workers and began to challenge the heartlessness of the employers. In 1926 he watched *cawl* (a traditional Welsh broth) served up to destitute families in the soup kitchens and men digging out coal from disused pits, with managers ignoring safety precautions. Now, as a convinced socialist with communist sympathies, he preached the left-wing message throughout the villages of north-east Wales, but faced an unwillingness to embrace radical change.

It was around this time that some religious institutions became nervous at the growth of an atheistic communism, which they believed threatened the moral state of the nation. The Communist Party was growing in membership and power, as more people voted for the party and its candidates gained seats on local councils. The NUWM, with its Communist leadership and fluctuating membership, had come closest to politicising the unemployed and providing them with support and an organisational framework. Yet the Communist Party of Great Britain had not gained control over the unemployed movement. As the parody of the opening lines of *The Red Flag* has it – 'The people's flag is deepest pink, it's not as red as people think'.[10]

The Communist Party was often at odds with the miners' leaders and the Labour Party, but many future Brigaders saw its class ideology as their best hope. Certainly the Welsh coalfields had their 'Little Moscows', and the Labour Party had lost the confidence of many miners. Communism seemed to provide the framework of discipline and political energy which was missing elsewhere. For intellectuals, the poet C. Day Lewis suggested, it was a substitute for a faith. Much was expected of a party member including attending meetings, trade union activities and selling the *Daily Worker* newspaper, which had 10,000 readers in 1931 when general secretary Harry Pollitt tried to make it more attractive. When Edwin Greening started attending Communist Party meetings at the time of the 1934 hunger march, they struck him as conspiratorial, utterly exciting, and provided the inspiration for agitation against war and poverty.

The last Britain-wide hunger march took place in October 1936, only a short time after the fascist uprising in Spain. Four of its leaders were to volunteer for Spain – Tim Harrington of Merthyr, D.R. Llewellyn of Blaengarw, Will Paynter of Cymmer, and J.S. Williams of Dowlais – and the marchers were reported to have sent a telegram to the TUC demanding that the British government abandon non-interventionism. The longstanding Welsh tendency towards internationalism was now becoming, in parts, an 'international socialism' akin to the 'workers of the world unite' cry from the Communist Manifesto.

Hywel Francis comments about a 'proletarian internationalism' in Wales with antecedents in a commitment to world peace, the brotherhood of man and international working-class solidarity.[11] This was nurtured in south Wales by the cosmopolitan nature of the coalfield and world trade, appositely exemplified by the growth of the Spanish community in Abercrave. Other heads turned to Russia to glimpse a vision of society liberated from the ills of capitalist Britain. Many of the British Left visited Russia: '…to have their opinions about what was wrong with Britain – the decay of capitalism, the class system, the searing inequalities of wealth and opportunity – confirmed…'[12] Most, including George Bernard Shaw and Malcolm Muggeridge, were unconvinced by what they saw, in spite of Russia's obvious sense of purpose. They were disappointed with the inefficient factories and the scarce and poor quality food, that led to starvation in some areas and despair in others. Welshman Gareth Jones, a former political secretary to Lloyd George, was the first journalist to document the existence and extent of the *Holodomor* (the state induced famine) which killed millions in the Ukraine in 1933-4. Nevertheless, this quest for an egalitarian utopia – eagerly promoted by Soviet propaganda – was certainly a driving factor behind the desire of those volunteering to fight fascism in Spain.

South Wales mining communities clearly contained many workers who were politically aware and politically active, and this awareness and engagement also played an important part in generating volunteers. For example, Brigader Jim Brewer of Rhymney came from a mining family, and described how politics and religion were always discussed at the hearth with his father, grandfather and uncles. A member of the Labour Party from his teens, he, like many others, was particularly moved by the Spanish government's brutal oppression of the strike and rebellion of the Asturian miners in 1934.[13]

Awareness of the growth of fascism abroad was sometimes evident in the language used by those in conflict with the authorities, or at the receiving end of police brutality. The police in Glamorgan were described as 'the gloved hand of fascism', and their counterparts in Lancashire as acting 'like little Mussolinis'.[14] Before the 1936 hunger march the chief constable of the Glamorgan Constabulary had prepared a dossier about the marchers describing future Brigader David Howell Jones of Maesteg as, 'a dangerous revolutionary who would resort to acts of violence should an opportunity arise', while Will Paynter was called a 'dangerous agitator and revolutionary'.[15]

Those young men who left south Wales to fight in Spain were clear that they would be fighting against a fascist state. Mussolini had named his ideology fascism, from the Latin *fasces*; bundles of rods or sticks which were symbols of power and authority in ancient Rome. For Mussolini, fascism was opposed to liberalism, socialism, trade unions, democracy, class struggle, internationalism and anything outside the state which threatens its unity and authority. The leaders of the 20th century European fascist governments – Mussolini, Hitler and Franco – were presented to their people as having the charisma, strength and means to rescue their countries from political and economic chaos. They ruled as dictators, demanding unquestionable obedience; used force and brutality to suppress opponents; rejected human rights; controlled the media; and distrusted intellectuals and freedom of expression in the arts.

In Britain, Oswald Mosley transformed his New Party into the fiercely anti-communist and anti-semitic British Union of Fascists (BUF) in 1932 after a visit to fascist Italy. In Wales, demonstrators heckled and fought with police when Mosley held meetings in Swansea, Cardiff, Pontypridd and other locations in the south. The best-known incident was at Tonypandy, in the heart of the militant Rhondda Valleys, which had seven Communist local councillors in 1936. Future Brigaders Will Paynter and Harry Dobson saw BUF leaders T.P. Moran and J.W. O'Neill address 2,000 people at De Winton Field. It had previously been argued that not even the ears of the sheep on the mountain should be defiled by the words of Mosley, and the crowd shouted the speakers down and sang *The Red Flag*. Paynter described how the fascists were forced to leave, but not before some pitched battles with their supporters which saw 36 Rhondda men receive prison sentences, and there is no doubt that the valley epitomised the international working-class solidarity that was later was to spawn so many International Brigaders.[16]

Another Rhondda Brigader, Alun Menai Williams, was at the 'Battle of Cable Street' in October 1936 when Mosley and his Blackshirts attempted to march through an area of London with a high proportion of Jewish residents, resulting in some ugly violence. Williams stated that the police were out in force to protect Mosley from the hatred of the people, and not to protect the people from the malignant objectives of Mosley's followers. The protestors surged forward, the police used their truncheons, and a riot ensued in which

Williams was knocked down by a horse and almost trampled.[17] Mosley's absurd claim in Cardiff that fascism, with its 'spiritual' appeal, could successfully express the Welsh character was given short shrift by the *Western Mail* editorial of April 16th, 1934.

Despite this rich seam of anti-fascism, some elements of the Welsh population were equally not supportive of left-wing ideologies. Historian Robert Stradling notes the dilemmas faced by Roman Catholics, who were genuinely disturbed by atrocities against the Church and the clergy in Republican Spain. The position of the Marquis of Bute, Roman Catholic and owner of much of Cardiff, was a delicate one. Lady Bute had published an article espousing 'liberation from the Reds', and the Marquis was rumoured to have generously supported Franco's war effort.[18] Harder evidence suggested that the Marquis had attempted to buy the docks of Cadiz, Malaga and Algeciras with funds raised from the liquidation of his Glamorgan estate. In parts of Wales the Catholic Church and some priests told their parishioners that the Republicans were a grave danger to the church in Spain, a view not always accepted by working-class Catholic communities in the docks of the port towns and across the south Wales coalfield.

The bitter and politically charged Welsh experience of deprivation, struggle and militancy against exploitation and injustice, particularly in industrial south Wales, provided the backdrop to volunteering for Spain. Volunteers came from communities that shared a similar economic situation, and knew what it was like to be oppressed. They came with the sting of the 1926 General Strike, the anger of the hunger marches, and a colourful history of working-class struggle. For Hywel Francis this 'flowering of an international working-class consciousness' was a unique coalfield development, and an internationalism of a new kind: '...essentially proletarian, extra-legal and extra-parliamentary'.[19]

They were also far better politically educated than many other volunteers. James Hopkins calls them a 'working class elite' arising from self-education and the web of educational bodies traditionally used by the miners.[20] Deprived of formal school studies, a miner might still have an impressive collection of Left Book Club volumes and a range of political pamphlets. He may have spent time in the library of the Miners' Institute or attended Workers' Educational Association lectures. Perhaps he had listened to a lecture on Spain given by Gwyn Thomas, a Rhondda writer, dramatist and student who had attended the University of Madrid. A heady mix of political awareness and engagement, vibrant coalfield militancy, enduring anti-fascism, communist directive, and pure empathy and compassion has produced a narrative of the Spanish Civil War, understandably romantic at times, but compelling and inspiring.

Notes

1. Juliet Gardiner, *The Thirties: An Intimate History*, London, Harper Press, 2010, pp.11-19.
2. Edwin Greening, *From Aberdare to Albacete*, Pontypool, Warren and Pell, 2006.
3. Hywel Francis and David Smith's book on the history of the south Wales miners maps out in detail the marches and other protests. See *The Fed*, London, Lawrence & Wishart, 1980.
4. For his story see the absorbing account by his grandson Richard Felstead, *No Other Way: Jack, Russia and the Spanish Civil War*, Port Talbot, Alun Books, 1981.
5. Will Paynter, *My Generation*, op. cit., p.51.
6. Ibid., p.49.
7. Leo Price's unpublished memoirs, Richard Burton Archives, Swansea University.
8. Hywel Francis & David Smith, *The Fed*, op.cit., p.106.
9. Read his story in: Pugh, Jane, *A Most Expensive Prisoner*, Llanrwst, Gwasg Carreg Gwalch, 1988; and Mark Metcalfe, *Tom Jones – A Fighter for Freedom and Working People*, Unite Education, 2014.
10. Juliet Gardiner, *The Thirties: An Intimate History*, op. cit., p.179.
11. For a discussion of this and for the definitive book on the role of the Welsh miners in the Spanish Civil War see Hywel Francis, *Miners Against Fascism*, London, Lawrence & Wishart, 2012.
12. Juliet Gardiner, *The Thirties: An Intimate History*, op. cit., p.216.
13. Jim Brewer, Imperial War Museum, interview, Reel 1.
14. Clive Emsley and Barbara Weinberger, *Policing Western Europe*, Santa Barbara, Praeger, 1991.
15. National Archives, HO144/20696 – 1936 Hunger March. Information kindly provided by Don Watson.
16. See article by Hywel Francis, 'Rhondda and the Spanish Civil War' in K.S. Hopkins (Ed.), *Rhondda Past and Future*, Rhondda Borough Council, 1973, pp.67-8. The defence counsel in Harry Dobson's trial was to claim: "A fundamental part of the life of this people is the deep-rooted feeling of antagonism towards the fascists."
17. Alun Menai Williams, *From the Rhondda to the Ebro*, Pontypool, Warren and Pell, pp.144-145.
18. Robert Stradling, *Wales and the Spanish Civil War*, Cardiff, University of Wales Press, 2004, pp.60-66.
19. Hywel Francis, *Miners Against Fascism*, op. cit., pp.260-2.
20. James Hopkins, *Into the Heart of the Fire*, Stanford, Stanford University Press, 1998, p.147.

3

To Fight Against Fascism

The International Brigades

Tarragona – one of many

On October 13th, 2013, the Roman Catholic Church held a ceremony of beatification in Tarragona for 522 people, mainly priests, who were killed during the Spanish Civil War. They were perceived as martyrs, and their killings were regarded as part of the religious persecution perpetrated by the Republicans. The other side of the Spanish coin is shown by the surviving air raid shelter in a little street called *Trinquet Nou*, where people huddled during the incessant bombing of the city from April 1937. In the fortnight before it fell on January 15th, 1939, Tarragona was the target of 33 attacks. From April 1937 onwards, 144 bombardments of Tarragona killed 230 people and left 607 buildings damaged.

   The military and revolutionary atrocities of Tarragona were replicated throughout the country and often described as Red or White Terror. Spanish historian Julian Casanova succinctly describes this 'veneration of violence'. In Nationalist-held territory, imprisonment, torture, repression and death awaited thousands of political leaders, trade unionists, councillors, mayors and those who opposed the 'glorious national movement'. In Republican territory, no mercy was shown to those implicated in the rebellion, including military officers, clergy, 'proven' fascists, and landowners. What was known on both sides as the *limpieza* (cleansing) often took the form of the *paseo*, a walk in the woods followed by a bullet in the back of the head. It was also an opportunity for 'settling personal accounts'. It was in response to events like those in Tarragona and elsewhere in the country that the volunteers of the International Brigades made their perilous way to Spain.

Recruitment and travel of the volunteers

The establishment of the International Brigade followed a complex Soviet political strategy. Stalin's intention from 1934 was to focus on bolstering the defence of the Soviet Union, rather than supporting world revolution. Following the Spanish uprising he had to consider both the threat of fascist domination in Spain and the need to avoid offending Britain and France as potential allies against fascism. He acted slowly and with caution, moving from assessments of the situation by agents in the field to a domestic propaganda campaign, then diplomatic and humanitarian actions and eventually, from October 1936, to shipping military equipment and personnel.

The Comintern asserted, in September 1936, that the fight was for 'a special state with genuine people's democracy', not a Soviet state but an anti-fascist one.[1] The 'bourgeois-democratic' revolution should not at this time become a socialist one, so collectivisation of land and industrial enterprises should take second place to victory over fascism. The first challenge was to integrate the loyal units of the regular army with the workers' militias, a move resisted by the anarchists. The role played in this by political commissars ensured overall Soviet control of the army but the consequences of this led to the suppression of the allegedly Trotksyist POUM. There was truth, as Brigaders would find out, in the disillusioned Franz Borkenau's acerbic comment that: 'in communist mentality, every disagreement in political matters is a major crime, and every political criminal is a Trotskyist. A Trotskyist, in communist vocabulary, is synonymous with a man who deserves to be killed.'[2]

An extraordinary meeting of the Politburo on August 26th, 1936, raised the possibility of helping the Republic by the creation of an international volunteer corps. Spanish historian Angel Viñas attributes this to the deterioration of the Republic's military situation once Franco's appeal for help led Hitler to betray his promise not to intervene.[3] Mobilising foreign support was organised through other national communist parties, a job given to the Comintern.

The nature of the Brigade concept has been widely debated. R. Dan Richardson makes a powerful case that the Brigades were not only a military force, but 'a significant political, ideological and propaganda instrument... used by the Comintern for its own purposes.'[4] This political role, along with the change of attitude towards the socialists which had enabled the Popular Front, was a temporary Soviet-Comintern tactic to meet the threat of powerful enemies. Certainly the Comintern had taken advantage of and exploited this idealistic democratic response, but this does not entirely explain how individuals and small groups from a range of backgrounds began to make their way to Spain. Neither does it diminish the idealism and sacrifice of the volunteers. It was only later that working-class organisations became aware of the need for a more structured approach. The Communist Party of France, no doubt under the watchful eye of the NKVD, the communist secret police, was given the central role in administering recruitment, with Britain assigned a quota to meet. André Marty, a devout Stalinist and brutal disciplinarian with an apparent paranoid obsession with spies and Trotskyists, was placed in political control of the Brigades.

The first Welsh volunteers tended to be unemployed miners who had found jobs in other industries. Some attempted to get to Spain independently, since there was no real apparatus for sending men from Wales until the beginning of December 1936. Hywel Francis describes in some detail the background to volunteering in Wales.[5] Some men had been enthused with crusading zeal by taking part in the hunger marches, and the Communist Party of Great Britain encouraged volunteering and recruited intensively throughout December 1936. South Wales miners, well used to acting in an 'extra-parliamentary' manner, began to respond. Most Welsh volunteers were Communist Party members. District recruiting officers worked discreetly at first, then secretly after February 1937 when recruiting for Spain became illegal.

The initial response was slow. Dave Springhall, the political commissar of the British Battalion, wrote in early 1937 that the Welsh contingent was 'incredibly small'.[6] No doubt, many Welsh activists were preoccupied with the hunger marches, while men with military experience and working-class backgrounds were preferred as volunteers, and with each volunteer having a slightly different story to tell. Some left without telling their families to avoid causing uncomfortable situations, such as Tom Jones, who knowing his family would be upset if he revealed where he was going, told his family he was going to Colwyn Bay for the weekend. Lance Rogers of Merthyr Tydfil left home without saying a word to his parents or anyone else, while Leo Price of Abertridwr said the hardest thing he ever did was to put his daughter to bed before leaving her, travelling to Caerphilly and staying the night with his sister to avoid his wife.[7] While the routes they took to Spain varied, there was a fairly common pattern. The Brigade's organisational centres in south Wales were in Cardiff, mainly at the rear of shops in Charles Street and the Castle Arcade. The early volunteers travelled more directly and freely, until the Foreign Enlistment Act of 1870 was applied to Spain.

When being recruited, men were usually interviewed about their motives for volunteering and political affiliations, with some rejected because of lack of previous military experience, or on medical grounds. Those accepted would meet on the weekend in Cardiff, looking very conspicuous in their cheap suits, and were escorted to London where they were taken to the secret meeting place for Welsh volunteers, a café in Denmark Street. Here they were questioned

Harry Stratton (seated) is seen here with Welsh volunteers Jack Williams of Dowlais, Bill Morrisey of Cardiff and Lance Rogers of Merthyr. (© Richard Burton Archives, Swansea Univ.)

again about why they wanted to go. Motivation, physical fitness and experience were all important features. The core organisers based themselves in Paris and were initially flexible with recruitment, but with political commitment as the overriding feature along with a successful medical examination the process resulted in the recruits gathered in Paris coming from a wide range of backgrounds; from miners, seamen, and labourers to intellectuals, writers and artists.

Some early volunteers from Wales had a fairly uneventful journey into Spain compared to those who went later. The three Ammanford volunteers, W.J. Davies, Sammy Morris and John Williams, crossed the border from Perpignan without the police checking their passports. Later, most volunteers found their journey restricted and had to do it the hard way – walking the goat trails over the Pyrenees. Many volunteers from Wales reached Paris with a weekend tourist ticket which required no passport. They travelled from Victoria Station in London, where members of the Special Branch would interrogate them and try, rather half-heartedly, to change their minds. However, Edwin Greening was told by a Special Branch officer that he had better be back from his jolly weekend in Paris by Monday, or he would be in trouble.[8] In France, the approach was usually more relaxed. Will Lloyd and Bob Condon, both from Aberaman, left the *Gare du Nord* on what Lloyd called a 'troop train' with wooden seats, with wives and sweethearts saying goodbye to their men. They still had to be careful since they were accompanied throughout the journey by people apparently trying to listen to their conversations. Lloyd had a more direct journey across the border, by lorry to Figueras, then to Barcelona, with a march through the city before moving on to the base at Albacete.[9]

Another with a fairly straightforward trip was Harry Stratton of Swansea.[10] A taxi driver who had done a lot of ferrying around of foodstuffs, clothing and medical supplies for the Spanish Aid Committee, he told his family he was off to a new job in Southampton. Looking back from the top of Pyle Hill, he wondered if he would ever again see the winking light of the Mumbles Lighthouse. At Victoria Station he carried a copy of *Tit-Bits* magazine and waited alongside the working model of the new Dover-Dunkirk train ferry. Once in Paris, Harry was taken to the headquarters of the French Communist Party. From there, a 19-hour journey on a train with 'wooden lath seats like park benches' took him and two companions to Perpignan, where they were met by a coach that drove them unchallenged across the border into Spain.

Jim Brewer was a committed and resilient member of the Anti-tank Unit in Spain, and regarded as a good example to other men. (© Tamiment Library, New York)

Jim Brewer, an ex-miner from Rhymney who had studied at Ruskin College, Oxford, was influenced by the hunger marchers, but initially deterred by the Brigade's requirement for military experience. He tried to get his fellow Iberia-bound travellers to be more careful and not congregate while waiting at Victoria Station, and realised that a Special Branch detective had followed them on the train, all the way to the café where they stayed in Paris.[11]

Yet, while approaching other passengers, the sympathetic *gendarmerie* did not ask for their passports on the train. Once met in Paris, volunteers were normally taken to various cheap hotels and disguised in French clothes. Each was given ten francs a day, while their British money was taken from them. They left for Spain from the *Gare du Nord*, accompanied by a guide, each man carrying his belongings in a brown-paper parcel. Their destination was normally Perpignan or Beziers.

Jack Roberts had volunteered soon after returning from the 1936 hunger march. Initially turned down for lacking military experience, he tried again in January 1937 along with unemployed Abertridwr miner, Wyndham 'Windy'

Watkins. Once accepted, they travelled by boat to France followed by the train to Perpignan, where they shared a house with six other volunteers. These included Alun Menai Williams of Penygraig and Tom Picton of Treherbert, a product of the fighting spirit of the coalfield in more ways than one, who was to be shot in prison in Bilbao in 1938. Wandering the streets of Perpignan, the group, apart from Roberts and Williams, was picked up by the *gendarmerie* and imprisoned for 15 days. Taken to the British consulate in Marseilles, Roberts and Williams, as lawbreakers, were refused help but made it home after being sent enough money for the journey home following a plea to the Clerk of Caerphilly Urban District Council.

Roberts and Leo Price repeated the journey a couple of months later, meeting other volunteers in Paris before travelling on to Arles in southern France, where they were billeted in the town hall. This time the French authorities turned a blind eye to their movements, and the socialist mayor involved them in the May Day celebrations. Next was a taxi journey to the foot of the Pyrenees, and the tortuous climb up steep rocks in strict silence and total darkness. They aimed to reach the summit before dawn, when the soil, vineyards and olive trees of Republican Catalonia would be in view below them. There were some scary moments and, to Jim Brewer's horror, the three parts of his razor fell out of his pocket, hitting the metal struts of a railway bridge they needed to crawl across; 'like a rifle shot in the silence'. As they climbed, the fierce wind ripped into them, the stones made their feet bleed, and the ascent was exhausting. During the horrendous night-long climb, stumbling and gulping for air, Morien Morgan of Ynysybwl, worked out the best way to walk – lowering your head, putting your hands behind your back, leaning forward and taking short steps.[12]

Billy Griffiths of Llwynypia, Rhondda, was enjoying the power, status and responsibility that came with an ever-widening circle of political activity. Yet in March 1938 he volunteered, resentfully at first, when recruits were desperately needed following losses at Teruel and the Aragon retreats. His task was to build up party strength and discipline. At Paddington he met fellow Rhondda-man, Jack Jones of Blaenclydach, and was helped to find digs for the night. He passed the medical examination in Paris – such was the need by this time, most were passed fit after a hurried medical consultation – but made his first big mistake in the fort at Figueras, where most volunteers had their first experience of Spain. While the majority of volunteers furtively tipped the foul-tasting rice cooked in rancid oil onto the ground, Billy returned his untouched first course to the kitchen expressing his willingness to eat the second course of roast mule! This led to his immediate arrest for wasting food when there was a shortage, amid fears of fifth columnists agitators stirring up trouble.[13]

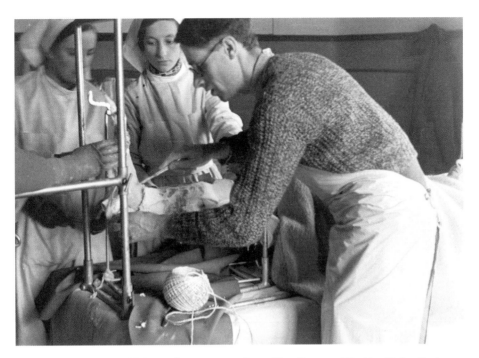

Thora Silverthorne (middle), a volunteer nurse from Abertillery, and Dr Alex Tudor Hart, who worked as a general practitioner for the Llanelly (sic) Miners' Medical Aid Scheme, photographed while operating in Spain. (© Imperial War Museum)

Thora Silverthorne, a nurse from Abertillery, remembers standing with a group of fellow nurses in their uniforms outside Victoria Station before being given a great send-off by banner-waving supporters, who gave them bunches of flowers and wished them a good journey. 'We were done up in little round nurses' hats, blue mackintoshes, black shoes and stockings'.[14] She and fellow Welsh nurse, Margaret Powell, volunteered through the Spanish Medical Aid Committee, in August 1936. The group's first task was to clean up a huge, filthy rat-infested former doctor's house in Granen, near Huesca, which was scrubbed to accommodate an operating theatre and wards.

Bob Peters was to live to be the last surviving Welsh volunteer.[15] He had grown up in Penarth, near Cardiff, and in 1931 left Wales to live in Canada, where he encountered poverty and homelessness as a result of the Great Depression. He empathised with Spain's poorly paid land workers, and was angry at the involvement of German and Italian fascists. After quizzing him about his political thoughts and beliefs, the Canadian Communist Party agreed to send him.

Alun Menai Williams later volunteered as a medical worker and attended to the injuries of many of the Welsh Brigaders. (© Alan Warren)

Routes to Spain were various and in some cases a little unclear, as are many of volunteers' recollections. Alun Menai Williams, son of the poet Huw Menai Williams, was born in Gilfach Goch. After working at the local colliery he moved to London, joined the army and trained as a medic, serving in Egypt with the Royal Army Medical Corps. In his autobiography he tells how his journey to Spain almost ended in tragedy for him, and killed more than 60 other volunteers.[16]

He recounts that he was on board the unarmed Spanish liner, *Ciudad de Barcelona* (City of Barcelona), carrying a few hundred International Brigade volunteers from Marseille, when it was torpedoed on the afternoon of Sunday May 30th, 1937, by a modern Italian submarine, *General Sanjurjo*, and sank off the coast just north of Barcelona.[17] Within ten minutes the ship began to sink, tipping lifeboats full of men into the sea. Some jumped into the sea and started swimming until fishing boats arrived to pick up survivors and take them to the little town of Malgrat. Williams and the other five Welsh volunteers on board – Harry Dobson of Blaenclydach, Pat Murphy of Cardiff, Alwyn Skinner of Neath, Emlyn Lloyd of Llanelli, and Ron Brown of Aberaman – all survived.

Tom Jones, who'd told his mother and father that he was just going to Colwyn Bay for the weekend, left Britain on April 3rd, 1937.[18] He made it to

Paris, and was met by Charlotte Haldane who was wearing a large red rose in her coat lapel. Haldane, the journalist, feminist and communist activist, was one of the organisers responsible for receiving the volunteers and arranging their transport from Paris. On the last leg of the journey to the Spanish border, Jones' taxi group was stopped by armed French police, and he was arrested and imprisoned for three weeks at Perpignan. On his release he managed to board a Spanish ship docked in Marseilles and sailed to Barcelona with many other volunteers. Packed with guns and tanks, the ship floundered in mud as it hugged the coastline, but eventually docked to the rapturous cheers of the citizens of Barcelona.

The old fortress at Figueras, birthplace of artist Salvador Dali, is near Spain's border with France and gave volunteers the chance to recover from the journey across the Pyrenees while enjoying some well-earned food – described as anything from beans, to sardines in olive oil, to artichokes washed down with a mug of *vino* – which tasted better when accompanied by the revolutionary songs of various countries. Author Laurie Lee spent ten days there. He describes a white acropolis on a bleak naked hill above the town, with a courtyard and a mix of volunteer nationalities.[19] To him, they looked a ragged lot, dressed in clothing ranging from civvies to military blankets. He heard a huddle of men talking in Welsh, and was surprised at the fragmentation of national groups scattered around the courtyard. At this starting point he sensed mixed motives and a coming test of nerves. For Jack Roberts, billeted in the underground stables, it was a stark reminder of the imprisonment and torture, in those same stables, of hundreds of Asturian miners following their revolutionary uprising in 1934.

Jim Brewer remembered an early morning arrival at Figueras after the climb over the Pyrenees. Following a breakfast of coffee and bread he was expecting a rest, but had first to hand over his civilian clothes and don a uniform. Then 'some bright Herbert' had the idea of playing football, and the combination of the climb over the mountains and the hot sun produced some very weary limbs the next morning.[20] Yet this was no excuse for avoiding the drills with ancient-looking rifles, used in a mock-storming of the fortress.

Albacete

Arriving volunteers were taken for training to Albacete in south-east Spain, a modern commercial and industrial centre which was the headquarters of the International Brigades. At first, the arrangements were hopelessly inadequate, and the town seemed ill-suited to accommodate the influx of volunteers. Recruits were marched into the bullring, focus of the town's autumn fiesta, interviewed

The bullring in Albacete, where the volunteers were registered, is still used for bullfights. (© Author)

and registered. Early experiences indicated a lack of organisation, discipline and commitment, low morale and poor equipment, with uniforms acquired from as many different countries as the volunteers. Many were kitted out in khaki uniforms, French steel helmets and cavalry bandoliers, but the brown boots were the best.[21] Laurie Lee remembered little formal discipline and parading through the streets to keep warm, holding up clenched fists and shouting newly-learned slogans such as *No pasarán* (they shall not pass) and *Muerte las fascistas* (Death to the fascists).[22] As the barracks overflowed, and public buildings such as the bullring were requisitioned, men were dispersed to nearby towns, with recruits from Britain taken to nearby Madrigueras and later to Tarazona de la Mancha, about 11 kilometres north west of the International Brigades headquarters.[23]

Albacete saw a lot of drilling and marching. Days were long – sometimes from six in the morning to six at night – and building discipline in the ranks was a chaotic process. Weapons and equipment were scarce, and varied in quality. Will Lloyd had only a wooden stick until two days before going into action, when he was given a rifle which was about 60 years old. Leo Price was given one with a barrel 'four feet long'. Most of the guns would not fire anyway, he said, and he ended his training more confused than he'd been at the beginning, such as when they'd taken apart a machine-gun with no one knowing how to put it back together again.[24] However, there was no one better at digging good trenches than a Welsh miner, and apparently no one better with a machine-gun than Jack Roberts. Yet, his comrades claimed jokingly that his left-handedness made his aim with a rifle rather unpredictable.

Archie Cook of Ystrad, Rhondda, was given a rifle on arrival in the Battalion and sent straight to the front. He remembered that his only practice with the weapon was to fire five rounds of ammunition. Some chaps, he said, were not given even that opportunity before they were in action.[25] Bob Peters, who arrived in March 1937, remembered the lectures and political discussions and the range of uniforms on offer, from woolly alpine hats to a variety of jerkins. It was in nearby Madrigueras, the training base for the British volunteers, that it was possible to touch grenades and machine-guns as well as listen to lectures. Locals, although extremely poor, would invite men in for dinner or offer to do their washing.

The volunteers were given elementary training in the use of their rifles, yet there were often not enough to go around. (© Tamiment Library, New York)

Edwin Greening's experience towards the end of 1937 did not indicate any improvement in weapons training. He had no experience of guns until one day in early January 1938, when, wearing new uniforms, his group was taken to the firing range at Tarazona de la Mancha and instructed in the use of the Russian rifle.

In his explicit unpublished memoirs, Will Lloyd admitted to a number of unpaid bills and drunken episodes in Albacete, one of which led to a three-day imprisonment. Yet there was also intelligent discussion about political issues, and great friendships and camaraderie grew among the diverse units.

It did not take the Nationalists long to realise that Albacete was the International Brigades' centre, and the town and the surrounding area were often bombed.[26] Madrigueras, a small village with three cafes and a small cinema (still today partially intact and serving as a garage area behind a row of houses), had been taken over by the British for training. Amid the poverty and squalor stood a large, beautiful church which had been ransacked and burnt out and was now used for cooking and transport. The story was told that the priest had hidden in the belfry and taken pot shots at villagers in the square. Two brothers had climbed the belfry, disarmed and hanged him.

The church at Madrigueras, seen here in a photo from 1930, was used by the volunteers for cooking. Some locals still have memories of this from their childhood. (© Juan Carlos Talavera, Mayor of Madrigueras)

Jack Roberts' memories of Madrigueras were vivid.[27] He recalled the poverty of the village with its dusty plaza, narrow exits, iron balconies and monumental church. Increasing anti-clericalism had closed the church, and peasants watered their mules at the well in the centre of the village and tilled and planted with ancient tools. The days were long with *Reveille* sounded at 5.30am, and after a cold water wash and a breakfast of coffee and dry bread, the men fell in at 6.45. There was parading on the village square, morning drill, the political commissar's pep-talk, manoeuvres over open country and wheat fields and lots of digging of holes.

Food was plentiful, as was the ever-present olive-oil. The proverbial saying *'No hay mal que el aceite no cure'* ('there is no ill that oil cannot cure') was never more real. It was Leo Price who insisted one day that he had his rice on a separate dish, before adding goat's milk to produce the tastiest rice pudding he could remember (*'Arroz con leche'* – 'Rice with milk'). He was also a frequent visitor to a café in Madrigueras owned by a lady called Matilda and her husband Leon. The day before he left for action at Teruel they let Leo sleep in their bed, and gave him a special breakfast of eggs, tomatoes, bread, grapes, orange and coffee.

The locals were similarly kind to Harry Stratton, who was billeted with five other comrades in a hay loft belonging to a peasant family who often invited him into the house. When some British soap arrived from home the men found it was in great demand by the locals, in return for a traditional Spanish tortilla.

Training was initially of a very elementary standard and only a few rifles were available for use on the two firing ranges on the outskirts of the town. However, as time went on, weapons such as Russian rifles, anti-tank guns and other equipment, began to appear. Fred Copeman,

During World War I Tom Picton served in the Royal Navy and was light-heavyweight boxing champion. (Courtesy Richard Havard)

Tom Picton: a larger than life character. A bare-knuckle mountain fighter and passionate anti-fascist he was killed in a Bilbao prison. (Courtesy Richard Havard)

The Cuidad de Barcelona *was carrying International Brigade volunteers when it was sunk near Barcelona. The five Welsh volunteers who were on board all survived. (© Wikimedia Commons)*

later commander of the British Battalion, arrived in Madrigueras when the British 16th Battalion was being formed. At that time its commander was Wilfred McCartney, with Tom Wintringham second-in-command. Copeman discovered that only a few rifles had been acquired for his battalion – at one time just six between 700 men. This restricted practice severely until new Russian rifles, a godsend in spite of their low quality, arrived. Lewis machine-guns were also replaced by German Maxims which were efficient, but mounted on wheels and difficult to handle. More uniforms arrived, but there were still incidents of drunkenness, petty crime and fighting among volunteers.

When Jack Roberts and Leo Price, both of Abertridwr, arrived at Madrigueras they came face to face with the man Roberts called "the mad Taff" – Tom Picton from Treherbert, the 52-year-old mountain fighter and former Navy light-heavyweight champion. Supplementing his miner's wages with bare-fist mountain fighting, he had lost his teeth by the time he went to Spain. Sitting awkwardly astride a mule and holding his clenched fist high, Picton boasted that, despite his imprisonment in Perpignan, he had managed to get to Spain before Roberts. Tom's stay in Spain was a colourful one, and his battalion records indicate frequent indiscipline and drunkenness.[28]

On one occasion he was expelled from the Battalion and sent to another one, with the recommendation that he be deported. This did not stop him

A Pilon (water trough) in Madrigueras which the Brigaders would have used during their stay. (© Juan Carlos Talavera, Mayor of Madrigueras)

from declaring, in a letter to George Thomas of Treherbert, that he was in the 'greatest army of comradeship the world has ever seen' and that 'if some people could see what happened out here they would be here with us.'[29] In other letters his enthusiasm was infectious, as he described having the 'buggers on the run' and making sure there is 'no pass around'; his version of *No Pasarán*! It was his unwillingness to conform and accept what fascism dealt out that led to his being shot in cold blood in a Bilbao prison. It is not clear why he was executed but W. Nathan, an English volunteer also imprisoned, described how they dragged Picton outside, along with an American named Dorland. They beat Dorland up, but pushed Picton against a wall and shot him.[30] It would appear that Picton had intervened in an attempt to protect Dorlan.

It was while Jack Roberts was at Madrigueras that Harry Dobson arrived, following his escape from the torpedoed *Cuidad de Barcelona*. Jack recalled that when Harry arrived at tea-time on June 4th, and told them of the loss of life, the canteen stood for two minutes' silence and some men wept openly.[31] Harry Dobson was a coalminer at Blaenclydach Colliery, Rhondda, an active trade unionist and fierce communist opponent of fascism.

Henry 'Harry' Dobson, one of the most valued and respected of the Welsh Volunteers. (© Richard Burton Archives, Swansea Univ.)

As the number of rifles accumulated, and the machine-guns and tanks appeared, these small units of men armed with varying weapons were gradually trained into brigades ready for their first major action. James Watt of Swansea, later to die at the Ebro and epitomising the inexperience and vulnerability of many, wrote that: 'Up to coming to Spain I had a dread of firearms but I no longer fear them as I know I have got to master them.'[32]

The strength of the volunteers was not, however, to lie in military prowess and experience, but in their unified stand against the forces of fascism. The first English-speaking battalion of the International Brigade came into existence on December 27th, 1936.[33] The British 16th Battalion consisted of more than 150 men divided into two companies. Part of the 15th International Brigade, it was incorporated into the Republican Army in January 1938. As the Battalion became more organised it was divided, in early 1937, into four companies, each with about 160 men. Three companies were infantry, and one machine-gunners, with No.1 company led by Jock Cunningham, No.2 – the machine-gunners – by Tom Wintringham, No.3 by Bill Briskey – a trade union activist from London – and No. 4 by Bert Overton, who had served in the Welsh Guards.[34] However, the old problems of lack of weapons, shortage of uniforms and of equipment remained. There were also tensions between those with military experience and others who had found themselves in leadership roles without appropriate skills. Confidence rose and morale improved when Soviet advisers helped with training, Russian weapons began to appear in numbers and each man had his own rifle.

It was at this time that the need for greater care in the choice of volunteers was communicated back to supporters like Harry Pollitt.[35] Political commissars were established at brigade, battalion and company level to focus attention on the anti-fascist character of the Brigades. Regarded as the 'political soul' of the volunteer army (and known by some as the 'political comic stars'), the commissars were very much part of the military units, equal in rank to the commanders as they sought to inspire and educate, ensuring that men understood the reason for military objectives. Their job was clearly set out.

Castelldefels is a largely 16ᵗʰ century castle that was used by the Republicans and International Brigades as a prison to punish indiscipline and desertion. (© Author)

They were to establish good relationships between officers and soldiers, engage in political and moral education and vigilance, train, clarify and strengthen the political consciousness of officers and soldiers and maintain their fighting morale. They were expected to secure respect and humane treatment for those imprisoned, yet there were reports of poor conditions, torture and executions at the prison at Castelldefels, south of Barcelona, with Matthew Nicholls of Cardiff listed as still being in Castelldefels in January 1939.

Some Welsh volunteers were appointed as commissars, but the role and concept remained controversial and ambivalent. With their pastoral responsibility came a vigilance role which required looking out for dissension, spies and Trotskyists, and at times they could be regarded as party bullies and ideological bores. Poor behaviour, drunkenness and indifference were seen as a product of deficient political development and a potential source of harm to the anti-fascist movement. This explains many of the harsh and often unwarranted political comments in files in the Moscow Archives of the International Brigades. Many come from the commission set up at the end of the war by secretary Billy Griffiths. However, some like Tom Jones who was made a commissar, thought that the system was very useful, since it gave men an opportunity to air grievances, take part in debate and discuss battle mistakes and future action.[36] However, communist proselytism was an issue, with the communist newspaper, *Mundo Obrero* often the only one to reach the front. Yet it was regarded by many in the government as a price to pay for Soviet aid and Communist Party support.

For Jim Brewer, commissars were 'political Johnnies', given too much power to waste people's time. 'When we should have been learning to be soldiers,' he noted, 'we were being preached at and indoctrinated.' Of Billy Griffiths, he commented: '...he couldn't stop preaching to save his life and he'd be there at you, he'd be telling you what Marx and Lenin said of this, that and the other....'[37] Further Soviet penetration of Spain and the International Brigades came in the form of the Soviet Secret Police (NKVD) and the Spanish Republican Secret Police (SIM). James Hopkins talks of the 'paranoid and murderous world of the SIM', and describes how promising party members in the Brigades were recruited by the NKVD for current and future undercover activities.[38] Brazell Thomas of Llanelli, included 'intelligence' as well as 'soldiering' when asked about his military duties for biographical information in his file in the Moscow Archives,[39] leading some to believe that he had been recruited.[40]

The Moscow Archives show that suspicion was sometimes cast on exemplary comrades. For example, Tom Howell Jones was tried by the Battalion Tribunal on June 19th, 1938, on a charge of 'spreading rumours with a view to disruption'.[41] Yet there was much worse than that for many other Brigaders at the hands of the NKVD or the SIM.[42] Arrests, imprisonment and executions were not uncommon for those accused of desertion, dissidence or the elastic term 'Trotskyist'. Methods of extermination included a walk in the trees followed by a bullet in the back, a firing squad, or being sent to an exposed position at the front to be 'killed in action'. André Marty admitted freely to the execution of many 'dissident' Brigaders and became known as 'the butcher of Albacete'. However Richard Baxell warns against putting a Stalinist gloss on such a rigid and hierarchical structure with its political orthodoxy, and that 'the notion that there was an army of NKVD agents operating throughout the Brigades, and Spain itself, is not supported by the evidence.' He cites recent research by Boris Volodarsky who has identified only 10 NKVD officers in Spain, and argues that the so-called overall presence of the NKVD in Spain is a myth. The intelligence gathering Russian GRU (*Glavnoye Razvedyvatel'noye Upravleniye*) had many more personnel than the NKVD in Spain.[43]

However, political paranoia remained an issue. One of Alun Menai Williams' records had 'Trotskyist tendencies' scrawled across it, while Edwin Greening was accused unjustly of desertion by the committee set up by his comrade Billy

COOK, Archibald SARGENTO   Age 30   *Britanico*   ✓ 6
Co.2.   Single.
Rifle No.
                              (Sister) Ruth Cook,
                                       ~~19, Tyntyld Road,~~
      Miner.   Ystrad, Rhondda,S.W.

      Joined Battalion 23-4-37.
      From **Nov.15th.1937** ~~until~~ March Ist. 1938, at O.T.School
      Confirmed as SARGENTO I4-5-38
      To. Hosp. 16/6/38. From Hospital 16.7.38.
      WOUNDED 26.8.38.

      ~~Hospital~~ ~~38~~

Information about many of the volunteers is found in the Moscow Archives of the International Brigades. Here is an extract from the file of Archie Cook. (© Deputy Director RGASPI, Moscow)

Griffiths, although the report does not have his signature. Further evidence of this dark side of the fight for democracy can be seen in this same committee accusing Greening of 'neo-Trotskyism' and of influencing another Brigader, William Thompson, to desert.[44]

Who were the volunteers and why did they go?

What motivated so many young men to align themselves to a cause which seems so remote from their lives in Wales? Who were they, and why did they leave their communities, friends and families knowing the dangers that lay ahead of them? Richard Baxell attempts to answer these questions,[45] and although statistics regarding the International Brigades should be treated with caution, most writers would accept that at least 35,000 men and women – including some 2,500 from Britain – served in the Brigades. However, MI5 records released in 2011 show that the Security Service tracked the movements of about 4,000 people trying to travel to Spain from Britain. Welsh volunteers made up about 6% of the British total. Most were between

A photo of Godfrey Price of Cardiff, taken from his International Brigade file. (© Deputy Director RGASPI, Moscow)

21 and 35 with just a few below 21 years of age. They came from various regions of the UK: the largest contingent came from the south east of England but many travelled from north west England and Scotland.

Most writers agree that the occupational profile of the British recruits was that of the industrial working class. Many were unemployed, and more than 60% were communists; some were members of the Labour Party and others claimed no political affiliation. The Appendix lists almost 200 'Welsh' volunteers of whom approximately 70% were members of the Communist Party, and more than half were miners. There were intellectuals, poets and professional people, but it would be a romantic fantasy to suggest that the majority fell into these categories. Yet, for a military force, there was an unusually high proportion of intellectuals. William Rust, the first editor of the *Daily Worker* newspaper, admits there was a spirit of adventure at work but describes the volunteers as 'crusaders in the cause of world peace and the advancement of mankind.'[46]

British volunteers tended not to see themselves as Marxist revolutionaries but, as Baxell powerfully states, 'they shared a hatred of fascism, which they combined with the willingness and determination to do something about it.'[47] This is true, despite the view of some that most volunteers were motivated by allegiance to the Communist Party, as opposed to Republican Spain. The anti-fascist motives of the Welsh volunteers were echoed by the comments of socialist leaders and politicians, and replicated in the debates and discussions of political groupings in the UK. For example Councillor Brinley Jones argued at a local council meeting in Llanelli on September 10th, 1936, that victory for Italy and Germany in Spain would mean the downfall of the British Empire and the end of a democratic chamber in Llanelli.[48] Paul Preston sums up the prevailing view when he writes: 'It was because they shared the collective fear of what defeat for the Spanish Republic might mean that men and women, workers and intellectuals, went to join the International Brigades. The Left clearly saw in 1936...that Spain was the last bulwark against the horrors of

Hitlerism…The volunteers believed that by fighting fascism in Spain they were also fighting it in their own countries.'[49]

Yet popular thinking in Britain often viewed them as adventurers, mercenaries or unemployed opportunists. Indeed, Harold Davies from Neath was described as 'a young man of no political opinions but he loved adventure.'[50] The miscellany of volunteering embraced criminal elements, Jewish opponents of Nazism, people like Tony Hyndman of Penarth who sought answers to personal problems, and those, such as Gilbert Taylor of Cardiff, who were dragged unceremoniously into the conflict. There is an honesty in men such as Michael O'Donoghue from Merthyr Vale who candidly states that his main reasons for going to Spain were poverty, no work, and a family to support. There were also other Merthyr men who

A photo of Lance Rogers of Merthyr, taken from his International Brigade file. (© Courtesy Deputy Director RGASPI, Moscow)

'had nothing to do and therefore this was the alternative of getting out of it.' O'Donoghue claims that a member of the ILP assured him that his wife would be 15s 3d better off and he would not have to be fed by his family if he were in Spain.[51] Yet these were not the motives of the majority, who journeyed abroad in their thousands at a time when such travel was rare, and to a conflict where they could be killed. Yet it is clear that some who arrived at Albacete were not suitable. Leadership there made it clear that they did not want 'drunks' and those not expecting a real war.

There is a common pattern to what some Welsh volunteers said about their reasons for going. Jim Brewer was convinced of the need to fight fascism as part of an international movement. He was very much influenced by Franco's treatment of the Asturian miners, which he called 'damned horrible', and was outraged by Hitler's military intervention in Spain. Many believed, like him, that Spain was the great burning moral issue of the time. For Brewer, 'to be silent in the face of injustice is to acquiesce.'[52] Having arrived in Spain he wrote to his parents that he had made the right decision – 'happiness for us is only possible when fascism is wiped from the face of the earth.'[53]

For Archie Cook, a Gelli miner, it was a recognition that the Spanish Republican Government was one, of the people, formed by the people and elected by the people. He volunteered to help that democratic government stay in power. To his dismay, in a medical examination on his return, his scar wound evoked the suggestion that he had been a mercenary.[54] Morien Morgan had interrupted the last year of his university honours degree to volunteer. A radical and intelligent thinker, he was appalled that Mussolini's actions went unchallenged, amazed at the Nazi's military might when he visited the Rhine, and felt helpless about German military expansion. He saw Spain as Hitler's testing ground for modern warfare, using bombers and tanks, while Britain had stood still militarily after World War 1.[55]

Will Paynter initially went to Spain, as the Communist Party organiser for Wales, in order to look after the British Battalion's interests in the International Brigade Headquarters. In a letter to *Miners' Monthly* magazine he wrote: '…a battle is in progress not merely to defend a people from a savage aggressor, but to destroy something that if allowed to advance will eventually crush the people of all democratic countries.…'[56] Writing to Arthur Horner (president of the South Wales Miners Federation) a couple of months after arriving in Spain, Paynter was moved by the suffering of the children, of the fleeing refugees and the queues for meagre necessities.[57] He was even more convinced of the menace of fascism to France and Britain.

Godfrey Price of Cardiff asked whether the people of his city realised that Hitler's bombers could easily strike against them from northern Spain.[58] Bob Peters and his friends were convinced that Spain's struggle was theirs too – a fight against international fascism. 'Maybe we were naïve, I don't know. We thought we could help and that's why we went.'[59] Active in his support of local, national and international industrial and anti-fascist struggles, Sammy Morris of Ammanford saw his war as one against international fascism. In his letters home he was particularly scathing about the church, which had joined the fascists against the government and allowed the use of church buildings as machine-gun nests and ammunition dumps.[60] All this resonated with the view of the Commissariat in Spain, expressed by Brigade Commissar Jean Barthel, in the Brigade newspaper *Our Fight*. The volunteers, he said, are fighting to 'conquer the hordes of that ominous triumvirate Hitler-Franco-Mussolini', and are 'fighting to defend Spain against a barbaric fascist triumph which would threaten the liberty and peace of the whole world.'[61]

A background of socialist political activism in the Labour Party led Tom Jones to empathise with the Republican struggle and who was appalled by the British government's attitude to the fascist powers. In a letter to the *Rhos Herald* he stated that fascism had nothing to offer the world except continuous war and a complete destruction of all culture, arts and learning.[62] Although opposed to both war and fascism, he believed that if men like him did not fight the latter it would spread throughout Europe and come to Britain. Alun Menai Williams would say that the emotions and motives for his decision were complex. Yet he wrote: 'I jettisoned a possible police career in favour of an impulsive act which this time coincided with a reason I had expressed many times in the past: the fight against fascism…there is a no-man's-land between conviction and action into which the majority of humankind never ventures.'[63]

Treherbert's Sid James agreed to accept the decision of the South Wales branch of the Communist Party of Great Britain when he and his brother Archie were asked by the Rhondda sub-district if they wished to be considered for Spain. Jack Roberts ('Jack Russia') came from the Nonconformist background common to many Brigaders. However, unlike most who had moved on to a more secular political philosophy, Jack's communist outlook derived from Marx and the chapel. 'The Sermon on the Mount told us that we all should get a fair share and the best way…is the communist way of taking over everything.'[64]

A similar view was expressed by Tom Jones, who felt that people in his community saw trade unionism, politics and religion as synonymous, such as when the hymns sung in chapel would also be sung at political and trade union meetings. This is why he faced huge personal difficulties when involved in the Republican's destruction of churches.[65] In a similar vein, David Llewellyn of Blaengarw said religion had instilled his principles of the brotherhood of man and a sense of justice. For some volunteers there was an internal struggle involving their religious and ethical values and the Republican cause of freedom and democracy. Conversely, some like Jim Brewer felt that the Catholic church was the problem – the men ate in a church in which the priest had killed 30 people with a machine-gun. To Brewer, feeding the Battalion was the 'first time it's been put to decent use.'[66] Lance Rogers acknowledged the personal crisis that he had to meet head on. He had always been more pacifist than militarist, but was committed to the job that had to be done, although it almost broke him in the end.

However, there is another story to tell about the first Welsh volunteer to engage in battle in the Spanish Civil War. Frank Thomas was born in Pontypridd and brought up in Cardiff. Bored with life as a travelling salesman he was attracted to Spain by his 'thirst for adventure and glory'.[67] Politically right-wing and strongly anti-communist, he wrote that he was touched by the sacredness of General Franco's cause and joined *El Tercio*, the Spanish Foreign Legion, linking up with them in October 1936 before the attack on Madrid. Not many of his countrymen would have appreciated his presence in Madrid's *Casa de Campo,* the *Parque del Oeste* or the university, throwing bombs at the members of the International Brigades who were bravely defending the city. They would not have been impressed to hear that, at the Battle of Jarama, Thomas' company had taken the village of San Martin de la Vega, a stone's throw from the British Brigaders at Morata de Tajuna. He writes: 'I had a splendid opportunity of examining the many enemy dead the next day and from passports and other papers found on them…had good reason to suppose they belonged to the 16th Battalion of the International Brigade".[68] Nor would the Welsh in the Battle of Brunete have enjoyed knowing that at Villanueva de la Cañada, Thomas had been strengthening the barbed wire defences before their attack. Frank Thomas was a Welsh volunteer for the Francoist cause who, by his own admission, deserted and returned home with O'Duffy's Irish Brigade. His ideology had little to commend it then, and even less currency today.

Notes

1. See E.H. Carr, *The Comintern and the Spanish Civil War*, London, Macmillan, 1984, p.20.
2. Franz Borkenau, *The Spanish Cockpit*, Michigan, University of Michigan Press, 1937, p.79.
3. For a fuller discussion see 'September 1936: Stalin's Decision to Support the Spanish Republic' by Angel Vinas in Jim Jump (Ed.), *Looking Back at the Spanish Civil War*, op. cit. Ed. Jim Jump, Lawrence & Wishart, London, 2010.
4. R. Dan Richardson, *Comintern Army*, Kentucky, The University Press of Kentucky, 1982, p.2.
5. Hywel Francis, *Miners against Fascism*, op. cit., pp.156-178.
6. Ibid., p.160.
7. All descriptions from the *Colliers Crusade*, BBC documentary, 1979.
8. Edwin Greening, *From Aberdare to Albacete*, op. cit.
9. *Colliers Crusade* and *Will Lloyd Unpublished Memoirs*.
10. Harry Stratton, *To Anti-Fascism by Taxi*, Port Talbot, Alun Books, 1984, pp.29-31.
11. Jim Brewer, Imperial War Museum, interview, Reel 3.
12. Ibid., and *Colliers Crusade*.
13. Unpublished memoirs, Richard Burton Archives, Swansea University.
14. 'The First Medical Unit' in Jim Fyrth & Sally Alexander, *Women's Voices in the Spanish Civil War*, London, Lawrence & Wishart, 1991, p.55. Thora Silverthorne was part of the first team from Britain to be sent by the Spanish Medical Aid Committee. It consisted of four nurses, four doctors, four student doctors and six drivers.
15. For his story see Greg Lewis, *A Bullet Saved My Life*, Pontypool, Warren and Pell, 2004.
16. Alun Menai Williams, *From the Rhondda to the Ebro*, op. cit.
17. However, in an interview with Hywel Francis (South Wales Miner's Library), Alun Menai Williams claims that he was on the boat after the one that sunk. In fact he is not on the list of survivors recorded in the Russian archives.

18. Read his story in Jane Pugh, *A Most Expensive Prisoner*, op. cit., and Mark Metcalfe *Tom Jones – A Fighter for Freedom and Working People*, op. cit.

19. Laurie Lee, *A Moment of War*, New York, The New Press, 1991, p.23ff.

20. Imperial War Museum, interview, Reel 3.

21. Leo Price, unpublished memoirs, op. cit.

22. Laurie Lee, *A Moment of War*, op. cit., p.75. In August 1936 John Summerfield and John Cornford found the drilling and the running around ploughed fields tough. It also seemed that each nationality – Spanish, Polish, German, Hungarian and Italian – did a right turn in a different way. (John Sommerfield, *Volunteer in Spain*, New York, Borzoi Books, p.23). The Thaelmann Battalion was regarded as the most disciplined marchers and the Lincolns as the best equiped on arrival.

23. For a fuller discussion see especially 'Three months in Spain: The British Battalion at Madrigueras and Jarama from January to March 1937' in Jim Jump (Ed.), *Looking Back at the Spanish Civil War*, op. cit.

24. Comments from both Will Lloyd and Leo Price in the *Colliers Crusade*.

25. Words recorded, on his return home, in the *Glamorgan County Times*, December 17th, 1938.

26. See the account of Fred Copeman in *Reason to Revolt*, London, Blandford Press, 1948, pp.79-84.

27. Richard Felstead, *No Other Way: Jack Russia and the Spanish Civil War*, op. cit., pp.64ff. My visit to Madrigueras revealed a strong interest by local historians in the presence of the British and an historical route has been produced for visitors. It is possible to see the cinema and balcony behind a row of houses, walk along Avenida Brigada and visit a memorial to Tom Wintringham. Local historian Caridad Serrano has written an online book of oral histories on Madrigueras – *'Recuerdalo Tu'* [http://www.brigadasinternacionales.org/images/stories/Documentos/recuerdalo]

28. RGASPI (Moscow Archives) 545/6/185.

29. Letters of Tom Picton, Richard Burton Archives, Swansea University. For a fascinating essay on two very different Welsh soldiers see Robert Havard, 'Thomas Picton and Sir Thomas Picton: Two Welsh Soldiers in Spain', in *Transactions of the Honourable Society of Cymmrodorion 2000*, Vol. 7, 2001.

30. *Rhondda Leader*, October 29th, 1938. The *South Wales Echo*'s headline at the time read: 'Welsh Boxer Shot Dead in Spain'.

31. *Colliers Crusade*, op. cit.

32. Letter from James Watt to Amos Moule, April 1st, 1937. Richard Burton Archives, Swansea University.

33. Tom Wintringham, *English Captain*, London, Faber and Faber, 2011, p.40.

34. Bill Alexander, *British Volunteers for Liberty*, London, Lawrence & Wishart, 1982, See especially the chapter 'The Formation of the British Battalion'.

35. RGASPI 545/3/450. Suitable recruitment was always an issue. A letter from Figueras in February 1937 stated that men were being kept back for a number of reasons – too young; too old; a liability; poor eyesight; weak physically,

etc. (RGASPI 545/6/89). Even as late as December 1937, strong – even vitriolic – comments, were made, for example: 'Drunkards, down and outs, criminals … are not wanted…there should be a stop to recruiting in hostels and parks….' The call was for men from the best sections of the working class. (RGASPI 545/6/87).

36. Jane Pugh, *A Most Expensive Prisoner*, op. cit., p.60.
37. Interview with Hywel Francis on November 29th, 1969, South Wales Miners' Library.
38. For a fuller discussion see James Hopkins, *Into the Heart of the Fire*, op. cit., pp.259-90.
39. RGASPI 545/6/207.
40. Richard Baxell, *Unlikely Warriors*, London, Aurum Press, 2014, p.245.
41. RGASPI 545/6/155.
42. See R. Dan Richardson: *Comintern Army*, op. cit., pp.159-76.
43. 'Myths of the International Brigades', *Bulletin of Spanish Studies*, Volume XCI, Numbers 1–2, 2014.
44. RGASPI 545/6/207.
45. Richard Baxell, *British Volunteers in the Spanish Civil War*, Pontypool, Warren and Pell, 2007, pp.30-50.
46. William Rust, *Britons in Spain*, Uckfield, The Naval and Military Press Ltd, 2007.
47. Richard Baxell, *British Volunteers in the Spanish Civil War*, op. cit., p.50.
48. *Llanelly Mercury* (sic), September 10th, 1936.
49. Paul Preston, *The Spanish Civil War*, op. cit., p.6.
50. George Eaton, *Neath and the Spanish Civil War*, self-published, 1980.
51. Interview with Hywel Francis, 1969, South Wales Miners' Library.
52. Letter to his principal in Harlech, quoted in *Miners against Fascism*, p.282.
53. Letter to his parents, in *Miners Against Fascism*, p.274.
54. Interview with Hywel Francis, 1969, South Wales Miners' Library.
55. Imperial War Museum, interview, Reel 1.
56. Will Paynter, *My Generation*, op. cit., p.68.
57. Hywel Francis, *Miners Against Fascism*, op. cit., p.273.
58. Letter to his wife, in *Miners Against Fascism*, p.291.
59. Greg Lewis, *A Bullet Saved My Life*, op. cit., p.21.
60. Information kindly provided by Terry Norman of Ammanford.
61. *Our Fight*, No.25, April 14th, 1937.
62. Hywel Francis, *Miners Against Fascism*, op. cit., p.212.
63. Alun Menai Williams, *From the Rhondda to the Ebro*, op. cit., p.148.
64. *Colliers Crusade*.
65. *Colliers Crusade*.
66. Letter to his parents, May 29th, 1937, in *Miners Against Fascism*, p.274.
67. Robert Stradling, *Brother Against Brother*, Stroud, Sutton Publishing, 1998, p.4.
68. Ibid., p.94.

4

Baptism of Fire

Madrid and the Jarama Valley

Madrid and the International Brigades

Today, *Gran Via* in Madrid has an intensity and grandeur. The Telefonica Building, which rises to a height of 89 metres, was used by the Republican Government during the Civil War to observe the whereabouts of Nationalist troops. British war correspondent Geoffrey Cox described Madrid in the autumn of 1936 as a nervy and dangerous city.[1] Although regular community life went on, with the cinemas and cafes open, the city had been bombed, rifle shots would go off in the night, guards were on the corners of the streets and requisitioned cars and lorries inscribed with the initials of the unions and militias. A number of hotels had also been turned into workers' kitchens or hospitals.

The Gran Via in Madrid, with the landmark Telefónica building, one of the first skyscrapers in Europe. (© Author)

Cyril Cule of Swansea, who was in Madrid, recounted the time he encountered militia fighters rounding up fifth columnists and found himself looking down the barrel of a gun held by someone itching to use it.[2] Madrid had felt what Dolores Ibárruri, the fiery Spanish Communist Party leader known as *La Pasionaria* ('The Passionflower'),

Isidora Dolores Ibárruri Gómez, known as 'La Pasionaria', was a Spanish communist politician and heroine of the Civil War to whom is attributed the slogan "No Pasarán!" – "they will not pass". (© Alan Warren)

called "the foul breath of the beast in its face". Cule had encountered the double-edged sword of civil war and revolution, the latter spearheaded by the anarcho-syndicalists of the CNT and FAI. For revolutionary groups, a combination of military action and revolution was the formula required to defeat fascism. Their desire for a dictatorship of the proletariat challenged the ideological communist and socialist aspiration of a bourgeois-democratic revolution. In spite of Moscow's wishes, a revolutionary process was already attempting to restructure society through the collectivisation of farms and expropriation of factories.

What Julian Casanova described as 'this melting pot of armed powers' boiling up in the first few months of the war, was best exemplified in Catalonia. In Barcelona, George Orwell saw a place in which 'the wealthy classes had practically ceased to exist', with almost every church gutted, shops collectivised, trams and taxis painted, and anarchist red and black and revolutionary posters and flags everywhere.[3] People wore the *mono azul,* the workers' blue overall, and there were no hats (symbols of pride and privilege to the anarchists) or other indications of wealth. Franz Borkenau, who wrote his diary of the Spanish revolution a year after its outbreak, described 30% of the males walking down *Las Ramblas* carrying rifles and watched a church burning silently, the people strangely indifferent.[4]

It was along *Gran Via* on November 8th, 1936 that the hearts of the people were raised, as men of the International Brigades marched to join the defence of Madrid. This time the planes in the air were Soviet I-15 biplane fighters with Republican markings, which dipped their wings in salute to their new allies in combat. The people shouted *"Vivan los Rusos"* ("Long live the Russians") from the balconies but the Battalions, a huge boost to the morale of the city and its defenders, were made up of French, Germans, Poles, British and Americans. This was the 11th International Brigade, under the leadership of General Kleber, including some early British volunteers in the *Commune de Paris* Battalion. Among them were the writers John Sommerfield, Bernard Knox and John Cornford, and the attention given to them often gives rise to the mistaken view that this was a war fought mainly by intellectuals and writers.

The attack on Madrid

Advancing from the south of Spain with his Army of Africa – Moors with a reputation for ruthless savagery – Franco diverted to relieve the Republican siege of the Alcazar in Toledo. This was less a strategic error than a first indication of his desire to wage a war of attrition which would systematically purge the country of adversaries. He moved against Madrid at the beginning of November and, with the city expected to fall, the government left for Valencia. As the Nationalists approached from the south-west, the inhabitants were subjected to artillery bombardment but defended with all their energy, building barricades in the streets and fighting hand-to-hand as the militia desperately resisted machine-gun fire with whatever weapons they had.

Nationalist machine gun post in the Parque del Oeste, Madrid. An indication of how close the frontline was to the centre of the city. (© Author)

Having effectively lost its authority, the government handed out arms from its military depots and barracks in a bid to set up a volunteer army recruited by trade unions and Leftist groups and parties. This was the context in which *La Pasionaria*'s slogan *No Pasarán* (they shall not pass) came to the lips of the defiant citizens of Madrid and the Welsh volunteers.[5] The people joined with the militias in a battle which was hopelessly one-sided, their remarkable spirit mocking General Mola's boast that he would take coffee in the cobbled square of the Puerta de Sol by July 19th. The empty table reserved that day for the Nationalist General was never taken, and the coffee went cold.

To the east of the Royal Palace and beyond the river Manzanares lies Casa de Campo, now the largest urban park in Spain. It was from this direction that the Nationalists attacked, and here the Republicans repelled them in an intense and bloody struggle. The first Welshman engaged was Frank Thomas of Cardiff, who was fighting for the Nationalists. He had entered the park through breaches blown in the 12-foot high walls, and described with some satisfaction how his unit came across a Russian tank which they destroyed before the occupants realised their presence.[6] However, most of the park was eventually recaptured and the Nationalists were forced to abandon their direct attack on the city on November 23rd, with Franco withdrawing to prevent further losses of his best troops to a well-organised and determined defence. Yet the cost was high. That single week left a third of the 11th Brigade dead or dying in battle, and Madrid remained a city under siege from Nationalist artillery bombardment, air raids and militiamen in the streets.

Claude Cockburn, covering the war for the *Daily Worker,* was in Madrid at the beginning of November.[7] His chilling account tells of a single German Junkers dropping leaflets warning people of what was to happen, and the city bracing itself for the bombing. Fascist gunmen and militiamen fought in the streets as searchlights on the Capitol building in *Gran Via* sought out the planes, which regularly made seven attacks per day. Children playing and women in milk queues were machine-gunned, and bombs filled with bullets tore people to shreds. Fascist fifth columnists added to the horror by throwing bombs from the windows of buildings. In other despatches Cockburn described how the attacks had driven families to live, in the piercing cold and the biting wind of a Madrid winter, on the platforms of underground stations. Others with homes queued for hours for pieces of wood to burn.

Another moving account was given by Henry Buckley, the *Daily Telegraph's* correspondent in Spain.[8] After buying a newspaper on *Gran Via* at about 9.00pm on November 17th, 1936, he was shaken by a huge explosion at Carmen Market, one hundred yards away. This was the beginning of a five-hour onslaught, with thousands of incendiary bombs causing raging fires throughout the city. People were killed sheltering at Puerta del Sol underground station, the Savoy Hotel was gutted and the Prado museum took a direct hit. Rows of houses were on fire, and eight-story properties destroyed at a stroke by German Ju-52s. Nor were hospitals spared the bombing where injured and homeless people desperately sought shelter.

Jack S. Williams of Dowlais, in hospital in Madrid in June 1937, witnessed the city's continued suffering. He saw hundreds of women and children sleeping in metro stations and lay helpless at night in his hospital bed as fascist planes dropped their bombs, pursued by Republican planes. He wrote home: 'If British workers could experience this they would get together as they did in 1926 during the struggle against the means test in order to end the farce of non-intervention.'[9]

The early Welsh volunteers

Hundreds of volunteers from outside Spain had attached themselves to various militias – communist, anarchist and POUM – before the International Brigades were set up. James Albrighton, a student from Salisbury, enrolled in the Republican Army on October 2nd, 1936, and wrote a diary of those early experiences in which he mentioned a Welshman named Sydney Lloyd Jones, who had joined a couple of days later.[10] They became part of the Spanish MM (*Muerte es Maestro*) Centuria who were involved in 'special duties', including searching out and executing fascist spies in Madrid. They also fought at San Martin de Valdeiglesias and Navalcanero in the attempt to stem the Nationalist advance from Toledo to Madrid. Sydney Lloyd Jones died on October 14th, in action against the Moors and the Spanish Foreign Legion at Chapineria, about 30 miles west of Madrid. Albrighton described how three men, Sidney Lloyd Jones among them, were killed while repulsing a fascist attack on their flanks. He wrote: 'Their bravery and courage in continuing their fighting, despite all

A No Pasarán! banner – photographed in 1936 – in Calle de Toledo which leads into Madrid's main square, Plaza Major. (© Wikimedia Commons)

being wounded, was not in vain – it gave the new Centuria time to reach us.'[11] Sydney Lloyd Jones, about whom nothing else seems to be known, was the first Welshman to die in combat against fascism in Spain. He was buried with his comrades in a ditch that ran through the grove where they were fighting.

Of the others we know that Will Lloyd and Bob Condon of Aberaman, and Pat Murphy of Cardiff, had joined a battalion of French volunteers. They were in a unit which was sent, on Christmas Day, by train to the Cordoba front and, in January, to Las Rozas. However, it was not until December 1936 that the unit began to expand. When the newly formed British Battalion went into action at the Battle of Jarama in February 1937, there were probably about 30 Welsh volunteers among the 600 British troops. Among these early arrivals were Billy Davies of Tonypandy, David Joseph Jones of Penygraig, W.J. Davies, John Williams and Sam Morris of Ammanford, Tom Davies of Bedlinog, Michael O'Donogue of Merthyr Vale, Will Lloyd and Bob Condon of Aberaman, Pat Murphy, Bill Coles and Jack Taylor of Cardiff, and William Foulkes of Treorchy. Others who had tried to get into service had failed medicals or been captured.

Bob Condon had travelled with Will Lloyd, leaving on December 5th, 1936. Both wrote regularly to the *Aberdare Leader* newspaper with news about their activity in Spain. On one visit to Madrid they were a little surprised to see people going about their work quite ordinarily. Condon – badly shell-shocked at Jarama, and still suffering from a severe nervous condition – remembered how on that day British workers met Spanish workers, and without understanding each other's language, they 'understood the comradeship and the brotherhood of man'.

Will Lloyd had been victimised in his role as a workers' committee man in Aberdare's Gadlys pit. Forced to seek work in London, he and a comrade had continued their communist activities. He described in documents now housed at the Moscow Archives how he arrived in Spain in December 1936, and saw action quite early at the Cordoba front with an English-speaking company which was sent on Christmas Eve to counter a Nationalist offensive.[12] It was in this five-day siege of Lopera, under attack from seemingly endless formations of planes, that John Cornford and Ralph Fox were shot and killed. Lloyd's Battalion also was sent, in a diversionary move, to Las Rozas in January. He wrote to his mother that they had come through the first test and were now in the barber's shop with three weeks of growth.[13] Will, from a staunch communist family background, returned to Wales five months later as the elected representative of the British Battalion. His tasks were to raise funds for the dependants of those killed in Spain, recruit new volunteers and counter *Daily Mail* claims that volunteers had been offered substantial financial inducements.[14] He also wanted people to know that the morale of the men, post-Jarama, was still unshaken.

The British Battalion at the Battle of Jarama

The Republican forces had defeated the Nationalists' direct frontal assault on Madrid, and it was clear that the offensive had come to an exhausted halt. The Republicans had organised their fragmented forces well, and were also able to reinforce their position. The Nationalists turned to another battleground for their next offensive – a series of plateaux and valleys south-east of Madrid, including the Jarama valley. The river flowed along a wide flat plain about three kilometres wide, and beyond this were further steep slopes, hills and plateaux. Republican forces were slowly concentrating there for an offensive, but General José Miaja was reluctant to weaken his forces around Madrid in case of a surprise attack on the city.

The Nationalists aimed to stop supplies and isolate Madrid from the Republican Government in Valencia. This would be done by encircling the city from the south by crossing the river Jarama and cutting the Madrid-Valencia Road, followed by a further offensive to the north, at Guadalajara. Nationalist commander Colonel José Enrique Varela, an experienced and militarily distinguished campaigner, led five brigades with support from German troops and other battalions in reserve. About 25,000 Nationalists would confront 20,000 Republicans.

As dawn broke on February 6th, the Nationalists pushed from their initial front line, running directly south from Madrid, and drove the Republicans back with four thrusts over the next few days. During the first phase, from February 6th to the 10th, the Nationalists met varied levels of resistance and were hampered by bad weather. Phase two, from February 11th, saw them cross the river Jarama, first at Pindoque and then, at dawn on the 12th, in greater numbers at San Martin de la Vega, hiding under the bridge arches before taking the sentries by surprise. At this point, the 15th International

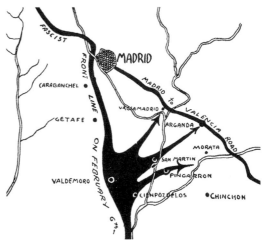

The three arms of the Nationalist front push forward towards the Madrid-Valencia road. (© Alan Warren)

Salute to a Comrade
and a Hero

W. COLES
WORKING-CLASS HERO

Died fighting Fascism at Jarama, Spain,
with the International Brigade.

Bill Coles, the first Welshman to fall at
Jarama, was a Labour activist from his youth.
(© Richard Burton Archives, Swansea Univ.)

Brigade, led by the Russian Colonel Gal, was deployed as an emergency force to prevent a breakthrough.

Bill Coles of Cardiff may have been one of the first Welshmen killed at Jarama, but it is not clear exactly when and how he died. The record of a meeting commemorating him, at Neath Street Hall, Cardiff, in December 1937 says that he died at Jarama Bridge, but does not specify whether it was Pindoque or San Martin. It described him as a very active member of the Labour movement, back to schooldays when he was known as the 'little Bolshie'.

His five years of military experience in the Welsh Guards had helped enormously in his role with the Republican forces. After leaving the army, he worked at East Moors Steel Works and, an avid reader of politics, was always raising important issues in the meetings of the Splott Labour Party and was instrumental in the formation of the League of Youth. His sister Nancy remembered how, when he was called by his mother for work, he replied: "I'm not going in today Mam – I'm off to Spain."[15]

For Bill Coles, Jarama was "one fight more, the best, and the last."[16]

The units of the 15th International Brigade at Jarama were the British 16th Battalion, the Slav Dimitrov, the German Thaelmann, the Italian Garibaldi, the Polish Dombrovski and the Franco-Belge Battalion, all under the 36th Division of the 5th Army Corps led by General Miaja. On February 7th, 1937, the British, including about 30 Welsh volunteers, left Madrigueras in a convoy of trucks. They assembled in the market place on a bitterly cold morning, and said their goodbyes to their comrades and personal friends. The mayor and local dignitaries stood, along with battalion leaders carrying the Republican flag, on a balcony overlooking the square. The mayor wished the men luck and victory over the fascists. George Aitken, the Battalion Commissar, responded and led three cheers of appreciation for the people of Madrigueras and their hospitality. Some villagers were in tears, and others cheered as the trucks left for the front.[17] Unfortunately, Will Lloyd departed in agony after

The farmhouse which was to serve as the Battalion's cookhouse. (© Author)

two unsuccessful teeth extractions, but had the problem treated in hospital and returned to the front line in the second day of the battle.[18]

The Battalion, now led by ex-public schoolboy, Oxford graduate and journalist Tom Wintringham, also received a warm welcome and food from the villagers of Chinchon, their destination near the front. The Battalion's four companies – three infantry and one machine-gun – were by now led by Kit Conway (No. 1); Harold Fry (No. 2, the machine-gun company); Bill Briskey (No. 3); and Bert Overton (No. 4).[19] Fighting alongside the Dimitrov and Franco-Belge Battalions, Wintringham had made last-minute preparations for the British Battalion, by issuing French steel helmets, getting water bottles filled and rifles cleaned and ensuring there were hot drinks and supplies in the Battalion cookhouse.[20] The men carried their recently-issued Russian rifles, which they had been working hard to master. The British Battalion had a full complement of more than 500 men and officers for its baptism of fire in battle. They, and the mostly Moorish infantry who opposed them, were to suffer heavy losses. The Nationalist air power was predominantly German – the Condor Legion which had so brutally destroyed Guernica.

The memoirs of Walter Gregory, who was brought up in Lincoln,[21] provide a useful detailed account of the major battles. He was present at Jarama until wounded by a rifle shot. He recounted how the British Battalion were first held in reserve at Chinchon, then on February 11th, hurriedly put on board a fleet of lorries which took them across the Tajuna Valley to the outskirts of Morata de Tajuna, a town in the foothills of the Sierra Pingarron. At sunrise on the 12th, a warm and sunny day, they began to march up the hillsides overlooking the town but were met by a messenger who warned them that the Nationalists had broken through.

Gregory described how they felt well-trained and ready for action, with every man clear about his position and duty.[22] Stopping for supplies at the farmhouse, which was to be the cookhouse during the campaign, the Battalion moved forward in the direction of the river, scrambling up a hill, across a plateau and dry valley and on to the next ridge. Wintringham was pleased with their movement and position – Briskey on the left, perfectly aligned with Overton in the middle, Fry behind Overton and Conway on the right. Then it all changed, as orders were given to change tactics and Wintringham became angry and fearful of the new deployment. Conway's company, initially to be held in reserve, was hurried to the line; Overton was told to swing over to the left and continue to the gorge of the River Jarama. The new formation saw gaps between the companies, who were now on what was later called 'Suicide Hill', begin to appear. Colonel Gal gave the orders to attack and the machine-gun fire got louder and nearer, as the bullets flew. The Moors then appeared, crawling expertly towards them, revealing that the Battalion was exposed on both flanks.

Jason Gurney, a British sculptor who had lived in Chelsea and served in Spain from December 1936 to August 1938, provided another perceptive eyewitness account.[23]

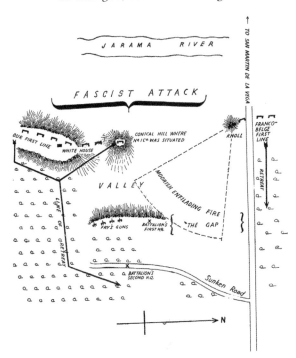

The positions taken by the Battalion – on the diagram the 'Sunken Road' is near the bottom and 'Suicide Hill' near the top. (© Alan Warren)

The 'Sunken Road'. (© Author)

He describes how numerous men, struggling with the climb and not expecting a long engagement, left belongings in the olive groves before they started climbing. He came across abandoned overcoats, ammunition, spares and books of all kinds, including Marxist textbooks, pornography, poetry and the works of Nietzsche. Over the ridge they crossed one of the many sunken roads created over centuries in Spain by mule and ox carts.

They then went down into the Jarama valley, under orders from the Battalion's headquarters to continue the advance. Yet there were problems. While there were plenty of machine-guns and light automatics, there were four different kinds, each requiring different ammunition. Many were discarded within the hour. Lack of maps, the inability to assess positions with any accuracy, poorly-maintained communication equipment and inadequate training all hampered their ability to cope with swift, skilful attacks by the Moors.[24]

Yet all seemed under control. The four companies held a superior position, commanding the slope down to the Jarama river, and felt that the enemy would be completely exposed if they attempted to cross the plateau in front of them. However, when the Battalion followed Gal's order to advance along the whole of the front, it came under such fierce attack that it was forced back to *Casa Blanca*, a white-washed farmhouse on top of the ridge. It was a catastrophic onslaught on the Brigaders, who had no answer to the artillery shells and heavy machine-gun fire, and were not equipped to deal with the elite troops of Franco's Moor army.

The volunteers' very basic training now left them extremely vulnerable and the lack of ammunition, which they blamed on British non-intervention, made things worse. There were reports that the wrong ammunition had been loaded into the belts of Fry's machine-gunners, leaving them only rifles to stem the tide of the Moors. The lorry, driven back after collecting the correct cartridges by a drunk Sergeant 'H' (Hornsby), was later found overturned in a ditch. Wintringham and Overton's report on the action would raise the possibility that the cartridge problem was an act of sabotage. Yet Fry's men retrieved some of the ammunition, and used it to halt the Moors' advance. Tony Hyndman of Cardiff was one of the group that dragged the ammunition boxes across two sloping ploughed fields. He recounts that the guns were on metal wheels, and each man held the side of the gun in one hand and a box of ammunition in the other. His partner in the team caught a bullet and had to be pushed off the gun. He also describes how 'the guns bubbled over with heat, drying up. For the final burst we all urinated into a steel helmet. Some liquid was poured into each gun as the light of the day ended.'[25]

A barrage of artillery and heavy machine-gun fire continued for about three hours. It concentrated first on the *Casa Blanca* hill, which became completely obscured in dust and smoke, with Company No. 3 taking the brunt along the nearby knoll. As Company No. 1 tried to dig down for cover, a steady stream of walking wounded and stretcher-bearers came from both positions. Company No. 4 also suffered the same fate. Gurney was, understandably, extremely critical of orders to hold the line at all costs on an exposed hillside, against heavy artillery and the advancing

George Fretwell of Penygroes was killed on the first day of the Battle of Jarama. (© Richard Burton Archives, Swansea Univ.)

What became known as 'Suicide Hill' is here seen from the 'Sunken Road'. The Jarama valley and the city of Madrid are in the background. (© Author)

Moors. He describes a broken Battalion, beaten by heavier firepower, superior numbers and superior skills. Talk of holding their ground after the battering they'd received seemed absurd.

George Ernest Fretwell of Penygroes was one of many killed on this tragic first day. A committed member of the Territorials with the rank of sergeant, his family did not know he had volunteered for Spain. He had asked his brother to look after his bicycle and then disappeared. They received one letter from him, and heard no more until they were informed the following year that he was 'missing believed killed'.

His village was shocked by his death, with many feeling proud of his heroism but many others resentful at the loss of such a young life. It was not until 1970 that they knew exactly how and where he was killed, thanks to fellow Welsh Brigader Tom Glyn Evans, who had been with Fretwell in Spain. On January 7th, 1991, a plaque was unveiled at a ceremony attended by more than 50 people in the Memorial Hall in Penygroes, Carmarthenshire. It reads, in Welsh: 'In memory of George Ernest Fretwell who lost his life whilst

Water bottles, some with bullet holes, found in the region of Morata de Tajuña.
(© Gregorio Salcedo Diaz)

fighting with the International Brigade in the Spanish Civil War 1936-1939 at Jarama Valley February 12th, 1937.'[26]

On the same day, Jack Taylor of Cardiff and London was seriously injured, and later died. James Prendergast explained in the *Irish Democratic* of November 20th, 1936, how, with Kit Conway in command of a number of companies, they moved upward from the sunken road and saw Taylor, drenched in blood, dressing a wounded comrade. "Hit bad?" he enquired. "Unconscious, thumbs up, I guess" was the reply. Prendergast noticed blood seeping through the back of Jack's trousers and asked him if he was hit. "Yes, but in a fleshy part", were his last words to Prendergast.

The British now had no alternative but to retreat to the plateau and the Battalion's headquarters. This took some time, and came despite orders from Gal to hold on at all costs. Two of the four company commanders were dead, one was out of action and only Harold Fry was left in position. Kit Conway had been shot while exposed, perhaps even standing up. Bill Briskey was also dead and Overton had lost his nerve and was seen away from his company, lying behind a ridge, weeping. As the men withdrew with their wounded, the Moors moved into their abandoned position on the ridge.

However, there was some retribution for the Battalion. The Moors did not know, as they charged over the ridge, that the machine-guns were now working. The correct ammunition had turned up, and was being loaded into the guns. Harold Fry and Fred Copeman had been racing against time to get the right ammunition and Copeman seems to have taken charge at this point. A battalion of Moors, in full dress with flowing cloaks and flashes of red from the linings, appeared from the hills expecting to mop up after the battle. Copeman recorded that his men were straining at the leash as the Moors advanced not knowing that the eight Maxims were now in action, and with plenty of ammunition.[27] The Moors charged across the valley in full battle cry, but the gunners were held back until they were in open ground. Then orders were given to fire, leading to a terrible and almost complete slaughter with piles of bodies left in the aftermath.

The offensive had been checked, yet about half of the Battalion had died in seven hours of fierce fighting. Of the 400 riflemen, only 125 remained. Some survivors lay horribly wounded on the battlefield or at the side of the sunken road; others were found huddled in a farmhouse or at the cookhouse, stunned and shocked from what they had experienced. Some took time to reform, after emerging from the olive groves, either at the Battalion's headquarters or the cookhouse.

The utter confusion of the day was illustrated by what Jason Gurney described as one of the ghastliest scenes he had ever seen. Making his way down the sunken road, he came across a group of wounded men who had been carried back from No. 3 Company's attack on the *Casa Blanca* hill to a hollow by the side of the road. They had arrived at a non-existent field dressing station and, instead of being taken to the hospital, had been forgotten. There were about 50 men on stretchers, all with appalling wounds, calling for help and water. Gurney wrote: 'I was filled with such horror at their suffering and my inability to help them that I felt I had suffered some permanent injury to my spirit from which I would never entirely recover.'[28] The *Brigade Handbook* admits the mistakes – the absence, all day, of the machine-guns, the bungling of the ammunition belts, the bad communications – yet the momentum of the enemy offensive was stalled because of the 'stubborn, not-an-inch stand of our men, their holding out against overwhelming fire superiority, their courage in untenable positions, their refusal to realise when they were beaten.'[29]

The town of Morata de Tajuna lies in the valley of the river Tajuna, about 35 kilometres south-west of Madrid. On the edge of the town the *El Cid* restaurant houses a museum set up by Gregorio Salcedo, an inhabitant who as a child started to collect scrap metal and artefacts of the war from the nearby battlefield.

It has a remarkable collection of bullets, missiles, weapons, photographs and other paraphernalia from the Civil War. Just a few kilometres outside the town is the sunken road which played such a major part in the battle. It now snakes through the countryside as a rough dusty path. What became known as 'Suicide Hill' is clearly visible from the road and it is still possible to see the neglected trenches and bunkers, some with deep tunnels featuring an entrance and separate exit. Men had slept, in great pain, on the sides of the sunken road with their moans and cries audible all night. Listening posts had been set up, sentries posted and, where there were picks and shovels, the volunteers dug in. Food and drink had appeared, but the cold chilled the bones. Those who managed to get some sleep were roused again at 3am when rifles were cleaned, ammunition loaded and water bottles filled. Fry's guns were out front, but secure with their flanks covered. They had fired at intervals during the night but, as dawn broke, the gunners observed enemy soldiers who had pushed forward and had rested for the night at the bottom of the valley. They were allowed to advance until they were close enough to be dealt with by the machine-gun fire. In the meantime, new Republican troops strengthened the British Left, but appeared very tired. Wintringham was also very aware of lack of cover on his right flank.

Other battalions were having a hard time as they engaged with reinforced enemy brigades. The rumour was that there was to be a Republican counter-offensive, with tanks and planes. Several orders were given to advance, but were ignored by Wintringham who regarded them as impossible. The tanks did not appear, and a waiting game began. The sunken road was sprayed with machine-gun fire, but to little effect. Although the Franco-Belge Battalion had lost all of its machine-guns, Fry's company was still active in front of the sunken road, but began to attract the attention of enemy artillery.

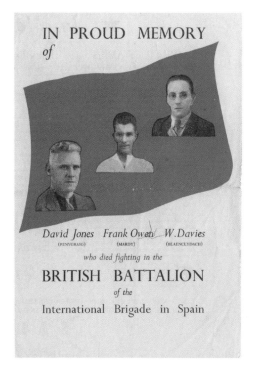

Memorial pamphlet for David Jones, Frank Owen, Willie Davies (© Richard Burton Archives, Swansea Univ.)

To take pressure off the other battalions, Wintringham and George Aitken took a party of about 40 men and headed south, away from the sunken road, before turning west to simulate an attack on the flank of the gunners who were attacking Fry. Movement and rifle fire from that direction kept up the bluff for some time, but the situation was deteriorating. There was no sign of any meaningful tank support, and the diversionary attackers returned to the sunken road. It was not long before the rebel artillery opened up in earnest on Fry's machine-gunners, leading to the disastrous capture of the company. How this happened is unclear, but it seems that Overton led his company into a frenzied retreat to the sunken road. This exposed Fry's right flank, allowing enemy soldiers to creep up on the high ground above the gunners and overrun them.

In the confusion, they were recognised as the enemy far too late. Bill Meredith described in the *Brigade Handbook* how, after returning from delivering a message to the Battalion's headquarters, he saw a number of fascists coming forward singing the *Internationale* and raising their fists in the anti-fascist salute. They were welcomed by men who assumed they were deserters, and reciprocated the salute. More swarmed over the top and then the firing began, bullets filling the air as the deception was made clear. Another account holds that members of the Foreign Legion, who had relieved the Moors after their heavy losses, infiltrated the gun positions and were mistaken at first for volunteers. Then the captured gunners began defiantly to sing the *Internationale*. When Will Lloyd entered the fray after his dental surgery he asked a member of the Battalion what the position was there. "A bloody shambles," was the reply. "The machine-gun company has been captured and no one seems to know what is happening."

It was on this day that David Joseph Jones, an unemployed miner from George Street, Penygraig who lived in London, was killed by a sniper. At the memorial meeting for him and two other fellow Welsh Brigaders – Frank Owen and Willie Davies – Jones, an ex-Grenadier Guardsman, was described as 'a splendid comrade, capable and reliable. His previous military training was utilised to the full in helping to train his comrades and sustaining their morale under fire. He carried his political convictions to the uttermost, making the supreme sacrifice.' [30]

On the morning of February 14th, the third day of the battle, the sunken road was still being held and was now the frontline. After a night of intermittent firing, the men were still there, hungry and exhausted, many on their third day without food because of the fragility of supplies. The commander of No.1 company wrote: 'On the morning of February 14th there was no breakfast, although I had sent four men to fetch it. They never came back.' [31] Franco's army made another attack, this time supported by tanks, and the line was finally broken as the Moors surged forward. It was a total slaughter, with the Spanish company taking the full brunt of the attack.

The Battalion records tell of a Welsh comrade, known to the men as 'Taffy', bravely defending his sector against a frontal attack.[32] He got quite near to the enemy, bayonet at the ready, but was shot down. This could have been 34-year-old Harold Davies of Elias Street, Neath, whose certificate of death, issued by the International Brigades and signed by Battalion Commissar George Aitken, shows he was killed on that day. George Eaton describes him as a young man with no political opinions, but a lover of adventure.[33] On the death certificate is written: 'His loss is mourned by all anti-fascist fighters serving with the International Brigades in Spain.'

Davies would have been buried in a communal grave. His parents wrote to Alwyn Skinner, who in turn wrote to Will Paynter, seeking information. Skinner reported different views from the men who fought at Jarama. Some thought Davies was killed, others that he disappeared on a ship that landed in Swansea, although Skinner was positive that no International Brigader landed at Swansea in this way. Harold Davies' death was reported in the *Neath Guardian* on October 1st. That the same article also reported a denial of persistent rumours of Alwyn Skinner's death by his brother epitomised the confusion both at home and in Spain.

Arthur Morris, from Cardigan, died fighting with the Irish Connolly Unit. He is said to have 'won their hearts' for being so cool and calm under fire. (© Anthony Richards)

With the Nationalists on the verge of breaking through to the Valencia Road, there was now no option but to retreat down the hill to the cookhouse. Men were scattered everywhere, straggling down the slopes dispirited and beaten, heartbroken at the loss of so many comrades. Will Lloyd wrote that what was meant to be an orderly retreat became total chaos as panic set in and men ran for their lives into the groves: 'I too began to run; a bullet struck my helmet and went spinning off in front of me. I hurtled down the hill and lay behind a large rock, looking around I saw the silhouette of an enemy on the skyline. I fired, and watched as he crumbled and collapsed.'[33]

There then took place one of the iconic moments of the British campaign, often called the 'Great Rally'. It was inspired by the commander of the 15th International Brigade, Colonel Gal, who praised the remarkable endurance of the Battalion, but explained the urgency of filling a dangerous gap to stop the Madrid-Valencia road being exposed. Jock Cunningham and Frank Ryan began an amazing rally, leading a gradual build-up of 140 blooded and tired men, some singing. They were joined, in amazement, by men from other battalions who had been lying around exhausted. From the swelling column came a rising volume of song until the ridge was reclaimed. Initially there was no plan, no sections, no companies, only cries of '*Adelante*' (forward) and individual determination to repel the fascists. Steadily, as they hugged the earth and inched forward, the volunteer's military training saw them reform as an effective fighting force which alarmed the rebel soldiers into thinking that these were fresh troops and a much larger force than they faced a day or so earlier. Unnerved, Franco's troops withdrew to their previous positions, and the Brigade held the line until Republican reinforcements arrived. Although

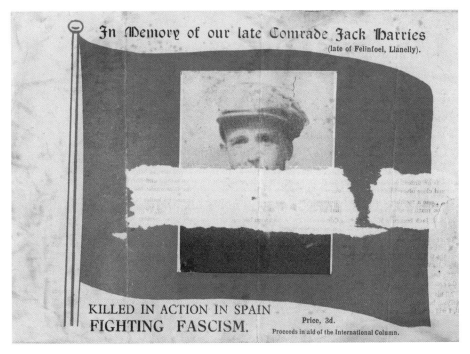

Memorial pamphlet for Jack Harries who was regarded in Llanelli as having tremendous enthusiasm for the cause of workers' rights. It is believed he died from friendly or fifth columnist fire.

there was further fighting, that was the position held by both sides until near the end of the war. It was an incredible rally.

Republican medical services reported that three of their mobile units had treated more than 2,500 wounded men at the front during the first few days of fighting. The Welsh wounded included Bob Condon, Billy Davies, William Morrison of Mardy, and William John Thomas of Aberavon. Both David Hooper of Gelli and Tony Hyndman of Cardiff went missing after suffering shell-shock. Harold Patterson of Penarth reported sick at Jarama, and then disappeared. Bob Condon was seen advancing towards the enemy in a dazed state and had to be held down while a medic injected a sedative.[34]

The victory at Jarama stemmed the fascists' advance on Madrid, but at enormous cost. Estimates differ widely, between 6,000 and 20,000 men lost by the Nationalists and at least 10,000 by the Republicans. Bill Alexander summarised the British Battalion's actions as brave and defiant: '...Jarama was its first major trial. The facts show that it came through with a record of individual grit, courage and determination which set standards for all its future fighting.'[35] Yet the Battalion was almost wiped out, with perhaps fewer than 100 men in any fit state to continue. Most of the political and military commanders were lost, positions that had to be filled from the ranks, and Spanish troops and new volunteers from Madrigueras were quickly drafted in.

There was a desperate need for volunteers and, as we shall see, Wales provided. Harry Stratton of Swansea was one of 80 volunteers to arrive in Morata de Tajuna on February 15th. He described how, although he had only done rifle drill with a stick, they were issued with Russian rifles. At dusk they were brought to some trenches, which they tried to improve as best they could.[36] Remarkably, one more military action was asked of the Brigade. As well as being controversial and unpopular, it took the life of Welshman Arthur Morris. He was born in Cardigan and grew up there until he was 21, emigrated to Canada where he served in the army, and then worked as a miner. Joining the Communist Party amid high levels of unemployment and harsh living conditions, he became a busy union activist.

Having enrolled in 1936 in the International Lenin School in Moscow, he followed the rest of the students to Spain and joined the Americans who formed the Abraham Lincoln Battalion at Albacete. He joined the Battalion as a motorcyclist on February 4th, 1937. On February 27th, a wet and dreary morning, Gal ordered them to attack on the front between San Martin de la Vega and the hills of Pingarron. In what was described as a poorly executed attack, they were shot to pieces by Nationalist machine-guns.[37] Fighting with the Irish Connolly Unit, Arthur Morris was described as calm and cool under fire. Although under orders to attack, he was remembered for his concern to rescue a wounded comrade. Unable to return to him during a lull in fighting, he was killed instantly by an explosive bullet through the head. It is clear that in his short time in Spain he was known as a popular and inspirational comrade.[38]

For the British the conflict continued, but shifted into a more trench-based warfare. The early diary notes of the volunteers and other accounts build up a picture of sporadic action, isolated incidents and periods of rest at the village of Morata. There was also a steady toll from sniper attacks, probably the cause of death of Jack Harries of Llanelli who died in the trenches following the major battle. A volunteer's diary entry for Friday April 2nd, recorded: 'Went up the line with Jock. On arriving, heard the news that Comrade Harries had been killed by a bullet in the neck'.[39] Michael O'Donoghue, however, suggests that it may have been the result of fascists working behind the lines. He mentions a Scottish volunteer sitting down beside him who took a bullet in the back of the neck – 'that shot never came from the enemy.' He says the explosive bullet that killed Harries was a ricochet off one of the olive trees which ripped out his throat.[40]

Aged 35, Jack Harries was educated at Old Road School and the Council School at Felinfoel, Llanelli. He was a mineworker at the Acorn Colliery, Llangennech which closed in September 1936, and had served in the Royal Engineers, but was unemployed during the economic depression. He was a great lover of music, a talented pianist who often performed at charity events, a leader in singing the Battalion's revolutionary songs and an avid reader of classical, economic and political literature. His last words at home were: "If I don't come back, it is because I have laid down my life for people like you. But if all goes well, I will come back, even if I have to swim."[41] On March 20th he wrote to his landlady from hospital explaining that his wound was only a scratch, and that he had to be back in the frontline soon.[42] In a letter on March 25th to Idris Cox, the Communist Party south Wales district organiser, he wrote: 'I am glad to inform you that all the Welsh boys are in excellent condition…we have always led the Battalion in singing revolutionary songs, cracking jokes, and generally being the foremost in any kind of fighting.' He died just a week later. Some of his possessions – a pair of spectacles, four shillings, unemployment insurance cards – were given to his brother Howell along with a letter of condolence from Harry Pollitt.[43]

Danger was everywhere. In one incident, following a bombardment on a flank occupied by Republican troops, D.R. Davies of Crumlin and two comrades went to investigate. When they came to the last section of the Jarama front guarded by the government's unit, they found the trenches were abandoned. Advancing down the trenches, they found a dead mule which had been used to deliver food, and then ran into a group of Nationalist soldiers. Uncertain if this was the enemy, they held fire until a grenade was thrown at them, then retreated into an olive grove and approached the rebels in a circular movement. The ensuing skirmish brought home the proximity of Nationalist units.[44] Davies volunteered with others to return to the scene of the morning's fighting and spend an hour digging trenches. On returning to the sector he stood next to a French officer who was very skilled with a rifle, but after a number of successful shots appeared to become complacent and took a bullet in the head.[45]

The notes made by the volunteers at the time are often brief but vivid.[46] Lice were a continuing problem. The men took advantage of mobile showers, and on one occasion their clothes were put into a large drum and the lice were gassed. Jack Murray of Nantyffyllon was writing a diary to be sent to his wife if he were to be killed. He was known as a warm-hearted Welshman devoted to his family, the thought of his son Ken bringing tears to his eyes.[47] For Bob Condon the military stalemate was an opportunity to dig a proper trench as opposed to the first one he had built on Christmas night at Cordoba – six inches deep with the aid of a pen knife.[48] Alec Cummings of Cardiff described a time when their position was flooded. Other diary extracts from the men read: 'my chest feels terrible; we have just finished burying the dead; grand concert this evening; had a bath today – needed it badly; had a surprise when reading *Daily Worker* – it reports my death; two comrades came over from the fascist lines; we have been in the front line now for 41 days without being relieved.'

Supplying food was a challenge, involving sliding from position to position in the mud and dodging bullets. Life was difficult and morale was low. Men had lost their comrades and their commanders. Many were exhausted and stressed, ill and demoralised. Harry Stratton remembers a short break at Morata when he was the 14th to use the same razor blade, and using the latrine when all he had to clean himself with was one cigarette paper.[49]

Sanitation became an issue and, although dysentery shows no favour, the British were more susceptible when they insisted on tea made in helmets with unboiled water. *Our Fight* journal,[50] described as the organ of the 15th Brigade at the front, stated forcefully that the efficiency of the Brigade would be hampered unless toilet habits improved, and suggested that suitable latrines should be dug and washing places established. The same edition complained about waste in the trenches, with food and clothing thrown away and too many olive trees destroyed for use in building shelters. These *chabolas*, made from branches, mud and grass were the idea of young Spanish conscripts brought in as reinforcements. A typical day's orders included breakfast at 7.30am, cleaning and inspection of billets, military exercises, dinner at 12.30pm, sick parade, baths and supper at 7.30pm. Other expectations were: no more than two blankets; only official latrines to be used; water bottles to be filled during the day; no less than 50 pesetas to be sent to home at one time; and each company to appoint a postman to oversee the mail.

Desertion was a major problem as men found their military position hopeless, their conditions intolerable, and with little hope of leaving the front line unless they went without permission. Those who suggested harsh measures for deserting, such as shooting, were shouted down since these men were not conscripts but volunteers, and the effect on further volunteering would have been disastrous. However, Battalion Commissar George Aitken had strong words for 'grumblers' and 'weaker elements' in the ranks who were decisively condemned by the vast majority.[51] Such grumbling was seen to weaken discipline and morale, making it easier for enemy agents to penetrate the ranks and continue their disruptive work. This paranoia regarding Francoist spies, Trotskyists and fifth columnists haunted the whole campaign. The *Daily Worker* of March 30th, 1937, published a speech by Stalin about 'the wrecking, divisive and spying work of the agents of foreign countries, among whom the Trotskyists have played an active enough role …have penetrated not only into the lower organisations but also into some responsible positions.'

Then there was the grim task of burying the dead, if there was an opportunity to do so, although many were not given their own resting place. Before leaving Jarama, graves were roughly dug with cairns of stones in the shape of the five-pointed star. Another song was written at this time, sung to the tune of *Red River Valley*, which was a satirical swipe at the time spent, in spite of promises, waiting in the trenches to be relieved. The first verse of which is:

> *'There's a valley in Spain called Jarama,*
> *That's a place that we all know so well.*
> *For 'tis there that we wasted our manhood,*
> *And most of our old age as well.'*

'Potato' Jones and the blockade runners

The spring of 1937 saw another battle involving Welshmen and Welsh ships,[52] motivated no doubt by a sound mixture of commercial enterprise and concern for the welfare of an oppressed minority. Once Franco announced that merchant ships were not allowed to enter ports in northern Spain, vessels taking supplies to Spain were intercepted by Nationalist warships. The Cardiff-based *Western Mail* carried numerous reports of Welsh ships caught up in this, with some captured by Franco's navy. The Cardiff steamer *Molton* and its crew of seamen from Cardiff docks was captured off Santander,[53] as was the Cardiff-registered *Candleston Castle*. The Swansea trader *British Corporal* was bombed, unsuccessfully, in the Mediterranean, but the Newport steamer, *St Quentin*, was damaged by

Nationalist aircraft at Valencia. More seriously, Heaton describes the sinking of the Cardiff-chartered *Andra* on April 5th, 1937, and ten other Welsh ships sunk by Nationalist forces in 1938-1939. The blockade of ports such as Bilbao was a blow to the Basque people already desperate for food. British ships could only be protected outside the three-mile territorial limit, while the British Admiralty accepted reports – later disproved – that the waters were mined and that it was too dangerous for any merchant ship to enter Bilbao. They instructed any ships in the vicinity to head for the French port of St. Jean de Luz.

Three of the ships that docked at St Jean de Luz were Welsh-owned and their captains soon acquired nicknames linked to their cargo: 'Potato' Jones, 'Corn Cob' Jones and 'Ham and Egg' Jones. 'Potato' Jones was captain of the *Marie Llewellyn* and carried a load of potatoes on top of, allegedly, a load of arms. He had no intention of obeying Admiralty instructions and at 4.00pm on April 15th, the *Marie Llewellyn* set out, pitching heavily on a swell, in the direction of the Spanish coast.

There are different accounts of what then happened from this point. *The Times* reported that 'Potato' Jones' ship was halted by a British destroyer before it could try to make port. Other accounts, strongly supported by eyewitness accounts from sailors on HMS *Hood,* suggest that he made it. They say that he successfully ran the blockade and was escorted in by British destroyers, with the *Hood* circling a Spanish warship to prevent interference. An interview with Percy Thomas Price, a gunner on the HMS *Hood*, corroborates those written accounts. He relates how the *Hood* was taken to 'follow the blockade of the stuff going into Bilbao. This ship was a runner because he had potatoes on board and they called him 'Potato' Jones and we had to go round there to let him in, get him in there. There was *(sic)* about three Spanish warships alongside come out to us and…the turrets just trained their guns and away they went – they shoot off quick *(sic)*.'[54]

Whatever the truth, the legend of 'Potato' Jones or *Juan Patatero* was born. There is no doubt, though, about the Captain Roberts and the Cardiff-registered steamer, *Seven Seas Spray*. On April 19th, at 10pm it slipped out of St Jean de Luz into the darkness without either permission from the harbour master or navigation lights. Warned by a British destroyer, *en route*, that he was proceeding at his own risk, Captain Roberts steamed ahead and sailed into Bilbao with 4,000 tons of food, finally escorted by Basque warships and planes and cheered by thousands of waving people. Both the British and the Nationalists were stunned by this success, and the Nationalists stepped up their patrols. Despite some skirmishing between British and Nationalist vessels, other ships were able to discharge their cargoes, including 'Corn Cob' Jones' *Macgregor*.[55] Captain Roberts of Penarth and his daughter Fifi enjoyed the hospitality of a people who were grateful that the myth of the mining of their harbour had been debunked.[56]

Notes

1. Peter Darman, *Heroic Voices of the Spanish Civil War*, London, New Holland Publishers, 2009, pp.80-86.
2. *The Spanish Civil War: A Personal Viewpoint,* Unpublished manuscript, Richard Burton Archives, Swansea University.
3. George Orwell, *Homage to Catalonia*, op. cit., pp.2-5.
4. For a fascinating study of the ways in which volunteers interpreted two potent cultural signifiers in Spain during the Civil War – dress and demeanour, see Elizabeth Roberts, 'British and American Volunteers and the Politics of Dress and Demeanour in the Spanish Civil War', *Limina*, Vol.14, University of Sydney, 2008.
5. Dolores Ibarruri, *They Shall Not Pass*, London, Lawrence & Wishart, 1966, p.252.
6. Robert Stradling, *Brother Against Brother*, Stroud, Sutton Publishing, 1998, p.66.
7. James Pettifer (Ed.), *Cockburn in Spain*, London, Lawrence & Wishart, 1986, p.115.
8. Henry Buckley, *Life and Death of the Spanish Republic*, London, I.B.Tauris, 2014, pp.264-6. Paul Preston describes the contribution made by other newspaper correspondents to accounts of the siege of Madrid in *We Saw Spain Die*, London, Constable, 2008, pp.22-61. Preston's view of Cockburn and Buckley's work is similar to many others: the former's writing was not always based on accurate information and the latter was a much respected correspondent who left an enduring record of the war.
9. Letter to Dora and Idris Cox, in *Miners Against Fascism*, p.279. In a letter to the *Aberdare Leader* (May 29th, 1937) Bob Condon describes how people were refusing to be intimidated by the bombing and are very welcoming to the Brigaders.
10. Marx Memorial Library, Box 50. The death of Sydney Lloyd Jones is also referred to in Bill Alexander, *British Volunteers for Liberty*, op. cit., p.53, and Richard Baxell, *British Volunteers in the Spanish Civil War*, op. cit., p.171.
11. James Albrighton, *Diary*, IBA Box 50, File L.
12. RGASPI 545/6/163.
13. *Aberdare Leader*, February 27th, 1937.
14. *Aberdare Leader*, April 25th, 1937, and also letter written from the International Brigade base in Albacete to *Comite Internationale d'aide au Peuple* asking them to help his return with no delay. (RGASPI 545/6/163).
15. See Robert Stradling, *Cardiff and the Spanish Civil War*, Cardiff, Butetown History and Arts Centre, p.88. According to Coles' sister they received one letter of reassurance from him, then someone told the family that he had died fighting at Jarama. Although they heard rumours that he been seen alive he never returned and they assumed that he had died in Spain.

16. Memorial service pamphlet, Richard Burton Archives, Swansea University.
17. Frank Graham, *Battle of Jarama*, Newcastle, 1987, p.9.
18. Will Lloyd, unpublished memoirs – http://crazydruid.net/Politicsandmedia Willmemoirs.html.
19. Richard Baxell, *British Volunteers in the Spanish Civil War*, op. cit., pp.71ff.
20. Tom Wintringham, *English Captain*, op. cit., p.60.
21. Walter Gregory, *The Shallow Grave: A Memoir of the Spanish Civil War*, London, Victor Gollancz, 1986.
22. Ibid., p.45.
23. *Crusade in Spain*, Newton Abbot, Readers Union, 1967. For an extremely detailed account of the battle from the perspective of a number of key individuals, see Ben Hughes, *They Shall Not Pass: The British Battalion at Jarama – The Spanish Civil War*, Oxford, Osprey Publishing, 2011.
24. Ibid., pp.101ff.
25. For Hyndman's short account of his experience in Spain see V. Cunningham (Ed.), *Spanish Front Writers on the Civil War*, Oxford, Oxford University Press, 1968, p.35.
26. See website.- http://www.nantlle.com/history-pen-y-groes-george-fretwell.htm.
27. Fred Copeman, *Reason in Revolt*, op. cit., pp.92-3.
28. Op. cit., p.114. One doctor with the 12th International Brigade describes the wounded on stretchers on the Chinchon road as being systematically killed by the Moors, a situation which led to the Brigades' stretcher-bearers pledging not to leave a wounded man on the battlefield if at possible – cited by Linda Palfreeman in *Salud: British Volunteers in the Republican Medical Service During the Spanish Civil War*, Brighton, Sussex Academic Press, 2012, p.87.
29. Frank Ryan (Ed.), *The Book of the XV Brigade*, Pontypool, Warren & Pell, p.53. The slaughter had been such that no communication from British survivors was allowed with the advancing Lincoln Battalion so that there would no effect on morale. (See Cecil D Eby, *Comrades and Commissars*, Pennsylvania, The Pennsylvania State University Press, 2007, p.56.)
30. Memorial service pamphlet for David Jones, Frank Owen and Willie Davies: Richard Burton Archives, Swansea University.
31. Frank Graham, *Battle of Jarama*, op. cit., p.22.
32. Frank Ryan (Ed.), *The Book of the XV Brigade*, op. cit., p.57.
33. Will Lloyd, unpublished memoirs.
34. Ibid.
35. Bill Alexander, *British Volunteers for Liberty*, op. cit., p.101.
36. Harry Stratton, *To Anti-Fascism by Taxi*, op. cit., p.35.
37. Richard Baxell, Unlikely Warriors, op. cit., p.161.
38. Research kindly provided by Anthony Richards of Pembrokeshire.
39. Frank Graham, *Battle of Jarama*, op. cit., p.64.
40. Interview with Hywel Francis, 21/09/69.
41. Memorial pamphlet in memory of Jack Harris, Richard Burton Archives, Swansea University.

42. Ibid.

43. *Llanelli Star*, May 15th, 1937.

44. Frank Graham, *Battle of Jarama*, op. cit., p.53.

45. Ibid., p.54. For an American Lincoln perspective on the incident see Cecil D. Eby, *Comrades and Commissars*, op. cit., pp.94-6.

46. Frank Graham, *Battle of Jarama*, op. cit., passim.

47. Ibid., p.28.

48. From a 'journal' written for the *Aberdare Leader* over five days from May 9th.

49. Harry Stratton, *To Anti-Fascism by Taxi*, op. cit., p.40.

50. *Our Fight* No. 13, March 1937. In addition to the obvious physical threat from military action, hygiene and disease protection was essential. The three main problems seemed to be sexually transmitted infections, malaria and typhoid infections; Linda Palfreeman, *Salud: British Volunteers in the Republican Medical Service During the Spanish Civil War*, Brighton, Sussex Academic Press, 2012, pp.83-4.

51. *Our Fight*, No. 1.

52. See especially P.M. Heaton, *Welsh Blockade Runners in the Spanish Civil War*, Risca, The Starling Press, 1985.

53. *South Wales Echo*, July 16th, 1937.

54. HMS *Hood* Association website.

55. It was after the blockade and the bombing of Guernica that the British government relented in allowing child refugees from the Basque country. Many came to impoverished Welsh communities where they were generously cared for. See especially Hywel Davies, *Fleeing Franco*, Cardiff, University of Wales Press, 2011.

56. For a graphic description of the arrival of the *Seven Seas Spray* and other vessels at Bilbao see the first-hand account of G.L. Steer in *The Tree of Gernika*, London, Faber and Faber, 2009, pp.197-209. The 2009 edition is an reprint of the 1938 edition.

5

A Brave Disaster

The Brigades At Brunete

Brunete and Villanueva de la Cañada

In mid-June 1937, the 15th International Brigade was withdrawn, for rest and recuperation, from the Jarama front to Mondejar in the province of Guadalajara. Fred Copeman recalls it as a comfortable time in beautiful countryside, with morale improving following the battering at Jarama.[1] The wounded men needed time to recover and those who were physically unscathed were exhausted. Many of their comrades hadn't been so fortunate, having died in action, while others opted to desert, of which most were quickly arrested and imprisoned. This was the time when Will Paynter was sent to Spain by the south Wales branch of the Communist Party in order to, as he put it, 'look after the Battalion's interests at the International Brigade's Headquarters and to deal with individual and other problems.'[2]

The main problem was repatriating those who wanted to go home because they were exhausted, wounded and traumatised.[3] He had become the 'friend of the weary, the sick and the halt'.[4] Many were being encouraged to return home by wives and family who were struggling to manage without them or their maintenance payments, and Paynter was sympathetic but firm, apparently showing greater understanding and compassion than other members of the Commissariat. He worked to establish a specific hospital for British volunteers and advocated repatriation for wounded men over 40. There were also problems, often due to personality clashes, in the leadership of the Battalion and indiscipline in the ranks.

Paynter arrived at the Jarama front to find them dug in after the horrors of the conflict. They needed a break from the trenches, but the lines had to be maintained. Harry Stratton of Swansea told Paynter that he'd had no contact with his wife, but had heard that she was not receiving any financial support and he wanted to return home at the end of July, after six months

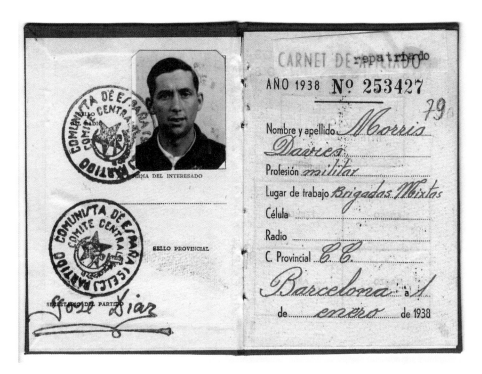

The International Brigade identity card of Morris Davies of Treharris. (© Deputy Director RGASPI, Moscow)

of service in Spain. As Jim Brewer explained, many volunteers thought they could also volunteer out, wanting to get home in any way they could after their experiences in the frontline. Some broke down or panicked, but later returned as better soldiers.[5]

The bitterness and anger of many men Paynter worked with often changed to a more positive attitude, and most returned to the battle front in good spirits. His advocacy for imprisoned deserters led to the creation of a rehabilitation camp at which men from several battalions came together to discuss their issues. Paynter found that the main reason for desertion was the Battalion's refusal to allow home leave, leading men who had come as volunteers to feel that they had become conscripts and were not trusted to return. As a result he urged the introduction of home leave for those who had been in Spain for six months and more.[6] Later, after the Battle of Brunete, he also had to deal with the reorganisation of the Battalion's persistently problematic leadership.

At about this time Bob Condon enjoyed some unexpected leave – 10 days' stay at the seaside resort of Benissa in the province of Alicante – 'after months of gazing at shattered olive trees and shell torn earth'.[7] New recruits were now

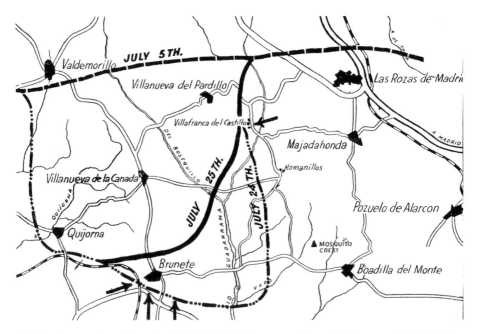

The battle scenario at Brunete. The British Battalion saw action at Villanueva de la Cañada. (© Alan Warren)

appearing, and the time was spent in training. Among them were men such as Jim Brewer of Rhymney, Archie Cook of Ystrad, Daniel Davies of Pentre, Morris Davies of Treharris, Harry Dobson of Blaenclydach, Sidney Hamm of Cardiff, Timothy Harrington of Merthyr, Morgan Havard of Craig-Cefn-Parc, Rhondda, Bedlington Jones of Tredegar, Tom Jones of Rhosllanerchrugog, Frank Owen of Mardy, Jack Roberts of Senghenydd, and Lance Rogers of Merthyr. They were encouraged by the visit of Clement Attlee, leader of the British Labour Party, who received a tremendous response. Fred Copeman asked him if he could use his name in the Battalion, and the No. 1 Major Attlee Company came into being.

The break from the frontline was not, however, to last long. Political disunity meant a change in the government leadership, and on May 17th, 1937, Dr. Juan Negrin replaced Largo Caballero as Prime Minister. Whereas Caballero was regarded as an 'impulsive revolutionary demagogue', Negrin was viewed as a 'cautious administrator and disciplinarian'.[8] There were also significant changes to the army which was reorganised under the control of the ministry of defence and, following the destruction of the POUM – denounced as 'Trotskyists' and 'fascist spies'[9] – the unity of the Republicans was restored.

July 1937 saw the launch of a large-scale offensive west of Madrid at Brunete. The aim was to relieve pressure by diverting Nationalist forces from the north of Madrid and threatening supply lines before a further attack from the south encircled the rebels. The offensive, led by General José Miaja, was ambitious, well-planned and well-located, attacking the Nationalists where they had detachments at strategic points rather than a continuous defensive line. The 15th Brigade was now led by Lieutenant-Colonel Vladimir Ćopić, a Croatian with vast experience of political and military struggle.

The Brigade was made up of six battalions, including the newly-formed Anti-tank Battery. They were grouped into two regiments: the first was the British, along with the Lincoln and Washington Battalions under the command of Major Jock Cunningham, with the second formed from the Franco-Belgian, Dimitrov and Spanish Battalions under Major Chapaiev. Fred Copeman commanded the British Battalion, which now included about 70 Welsh volunteers. Copeman believed that the concerts, sing-songs and other forms of entertainment had made a big contribution to morale: 'Many were the times when a thousand men, including groups from thirty nationalities, would sit round listening to the singing of a dozen Welsh miners.' Equipment too was plentiful compared to the scarcities of the past.[10]

At Brunete they were joined by the British Anti-tank Battery, a special group

Vladimir Ćopić was formerly a Croatian politician and communist leader, before becomming the commander of the 15th International Brigade. (© Alan Warren)

Fred Copeman was wounded at Jarama but recovered sufficiently to lead the British Batallion at Brunete. (© Alan Warren)

George Baker, an unidentified volunteer, and Tom Jones relaxing in Barcelona, 1938.
(© Keith Jones)

of about 40 men formed in May 1937. This unit included Welsh volunteers Jim Brewer – who was appointed quartermaster – George Baker of Gelli, Archie Cook of Ystrad, Tom Jones of Rhosllanerchrugog, Morgan Havard of Craig-Cefn-Parc and Victoriano Esteban of Abercrave. Fred Thomas (who was not Welsh), one of the Anti-tank Battery, wrote a memoir of his battle experiences.[11] He was taken from Madrigueras to the barracks at Albacete for special training with Soviet 45mm guns which were capable of firing armour-piercing and high explosive shells. This was state-of-the-art technology and with the help of Russian instructors made them a highly efficient elite unit, personally selected by Captain Ronald Dunbar. Jim Brewer praised the quality of officers, regarding Dunbar as a magnificent soldier, and well-disciplined comrades from a variety of backgrounds.[12]

Manhandling the heavy guns was hard work when they needed to be lifted, heaved over mounds and pulled through fields. They could be aimed with great accuracy, while the flat trajectory of the shells and an efficient sighting mechanism meant that they could attack small targets. Fred Thomas described how they started loading up on July 3rd at 4.30am, and later connected with the British Battalion about 15km from Madrid. After negotiating hairpin bend after hairpin bend on mountain roads crammed with troops and equipment, they took up their position overlooking the plain where battle was to commence at 3.15am on July 6th. The order for the 15th Brigade to move off came suddenly, just as men were settling down to a concert at the end of a

The old road leading into Villanueve de Cañada with the ditches used by the volunteers (© Author)

big sports event in the bullring at Albacete. It was too much for some after the horrors of Jarama, and there were predictable desertions.

The town of Villanueva de la Cañada is adjacent to Brunete. Its modern population of about 18,000 permanent residents is increased to around 30,000 by students attending nearby universities. It was completely destroyed in the fighting, but features recognisable from contemporary accounts – in particular ditches along the old road from the north – can still be seen along with bunkers along the main road to Brunete.

The Brigade was sent to reinforce another unit which was taking longer than expected to capture Villanueva de la Cañada, which appeared to be very strongly defended with trenches dug and parts extremely well-fortified. The men had only just completed their exhausting night-time journey, and from their high vantage point they watched an aerial bombardment, lines of infantry advance and tanks roll forward in clouds of dust. Then the artillery started up, and they heard the rifles and machine-guns crackling. General Miaja thought it essential to capture the village, and Franco was equally committed to holding it, so the order was given for the 15th Brigade to advance. Alec Cummings of Cardiff was in charge of No. 1 Company.

Republican tank in Villanueve de la Cañada (© Alan Warren)

On the morning of July 6th, the British and Dimitrov Battalions were ordered to attack the southern part of the town, which meant an arduous trek across country exposed to enemy fire. Writing in the *Aberdare Leader*, Bob Condon described their first big trial – the sun. The heat was blistering, there were no water bottles and the river bed was dry. There were already casualties as they approached the town, moving across flat cornfields with little cover. The aim was to reach the road between Villanueve and Brunete, and once this was done they took refuge in ditches alongside it. They were pinned back a little way outside the village and the number of casualties was increasing, with Cummings' company alone losing five killed and seven wounded. There was no option but to stay put until nightfall, when the wounded could be rescued. Before that, Copeman decided to do something about gunfire from the church tower. Taking four men, he zigzagged towards the tower as the machine-gun, supported by four enemy tanks behind the church, opened fire. Copeman and one survivor approached the tower and tried to smoke the enemy out, but had to retreat when the ruse was spotted by Nationalist infantry.

The memorial service pamphlet for Roman Roderiguez, a valued and active member of the Spanish community in Merthyr. (© Richard Burton Archives, Swansea Univ.)

Walter Gregory recalled, vividly and tragically, of the death at Villanueva of a Welsh brigader, known to him as 'Taffy': 'Throughout the march from the environs of San Lorenzo del Escorial, I had been in the company of a Welsh comrade. He had rabbited on interminably about how, when the war was over, I had to go and visit him and how he would take me to a pub which he knew in a green Welsh valley...when I had dived for the safety of the roadside ditch he had been right behind me and now, safe from the fire of the machine-guns, I turned to look for him. "Are you alright, Taff?" There was no reply. I worked my way back along the ditch and saw him lying on his face. I rolled him on to his side. He was dead. A bullet had gone through his forehead. His mouth hung open and was full of flies...it is a picture which has stayed with me for 45 years....'[13] Identifying this fallen Welsh volunteer is problematic but, knowing who else was in that unit, it could have been William Morris of Llanelli or Richard Horridge of Swansea. The nickname 'Taffy' would exclude Roman Rodriguez of Dowlais – who was killed on the first day of the fighting – and the 'pub in a green Welsh valley' could also rule out Robert Traill of Cardiff who is thought have died at Villanueva on July 7th.

Michael O'Donoghue saw Roman Rodriguez fall, alongside Fred Copeman, for whom he acted as interpreter,[14] and Lance Rogers has said that he also was right alongside him. Rodriguez, like Victoriano Esteban and Frank Zamora, was a Spanish immigrant, one of many who had come from the Bilbao area to make a better life and escape persecution for trade union activities.

He had lived in Dowlais for 21 years and was a popular figure in the Spanish community, known for his smile and happy expression, who had worked at the Dowlais Iron and Steel works but was now unemployed. He read widely on economics and politics and, along with other Spanish families, reinforced the community's strong socialist and communist activism. It was believed in the Spanish community that 'we had some of the finest trade unionists that these lodges have ever possessed'.[15] They were well respected craftsmen, strong trade unionists and very much part of the community.[16] Eaton suggests that many attributed the tradition of militancy at Abercrave to the Spanish influence.[17] Will Paynter said at Rodriguez's memorial service "There was never a more devoted, conscientious comrade...because of his knowledge of Spanish, he was attached to the Battalion Command and was at his duties day and night."[18]

Others from the Abercrave community had volunteered, but had been rejected. One who was accepted, but also later died, was Victoriano Esteban, who served as a member of the Anti-tank Battery and is often described as 'missing, presumed dead' at Brunete. However, it is not clear exactly how he met his end, and exactly where and when he died. His Moscow file suggests he did not arrive in Spain until September 1937 and a note reports him as still active in September 1938. Although Sam Wild – speaking at a homecoming reception for Brigaders attended by Esteban's brother – accused him of desertion, there is no record of him on any deserters' list or reason to believe that he did not fall in battle. Like other Abercrave volunteers, his family came from the Basque country to seek employment and, as skilled workers, to fulfil an industrial need. Esteban's father, Melchor – a well-known anarchist and atheist – is believed to have settled in the area after finding work with the Dowlais Iron Company.

The Anti-tank Battery were still watching from the heights, waiting for the order to attack and wincing as tanks went up in flames and planes bombed the village. Jim Brewer, driving to the *Intendencia* to pick up supplies, was regularly strafed but never hit. When the

Welsh brigaders Jack Roberts (right), with Leo Price (left) and Frank Owen (middle). Sitting is English volunteer 'Dickie' Bird. (© Richard Felstead)

order finally came, the following day, the village was little more than a shell. Jack Roberts described how, at dusk on that first day of action, a group of people were seen walking down the road towards the British position.[19] The men were taking cover in ditches, with Jack and four others taking shelter behind a dung-heap, when someone shouted not to fire since there were children coming out of the village. About 25 people – men, women and children – approached, led by a little girl of about ten years of age, an elderly woman, a boy of about 14 and a few old men. Behind them were younger men, probably Falangists, who shouted: *"Camaradas! Camaradas"* (Comrades).

Since they seemed to be refugees, they were called forward and Pat Murphy of Cardiff, who was nearest, told them to lay down any arms. In response, the men hiding behind the group, who'd been forcing the civilians forward with their rifles, started shooting and tossing hand-grenades. Pandemonium reigned as grenades crashed, guns fired and the women and children screamed. It was difficult to distinguish friend or foe. Murphy was wounded in the groin by a hand-grenade and Bill Meredith, the commander of No. 2 Company, was shot when responding to the cries of a wounded fascist. The reward for his help was a bullet through the heart.[20] They had fallen for an old and cruel trick of war, but had no option but to return fire, despite the presence of the villagers. Jack Roberts wrote: 'We could not help thinking about the brutality of fascism when we found the bodies of the little girl, the elderly woman and the two elderly men.'[21]

By now, all that was in the minds of the men was to move forward, finish the job and storm the village. They met the Dimitrov Battalion advancing from the other end of the village, and it was a case of taking control, street

"Man's dearest possession is life! And since it is granted to him to live but once he must live so as to feel no torturing regrets for years without purpose: so live so as not to be seared by the shame of a cowardly and trivial past: so live that dying he can say— 'All my life and all my strength were given to the finest cause in the world—the fight for the liberation of mankind' ".—LENIN.

FRED WHITE.

A loyal member of Penllwyngwent Lodge. A Pioneer of the Local Communist Party. Three times he marched to London in the struggle on behalf of the unemployed.

Fred White of Nant-y-moel – killed as the Battalion moved into Villanueve de Cañada – pictured in his memorial service pamphlet. (© Richard Burton Archives, Swansea Univ.)

by street. By midnight it was all over. There had been heavy casualties in the Battalion, with 50 men killed or wounded, and the village was in ruins. Leo Price, wounded in the earlier human shield incident by a rifle shot from close range, said that it felt like having the whole village thrown at him. The bullet had spun him around and another shot grazed his thigh and ankle. "I thank God he was a poor shot," said Price.[22] The bullet had also set alight some cartridges in his pocket and, although he'd tried to bandage himself, Price started slumping to the ground and woke up in a field hospital where he spent several weeks and saw no further action at the front.

Bob Condon remembers burned houses glowing in the eerie darkness, a family cowering in the cellar of a wine shop and fascist snipers still around the town.[23] Will Lloyd found half a dozen soldiers, seven women and two little boys – all giving the Republican clenched fist salute – hiding under a grating at a farmhouse. Later in the month he was to suffer a head wound from shrapnel.[24] Other Welshmen wounded in the battle were: Evan Ellis of Caerphilly, John Murray of Nantyfyllon, Charles Palmer of Llandudno, George Poustie of Treorchy, Wyndham Watkins of Abertridwr, Robert Watts of Swansea, and Rowland Williams of Trelewis.

The anti-tank soldiers felt like spectators watching a macabre game and wondering why they were not involved. At noon the following day they drove through the village, its buildings shattered and the streets littered with bodies of both sides as enemy bombers continued to attack the village and surrounding area. Welshman Bob Peters found some surprising items in the well-stocked Nationalists stores – brand new British Army socks – and was angered by this mockery of non-interventionism. 'Nevertheless, I soon whipped off my worn-out socks and replaced them with the new ones, courtesy of Franco and his British backers.'[25] Bert Williams of Abertillery, the Battalion Commissar, found hundreds of British-made tins of food and piles of clothes in the Nationalist stores.[26] As Bob Peters'

group moved on from the village, they were pinned down in a gulley by enemy fire and lay face down as bullets whistled above them. On his way back from a reconnaissance crawl, Peters noticed a friend in some distress. As he crouched to talk to him, a bullet slammed into his back. Fred Copeman stopped an ambulance full of wounded men and made sure Bob got on, although he had to stand in considerable pain. Surgeons at the University City hospital in Madrid found the bullet lodged against his spine and left it where it was. When he returned to the Battalion as a dispatch rider, the bullet worked its way up to his arm and was surgically removed in perfect condition under local anaesthetic! He would not serve in the frontline again, but continued to risk his life carrying messages in the motor bike section at Albacete. However, two Welsh Brigaders lost their lives on the first day of the battle at Villanueva were Fred White of Nant-y-Moel and Sid Hamm of Cardiff.

Sid Hamm of Cardiff also died during the fighting in Villanueve de Cañada. His memorial gathering took place in Queen Street, Cardiff. (© Richard Burton Archives, Swansea Univ.)

A loyal member of the Penllwyngwent Lodge, Fred White had marched three times to London in the struggle on behalf of the unemployed and Will Paynter addressed White's memorial service, held on Sunday November 27th, 1938, at the Workmen's Hall in Ogmore Vale. Money was raised for the Spanish Dependants Aid Fund and Lenin's words were read: '...so live that dying he can say – all my life and all my strength were given to the finest cause in the world – the fight for the liberation of mankind.' On the accompanying leaflet were the words: 'In his death is born a greater need to live, to make the banner stained a deeper red with blood, and cry that all the world may hear – they shall not pass.'[27]

Sid Hamm, an engineering student at Cardiff Technical College, was 19 when he volunteered for Spain. He was a member of Cardiff United youth movement, Heath Ward Labour Party and later the Communist Party, and active in the students' Spanish Aid Committee. Influenced by the plight of the people of Madrid and the heroics of Jarama, he left with a group of more than 20 men. His last words when leaving Wales were: "There is no victory without sacrifice."

His diaries indicate a fair amount of training with rifles and grenades, route marches, lectures on military strategy and time to enjoy a book and a sing-song.[28] Sent to the front after 18 days at Albacete, he wrote to friends about the amazing spirit of enthusiasm and sacrifice of the volunteers, many still wounded: 'I have never experienced anything like that before.'[29] Often ill, he usually worked through it. His diary entry for Friday July 2nd records a visit to the dentist in Madrid, and then back to the barracks. The last diary entry on, Tuesday July 6th, written by a student friend, reads: 'On this day Sid Hamm was killed in Brunete, Spain.' Tom Adlam, who had come to Spain at the same time, recognised his body lying on the road.[30]

Robert Traill of Radyr, near Cardiff (also of London and Moscow), was killed on the battle's second day, as the Battalion was moving through the area dealing with small groups of Nationalists in other villages. A Cambridge graduate and an enigmatic figure, Traill had travelled to Spain directly from Moscow where he had married a Russian named Vera, the daughter of a minister in the short-lived Kerenski government of 1917. Described as a 'British communist...from a respectable British family who knew nothing of the marriage or the birth of a daughter until after his death',[31] there is one intriguing glimpse of Traill's activity in Spain held in the Moscow Archive, where he is referred to as being much liked and with military tactics at his fingertips. The archive notes that he was commander of a group of around 40 British and Irish volunteers who were training to form No. 1 section of the Anglo-American Company, part of the 20th Battalion, while the British Battalion was entrenched at Jarama. Called to defend Pozoblanco against

On what was later called 'Mosquito Hill', because of the bullets flying continuously overhead, the Battalion suffered an appalling bombardment. (© Author)

a Nationalist offensive on March 20th, they found themselves pursuing the enemy by train along a single-track railway. Trapped and under artillery fire as the engine emitted plumes of black smoke, they retreated but were later involved in fierce exchanges with Moorish troops on the heights of Sierra Chimorra. Robert Traill was described as showing excellent leadership, and his company was the only one to suffer no casualties.[32] He was later promoted to the command of the 20th Battalion and to Brigade Staff, but left the rifle company reluctantly, not wanting to appear 'yellow'.

When dawn broke on July 7th, it was confirmed that the British Battalion had suffered many casualties, with 50 men killed or wounded, among them heroes of previous battles. Harry Stratton was working in a medical unit north of Madrid and described how casualties began pouring in at the start of the offensive. He was given the job of taking the details of the wounded. Ambulances were arriving continuously at all hours, while stretcher cases were lined up outside the operating theatre, along the corridor and out into the open. He recalls enemy planes harrying the ambulances, and near misses of the hospital.[33] Yet the battle had started well, and the Nationalists had lost Brunete by noon on the first day. The 11th Republican Division under Spanish General Enrique Líster struck at dawn on July 6th, advanced ten miles with support from artillery and planes, and surrounded the town. However, Nationalist reinforcements were rushed to the front and this, along with delays in Republican movements, slowed progress.

The Nationalists had now taken up new positions on the Romanillos heights, across the river Guadarrama, and the British Battalion supported the advance – led by the American Washington Battalion – towards the village of Boadilla del Monte, but dozens were killed in an attack by four of Mussolini's Caproni bombers. Their task was to secure the high point, later called 'Mosquito Hill' after the incessant buzzing of bullets overhead. The 15th International Brigade's records describe conditions during the advance on July 9th, with the enemy firing from high ground, as appalling. Food and water ran short, the lines of communication raked by snipers and machine-guns, and ration parties running the gauntlet.[34] First-aiders worked under intense fire and wounded were often left where they'd fallen until nightfall. Italian and German planes bombed the hillside as men hugged the earth and 'that awful whistle, scream and rush of the bombs, then the explosion. The whole earth

Charles Orr called this site below 'Mosquito Hill', where the brigade located its HQ, "a lovely spot for a picnic". (© Author)

was blasted into pieces. It heaved and rocked and swayed and roared and smoked, and the bombs kept coming down.'[35]

The Anti-tank Battery was also taking significant artillery hits, with No. 2 gun destroyed and two men killed. As the battery prepared to cross the river and move up to 'Mosquito Hill', planes had the guns in their sights and pinned them down for hours. Hugh Slater, commander of the Anti-tank Battery gives a vivid account of one pounding: '...our base was being violently bombarded. Some cases of ammunition were exploding in howling syncopation with the screaming of the enemy shells. The grass all around the guns and Cunningham's dugout was on fire.'[36] To Charles Orr are attributed the famous, often-quoted words about the Brigade HQ near a ford in the river below 'Mosquito Hill': 'It would be a lovely spot for a picnic.'[37] He also said that it seemed the Nationalists had three times as many planes as the Republicans, and that 'a fly can't move without a shell following him.'

The situation was grim. Each time progress was made over ridges, they were beaten back, seeking cover by burrowing into the ground and digging out shallow trenches. The heat was unbearable, men were exhausted and it was obvious that it would not possible to advance beyond some of the other ridges to occupy 'Mosquito Hill'. The Nationalists had been well-reinforced, with planes continuously attacked Republican troops and supplies moving

A position held by the British Battalion on 'Mosquito Hill'. (© Ernesto Viñas)

Alun Menai Williams (sitting) and his friend Billy Davies in Mondejar. Three days after the photograph was taken Billy Davies died at Villanueve de Cañada. (© Alan Warren)

towards the front. The dropping of incendiary bombs turned the fields into carpets of fire, and when they weren't bombing they were strafing.

Despite a firm determination to press steadily on from ridge to ridge, progress was painfully slow and the casualties were heavy. On July 11th, the Battalion was withdrawn and placed in reserve. Key people had been wounded and killed, with one huge loss being Major George Nathan, Chief of Operations of the 15th International Brigade. Jim Brewer described Nathan, killed by a fragment from a bomb dropped by a German Junkers while the Battalion was resting behind the lines, as a superb commander but excessively brave. Alun Menai Williams described how many of the men who'd died, often in his arms, were initially left where they'd fallen, and how, when the fighting subsided, they were buried close to his first aid post in the dry river bed at the bottom of 'Mosquito Hill'. They are still there, their remains unidentified.

Williams said that his saddest memory was meeting his life-long friend, Billy Davies, at Mondejar before the British advance. Davies was a political activist in Wales, sold the *Daily Worker* in London and was at the anti-fascist demonstration in Cable Street in London, where, with Williams, he threw marbles at Mosley's fascists. Amazed to see one another after four years, they went to a nearby village to be photographed together as a memento for the future.

Williams tells us that the future lasted only another three days, as Davies was killed during the storming of Villanueva de Cañada. The photo remained in Menai Williams' possession as 'a memento of a loyal and trusted friend, at a very unusual moment in our lives'.[38] In his last letter to his parents, Davies wrote: 'I was willing to pay the supreme sacrifice for my ideals and I knew to what I was coming – war, the most loathsome thing ever known. Although I have been wounded I still hold to my views.'[39] Having refused a discharge offered by the Medical Commission, Davies died at the front line against fascism, and an Irish comrade described how his clenched fist shot up in salute as his body fell, riddled with machine-gun bullets at his memorial service Will Paynter declared: "He was one of our best comrades, and his comrades fight on, inspired by his example." [40]

On the second day of the battle, Frank Owen of Mardy was killed. Jack Roberts, now emotionally and physically exhausted, had stumbled down the hill looking for water when he came across Owen's body under a tree. In shock, his mind turned to the photo taken in Madrigueras of Leo Price, Frank and their friend, Dickie Bird.[41] Owen was a member of the Communist Party and his working-class radicalism led to his being jailed three times. He had also marched to London three times on the hunger marches. In a letter written shortly before his death, to his wife and children, he talked about an ideal worth fighting for, and was still optimistic in July 1937 that there would be a 'smashing victory to the Spanish Republic...Franco is not expecting

Sammy Davies of Ammanford, who died in the arms of his friend Jack Williams. (© Terry Norman)

the reception which is being prepared for him, and I must say this, our side will leave very little quarter to the fascists, for the murder of women and children has been their game, at Malaga, Almeria, Guernica and Bilbao, etc.' He assured his family that the Republican Army was on the move, told them not to worry and that he was okay. Will Paynter told those gathered for Frank Owen's memorial service that he was a disciplined soldier, ready at all times to respond when a job had to be done, and had proved himself worthy of the revolutionary traditions of 'Red Mardy'.[42]

If the date (July 17th) on the death certificate issued by George Aitken, the political commissar of the 15th International Brigade, is correct, Sammy Morris of Ammanford was killed while the British Battalion was in reserve. It is possible either that he died on that day after being wounded in the earlier

Jack Williams of Ammanford died a few days after his friend Sammy Morris, probably in a push against the nationalist counter-offensive. (© Terry Norman)

action at 'Mosquito Hill' or, as described in Brigade Commander Ćopić's diary, the continuous bombing of the British position in reserve took Morris' life.[43] To many, Sammy Morris was a perfect example of the Welsh Communist miner in the inter-war years. He joined the Communist Party in 1925, was jailed for his part in the four-month-long West Wales Anthracite Strike, became chair of his miners' lodge and was active in his support of local, national and international industrial and anti-fascist struggles.

An obituary in his local paper said that, far from having embarked on a mad-brained prank, Morris was a man of mature discretion, who had carefully weighed all the consequences of his action. His letters home show a strong determination to defeat fascism and he returned to action following three months in hospital after he was badly wounded in the leg in December 1936. He refused to return home: 'Not,' he said, 'until we stop international fascism or I am wiped out.' In his letters there is a mix of fierce politics and thoughtful kindness: 'Share the wealth; share the land; share the rhubarb; share the tent,' and 'you must convince everybody of the justice of our cause, do everything in your power to bring about the unity of every peace loving individual into any campaigning that will help the Spanish people's victory.' Sammy Morris died in the arms of his friend, Jack Williams, with whom he had resolved to travel to Spain after attending a meeting organised by the Welsh Communist Party in Cardiff in 1936.[44]

Sadly Jack Williams was also killed a few days later. He too was a member of the local branch of the Communist Party, a carpenter by trade and acknowledged to be a splendid craftsman. It is possible that, like Sammy Morris, he was killed while in reserve, but likelier that it was when the Battalion returned to the front line to oppose the counter-offensive launched by the Nationalists on July 18th. There they stayed for the next week, pushed back gradually with the rest of the Republican forces and retreating over the river Guadarrama, until they were finally placed in reserve again.

There is more to the story of Jack Williams. Dai Jones, the only married Ammanford volunteer, had left for Spain after giving a goodnight kiss to his five-year-old son, but without telling his wife. Sent home with an injured hand, he planned to return when he had recovered. Jack Williams, Dai's best friend and a bachelor, insisted on going to Spain in his place.

Summing up the three weeks of battle, Richard Baxell notes that the Republic had gained more than 40 square miles of territory, but suffered disastrous losses with more than 25,000 casualties and a monumental cost in armour and aircraft.[45] Alun Menai Williams' unforgettable memories of the battles of Brunete as a first-aider were of soldiers dying from loss of blood, with swollen tongues filling their parched mouths for lack of water.[46] He also described the lack of proper treatment facilities, the shortage of medical equipment and the insufficient medical expertise of those drafted in to provide assistance. The soldiers saw women and children lying dead in the streets from shells and bullets, and of course their own colleagues dying alongside them. The loss of key figures, with Fred Copeman cracking up under the strain made the request, on July 28th, for volunteers to go back into the line an almost impossible dream. The Battalion was now down now to about 200 men, most exhausted by their ordeal and the lack of food. The order was resisted vehemently by 60 to 70 of them.

Will Paynter wrote to Harry Pollitt on July 14th, arguing that the Battalion could not be put in the field without reinforcements. He estimated its strength at 150, including the slightly wounded.[47] Paynter saw two other major problems. First was political division among leaders, with senior battalion personalities criticising Republican battle strategy, and what was seen as the incompetence of officers. Second, an increase in the demand for repatriation, or leave, to Britain. Desertions remained a problem. Paynter admitted that a minority deserted at this point, and said he expected to interview ten in Madrid and seven in Albacete. Men like Jim Brewer were fiercely critical of 'quitters' who deserted at the most trying hours.[48] Paynter also took a hard line at this time, regarding desertion as 'an act of treachery which in a war can mean the death of one's own comrades.'[49] Some would-be deserters were picked up and imprisoned at Albacete; others made their way home on boats from Spanish harbours.

Paynter argued that these were not the normal category of desertion, but the result of frustration at the conflict among the Battalion's leadership. He believed that the commanders at Brunete had little or no experience or training in the strategy and tactics needed at Battalion level. Differences between them became violent arguments, and a group was recalled to London for discussions with Communist leaders. While Alonso Elliott argued, in his report on the

British Battalion, that Paynter could have done more to 'prevent or limit the leadership crisis among the English after Brunete,'[50] he and others took the lead to 'restore the British Battalion in numbers, morale and fighting ability, and finding a new leadership to do this. There could be no breathing-space in the fight against fascism.'[51] Indeed, Paynter remarked, in the same letter to Pollitt, on the improvement in the Battalion due to better political work and 'the infiltration of new men, mainly, I say, with national pride, of the Welsh variety.'[52]

Notes

1. Fred Copeman, *Reasons in Revolt*, op. cit., p.120.
2. Will Paynter, *My Generation*, op cit., p.65. Also *Our Fight* No.36, May 7th in which Will Paynter and Ted Bramley of the London District of the Communist Party are welcomed.
3. See James Hopkins, *Into The Heart of the Fire*, op. cit., pp.255-6, and for a fuller discussion of desertion, repatriation, and disciplinary issues, Richard Baxell, *Unlikely Warriors*, op. cit., pp.240-64.
4. Letter to Pollitt, May 30th, 1937, Marx Memorial Library, Box C:13/8.
5. Imperial War Museum, interview, Reel 5.
6. Letter to Pollitt June 9th, Marx Memorial Library, Box C:14/5.
7. *Aberdare Leader*, June 8th, 1937.
8. E.H. Carr, *The Comintern and the Spanish Civil War*, op. cit., p.45.
9. See Paul Preston, *The Spanish Civil War*, op. cit., pp.253-265, for a fuller discussion of the end of the POUM and George Orwell, Homage to Catalonia, op. cit., pp.209-221, for his POUM perspective.
10. Fred Copeman, Reason in Revolt, op. cit., p.123.
11. Fred Thomas, *To Tilt at Windmills: Memoir of the Spanish Civil War*, East Lansin, Michigan State University Press, 1996.
12. Letter to Ben Bowen Thomas, Warden of Coleg Harlech, June 20th, 1937 – *Miners Against Fascism*, p.276.
13. Walter Gregory, *The Shallow Grave*, op. cit., pp.69-70.
14. Interview with Hywel Francis, South Wales Miners' Library.
15. Interview with Dick Beamish, South Wales Miners' Library.
16. For more information about the Spanish community at Abercrave, see the 'Memoirs of Leandro Macho', Richard Burton Archives, Swansea University.
17. George Eaton, *Neath and the Spanish Civil War*, op. cit., p.79.
18. Memorial service pamphlet, Richard Burton Archives, Swansea University.
19. Frank Ryan (Ed.), *The Book of the XV Brigade*, op. cit., pp.141-2, and in *Our Fight*, the Journal of the 15th Brigade, No. 32 August 19th, 1937.
20. Later Will Lloyd wrote to the *Aberdare Leader* suggesting that Murphy had been killed.
21. Frank Ryan (Ed.), *The Book of the XV Brigade*, op. cit., pp.141-2.

22. *Colliers Crusade* and Leo Price's memoirs, p.29.

23. *Aberdare Leader*, July 31ˢᵗ, 1937.

24. *Aberdare Leader*, September 4ᵗʰ, 1937.

25. Greg Lewis, *A Bullet Saved My Life*, op. cit., p.35.

26. In the *South Wales Echo* report of Williams' repatriation.

27. Memorial service pamphlet, Richard Burton Archives, Swansea University.

28. Robert Stradling, *Brother Against Brother*, op. cit., pp.155ff.

29. William Rust, *Britons in Spain*, op. cit., p.132.

30. *Colliers Crusade*.

31. Peter Day, *The Bedbug: Klop Ustinov: Britain's Most Ingenious Spy*, London, Biteback Publishing, 2015.

32. RGASPI 545/3/478. See also for more details of the action, Bill Alexander, *British Volunteers for Liberty*, op. cit., pp.111-14.

33. Harry Stratton, *To Anti-Fascism by Taxi*, op. cit., p.45.

34. Frank Ryan (Ed.), *The Book of the XV Brigade*, op. cit., p.142ff.

35. Ibid., p.146.

36. Ibid., p.151.

37. Ibid., p.153.

38. Alun Menai Williams, *From the Rhondda to the Ebro*, op. cit., p.169. Davies' words to Williams were: "Good God, Alun, what the hell are you doing here?" His reply was: "The same as you Billy". This brought a smile to his face.

39. Memorial service pamphlet, Richard Burton Archives, Swansea University.

40. Memorial service pamphlet, Richard Burton Archives, Swansea University.

41. Richard Felstead, *No Other Way: Jack Russia and the Spanish Civil War*, op. cit., pp.83-4.

42. Memorial service pamphlet, Richard Burton Archives, Swansea University.

43. RGASPI 545/3/467.

44. Information about Sammy Morris, Jack Williams and W.J. Davies, including the death certificate, is kindly provided by local Ammanford historian Terry Norman.

45. Richard Baxell, Unlikely Warriors, op. cit., p.234.

46. Alun Menai Williams, *From the Rhondda to the Ebro*, op. cit., p.168.

47. Marx Memorial Library, Box 21. A scribbled note in the Moscow Archives records 'English wounded 201, killed 79'. (RGASPI 545/3/486).

48. Letter to Ben Bowen Thomas, *Miners Against Fascism*, p.275.

49. Letter to Harry Pollitt, Marx Memorial Library, Box C:14/5. There was confusion among the men who had at first volunteered but now were regarded as conscripts. At this time repatriation was being refused and then, from September 1937, were told there was no return until the defeat of fascism.

50. RGASPI, 545/6/22. Alonso Elliott worked at the headquarters of the political commissars in Madrid. He wrote a report, produced in French in the Moscow Archives, about the British volunteers.

51. Bill Alexander, *British Volunteers for Liberty*, op. cit., p.132.

52. Letter to Harry Pollitt, Marx Memorial Library Box C:14/5.

6

A Long Way Back

The Aragon Front

Following the failures at Brunete the Republicans looked towards an offensive in Aragon, with the aim of capturing Zaragoza. There were both military and political reasons for this move. Militarily, the capture of Zaragoza – a key Nationalist communications centre – would slow down Franco's gains in the north after the fall of Bilbao, the merciless bombing of Guernica and with Santander coming under increasing military threat. Politically, Zaragoza was also the home of anarchism in Aragon, and the Republicans wanted to end the anarchists' dominance in that part of their front line. The Civil War had focussed on the capture of key towns and positions, rather than controlling wide areas of countryside, and Zaragoza was near a 300-kilometre front guarded by only three of Franco's divisions, with the rest of his troops located in the towns. The Republican plan was to break through at seven points on the 100-kilometre stretch from Zuera to Belchite, avoiding the error made at Brunete of offering too many targets for bombing and strafing. Although it was only six weeks since Brunete, Republican commanders believed that they had superiority on the ground as well as in the air and that the action would be a success.[1]

Since Brunete, there had been changes affecting the International Brigades and the British volunteers.[2] First, Spanish Republican soldiers were incorporated into each of the Brigades – with a Spanish Battalion assigned to every one, and in each company a section of Spanish soldiers was drafted in. The 15th International Brigade was to be part of the Republican 35th Brigade, commanded by the Polish General Karol Wacław Świerczewski, known as 'General Walter', who was recognised as a hard but efficient commander. Peter Daly, a former Irish Republican Army (IRA) man, was made Commander of the British Battalion with Paddy O'Daire as his second-in-command, and the position of political commissar was assigned to Welshman Jack 'Russia' Roberts. New recruits had arrived from Madrigueras, and some men had returned from hospital treatment after being wounded at Brunete. Among the new recruits would have been Les Brickell of Tredegar, Reginald David of Ton Pentre, Archie Yemm of Pontypridd and Frank Zamora of Abercrave. The Battalion now numbered about 400 men of whom approximately 200 were British. The 15th Brigade commander was still Lieutenant-Colonel Ćopić, a Croatian with a history of revolutionary socialism. He was described as 'feared by the enemy, respected by the men, loved by the people – the mark of a real commander in any men's army'.[3]

The British had been in the Tajuna valley during the previous weeks, resting, enjoying the weather, bathing in the river and joining in a fiesta. There was even time to join some Spanish workers in reaping the barley harvest, and an opportunity to experience at first hand the crudity of the process.[4] Eventually, trucks took them to Valencia where they slept in the bullring and were issued new uniforms and some

Reginald David of Ton Pentre, one of the new recruits in August 1937. (© Deputy Director RGASPI, Moscow)

better equipment, including Dictorovs – light, Russian-made machine-guns. The rest of the journey to Caspe, and ultimately Azaila, was a slow one by railway trucks, allowing them to catch up on some sleep. They were now about 50 kilometres south of Zaragoza.

Quinto

The attack on Quinto began on the morning of August 24th, 1937. Of the 15th International Brigade, it was the Lincoln Battalion which had the task of engaging with Nationalist forces. First was a pounding by artillery, then aerial bombing, before tanks led the attack which captured the trenches outside the town, and pursued the Nationalist troops retreating into it. However, the houses were strongly fortified, with machine-guns and snipers deployed everywhere and, as so often in urban warfare, the town's church was used as a refuge by a large group of soldiers due to its tower being a perfect location for a machine-gun. The Anti-tank Battery was firing into the side of the church from wooded higher-ground and, as they tried to deal with a sniper, hit the bell in the tower. The accuracy of the Brigade's gunners was impressive as,

The imposing church, la Asunción de Nuestra Señora *(Assumption of Our Lady), at Quinto which was used by a Nationalist sniper. (© Author)*

even from such an acute angle, they fired through the open windows, and succeeded to silence the snipers inside. Evidence of their shells' impact on the inside of the church can still be seen today. Jim Brewer adds more details of the assault from his account.[5] After Tom Wintringham was wounded in the shoulder, Battery Commander Dunbar identified a sniper in the church tower, onto whom Brewer trained and fired the gun – hitting the metal casing of the bell. When the hill was finally captured the sniper was caught, while running away in civilian clothes, and placed before a firing squad.

Asked to join the squad, Brewer refused on a point of honour. He argued that there was a legitimate government which should try the 'civilian', and also that the sniper could easily have shot him when he'd earlier walked from the ambulance where he had taken a wounded comrade.

The town was eventually taken, street-by-street, as houses occupied by the Nationalists were overrun, and terrified families liberated and provided with food and drink. Will Lloyd described how he went into a barn with about ten other men and, hearing scuffling from a cellar under a trap door, he stopped

The strongly fortified hill at Purburell proved a daunting target for the Battalion. (© Author)

a comrade from throwing a grenade just as a woman lifted up two children, stiff with terror.[6] The troops occupying the church held out until a concerted bombardment enabled the Republicans to capture 75 enemy soldiers, including Carlists, falangists, Civil Guards and young Spanish conscripts. The latter happily shouted; *"Viva la Republica"* and *"Viva el Frente Popular"*. However, the officers were taken, lined up outside against the walls of the church, and shot.

The British Battalion's next objective was to take control of the heights overlooking Quinto. 'The terrain there was the very worst: bleak, exposed, unproductive, treeless hillsides which offered no protection from the elements and scant cover from enemy fire. It was a dreadful and dreary landscape which seemed to gnaw into one and erode the spirit.'[7] The British, tasked with attacking the conical hill called *Purburell*, believed from reports that it was not strongly fortified; but clever work from German engineers ensured the opposite was the case.

The hill was one of two between which the main road ran. Three companies, carrying only rifles and grenades, went down into a gulley connecting the hills, and began climbing the slopes. It wasn't long before a torrent of machine-gun fire came from Nationalist trenches near the top of the hill. It was obvious that, with the hill very strongly held, there was no possibility of advancing further. Casualties were numerous, including Jack 'Russia' Roberts who was wounded in the shoulder and Battalion leader Peter Daly who was wounded in the stomach and died a few days later in Benicassim. Taking over from Daly, Paddy O'Daire decided to hold the men back and use the welcome darkness to reorganise. That night some of Franco's troops came down the hill to search for the water they desperately needed and ended up surrendering to the Battalion. The information they provided, about dug-outs, machine-guns and artillery, was invaluable for the next day's attack. This was to be the last action in the war for Jack Roberts. He ran down the rear of the hill to locate a machine-gun company to cover the assault but, on his return journey, he didn't keep low enough to avoid a machine-gun burst which tore through his right shoulder. After having the wound cleaned and bandaged at the field dressing station, he was taken by ambulance to the railway station and joined a host of other wounded men waiting to be taken to the hospital at Benicassim.[8] He may well have been taken first to the forward hospital in which Welsh nurse Margaret Powell was based. This was an old farmhouse in which the slaughterhouse was used as an operating theatre. As usual in the field hospitals, the conditions were primitive, and medical teams worked miracles with operations, anaesthetics, sutures and sterilising. As the war progressed, the International Brigades Medical Services developed an impressive system aimed to reduce the time it took the wounded to receive treatment, whereby the casualties were stretchered to the Battalion Aid Post, where minor injuries would be treated. From there they went to a classification centre (perhaps in a dug-out or cellar) for injections, a blood transfusion or minor surgery. Then, hospitals nearer the front – often in out-buildings, caves and tunnels – dealt with more serious cases. In addition, trains were often used to transport patients to hospitals further away, for medical and post-operative care.

Margaret Powell – back row, left – of Llangenny volunteered with the British Medical Unit and is seen here in Poleñino, Aragon, in May 1937. (© Ruth Muller, Margaret's daughter)

Next morning the attack resumed, but this time the artillery prepared the way for the Battalion. The anti-tank guns were most effective, aiming continuous fire at the enemy trenches and destroying the machine-gun nests. Down the slope the men went again, then began the upward climb of the hill. The Lincolns and Spanish Battalions provided additional cover until about nine o'clock when the guns stopped firing, only for the sound of enemy planes to shatter the silence. The *Brigade Handbook* described how, as they hugged the ground, one of those ironic features of warfare took place.[9] Thinking that the hill was held by the Republicans, the Nationalist planes savagely bombed their own troops who, believing the planes were Republican, prepared to surrender. When they realised their mistake, they opened up again ferociously, causing many casualties, but the Republicans gained ground as the Anti-tank Battery continued to pound Nationalist positions. When the barbed wire defensive line was destroyed the final assault took place and, as the Battalion charged the trenches, they found defenders with their hands in the air shouting "*agua! agua!*" (water). Shots were also heard further down the trenches as officers committed suicide in preference to the likely firing sqad.

Belchite

Today, it is possible to enter the gates of the compound which is the now-abandoned town of Belchite, and walk into the broken streets and shattered buildings, imagining that the ghosts of those whose homes and lives were taken look on in disbelief. This was Belchite, left in its cadaverous state after the war. Reorganised plans meant the Republicans, *en route* to Zaragoza, were to attack the town. It was extremely well fortified with a German thoroughness, including an inter-locking network of pill-boxes, trenches, iron stakes, steel prongs and machine-guns strategically placed to cover all approaches.[10] Codo had been taken on August 27th after a short battle, with the Carlists who'd abandoned it leaving a message scrawled on a wall: 'When you kill a Red you will have a year less in Purgatory'.[11] Codo's inhabitants had long left for Belchite.

At this point the British were ordered to make a diversion to nearby Mediana, ten kilometres north of Belchite. The order, intended to hold back any Nationalist reinforcements, produced a negative response from some men so Paddy O'Daire called for discussion with the communist members of the Battalion, mainly Welsh miners, who agreed that it had to be done.[12] The advancing Republican front now ran for about 25 kilometres north of Belchite, with the Nationalists continually trying to break through it. The *Brigade Handbook* describes how the Battalion set out on trucks but, to avoid artillery fire, completed the journey on foot.[13] At about 3am they met an advancing Nationalist party, which retreated before them. Once at Mediana they were able to recapture the two hills which dominated the town, and further into the surrounding soft soil. The Nationalists counter-attacked and, for three days and nights, aerial and artillery attacks followed, with many skirmishes. However, the Brigade had done its job - the Nationalists were foiled in their attempt to retake Belchite.

It was here that Edwin Greening joined the Battalion after undergoing his training at Albacete and Tarazona, at first only with wooden rifles, but then loading and unloading Soviet ones until he could do it with his eyes closed. His preparation was insubstantial to say the least, and he relied on Morris Davies, Tom Howell Jones and a couple of others to help in what he called a harrowing and frightening experience. He was very much aware that he was not a trained soldier, and had only fired ten rounds in his life.[14]

Meanwhile the Lincolns, Dimitrovs and Spanish, along with the Anti-tanks, had been fully engaged in the battle to take Belchite. The Anti-tank Battery in particular played a big part. It was reported that the three Soviet-made guns fired 2,700 shells in the first two days. The number one gun was fired at such a rate that its barrel burst, and it had to be withdrawn from action. The end of the

The ruins of Belchite remain as a monument to those who suffered and died there. A new small town was built alongside it by Republican prisoners. (© Author)

fighting left the town in ruins. 'When darkness fell on the fourth night Belchite presented a picture of the horrors of war which no Hollywood film could ever give. Several large buildings were ablaze. Tongues of flame shot up into the black palls of smoke overhead. The summer breeze wafted across the countryside the stench, nauseating and strong of dead bodies, human and animal…it was war shorn of all its glamour, war cruel and bloody – but a war we had to win.'[15]

Dave Engels and Emanuel Lanzer's vivid first-hand account of the Brigade's main actions provide a fascinating insight to the battle.[16] The Government Army had already surrounded Belchite as the Brigade took up their positions in trenches about 400 yards from the town, which were so shallow that cover was ensured only by lying down. After a few days, the advance was made by fighting house-to-house and building-to-building, using rifles, grenades and sometimes twigs and petrol to set fire to buildings where there was resistance. As each house was captured, a piece of bunting or blanket was placed in the window as a signal to fellow Republican fighters.

The town's church and Convent of San Agustin dates back to the late 16th century – the church and bell tower in baroque style mixed with the Moorish influence often seen in Aragon – the battle torn remains of which remain today, as a memorial to the war. Inside, ribs of precarious arches, open to the sky, provide no protection for the remnants of frescoes that once stirred the emotions of worshippers. Outside, a shell is still lodged in the brickwork.

At the time of the attack, it housed Nationalist machine-guns and claimed the lives of 22 men of the Lincoln Battalion during the first assault. Before it was finally captured, the church was pounded by artillery and tank shells – during which the Nationalists ran outside into the safety of the town during shelling, only to regroup when there was a pause – as well as by machine-gun fire and numerous charges from the trenches. The town was in ruins when it was finally taken, and while Franco later used Republican prisoners to build a new town, the old town was left as it was.

Alun Menai Williams captured the horror of Belchite when recalling an incident during the storming of the church. A young Spanish Nationalist soldier was brought to the casualty assembly point with his clothes still smouldering, and his body described as one massive blister from head to toe. Realising the hopelessness of his fellow countryman's situation, a Spanish stretcher bearer bent down to him and spoke briefly, then took out his revolver and put him out of his agony.[17]

So what was the outcome of this campaign which lasted 13 days, producing widespread destruction and carnage? Most would say that little was gained – an advance of approximately ten kilometres and the reduction to rubble of a few villages and towns. The aim of the offensive, capturing Zaragoza, had

The remains of the church of San Agustin amongst of the ruins of Belchite. (© Author)

failed and the British Battalion was exhausted. Beevor argues that the Republican commanders were too obsessed with crushing every defensive position, instead of forging ahead and leaving mopping up to second-line troops. They made the same mistakes at Brunete, with the delays allowing the Nationalists to bring up reinforcements.[18]

Yet more action was in store for the 15th Brigade, a move against Nationalist lines near the town of Fuentes de Ebro on October 13th. In contrast to the sluggish nature of their previous engagements, a special feature of the attack was the Republicans' tactics of driving a large number of tanks through the enemy lines, followed by the infantry piling through the breach in the defences. Another audacious action saw Republican troops, mounted on the tops and turrets of Whippet tanks, travelling at 40 miles an hour, but failing to cling on and firing at the same time. The attack was a disaster. British losses included their Battalion Commander Harold Fry and Commissar Eric Whalley. They stayed another ten days at the front before being withdrawn.

A welcome break

They returned to Mondéjar, a town of around 3,000 inhabitants in the province of Guadalajara, for rest and recuperation. The rolling hills around it house vineyards of lush grapes providing, among others, a fine red Tempranillo and a versatile white Macabeo traditionally blended to produce a sparkling Cava wine. The town was approached along narrow cobbled streets, with the troops billeted in houses along the route. At a beautiful wrought iron fountain, children splashed their feet, and women and children filled large heavy stone jars with clear drinking water. Nearby, a huge stone church was being used as a garage for repairing vehicles.[19]

It was to be a period of change too. A decree from the Republican Defence Ministry brought the Brigades formally into the Spanish Army. Implications included the commitment of brigaders until the end of the war, limitations on the role of the base at Albacete, and better organisation, discipline and officer training. The Battalion, about 150 in number with Fred Copeman in command, became the 57th of the Spanish Army. Although it was not a comfortable existence in Mondéjar (some still lacked proper mattresses and adequate uniforms) these were relatively happy times as there was enough food and wine, some leave to Madrid was granted, and fiestas brought brigaders and locals together in song and festivity.

It was said that it was the first time that the local inhabitants had ever heard British music played on mouth organs and combs & paper. Leo Price, asked to sing *Ramona*, was rewarded by the local baker with a large bag of biscuits. The travelling cinema van helped to lighten the mood and there was a special sports fiesta which included grenade throwing, boxing matches and shooting events. Jim Brewer, a great friend of the talented Miles Tomalin, helped him in the production of a 'wall newspaper' very often pinned to a tree. Titled *Assault and Battery News,* the publication contained articles by the men and was eagerly ready by all, particularly the Americans, who came from far and near to read it. Brewer, known to be outspoken in his views, also wrote a regular column in the paper.[20]

Wall newspapers were an important way of letting men express their feelings humorously or through poems, cartoons and other articles. Obituaries of the dead troops and biographies of the wounded were also published as well as lighter, more entertaining articles. One such piece, the 'Honourable Sport of Butting', involving cigarettes, was published with rules of a game designated for the 'butter', 'butte' and the 'butt'.

The town square of Mondéjar saw two happy occasions, when a flag sent from Britain was presented to the Battalion in the presence of the mayor, and when the Battalion received a group from Britain which included the leader of the Labour Party, Clement Attlee. Men stood in the evening darkness with torches made from oiled rope and broom handles, with sacks dipped in tar on their ends. It was then that Fred Copeman suggested that a company be renamed the Major Attlee Company, causing a furore in the British Parliament. Following Attlee's visit, regular reports from the Battalion and No.1 Company were sent to the opposition leader's Westminster office.

Meanwhile, Republican commanders were planning a move which would involve the International Brigades in a costly and decisive battle. They had decided to attack the Nationalist town of Teruel, a salient probing like a finger into Republican Spain. Intelligence had indicated that Franco, after his success

Wall newspapers provided a welcome opportunity for the volunteers to express themselves and have some fun. (© Tamiment Library, New York)

in the north, was planning a major offensive against Madrid in the Guadalajara sector. To take Teruel would be a major distraction and help regain the military initiative.

On leaving Mondéjar, Commissar Bob Cooney emphasised the need to defend notable Republican victories and called for vigilance as Nationalist agents tried to penetrate the ranks with disruptive activities, exploiting every grumbler and weakling.[21] Yet there was also humour from him in the same edition of *Our Fight*. Offering hints for the journey, he suggested: 'If you don't wish to ride on a *camion* (truck) ask your political commissar to hire a taxi; If you want a drink on the journey, ring the bell for an attendant'.

Bob Clark provided a vivid account of activities leading up to the Battle of Teruel.[22] A long train journey into Aragon took the men through vine covered hills, orange groves and deep gorges with towering mountains to Alcaniz. They marched through this desolate, dusty town, with its people mostly gone and shops boarded up. It soon became clear that a long march to the front lay ahead. A demanding uphill hike accompanied by renditions of *It's a Long Way to Tipperary* resulted in frequent rest periods and linking up with anarchist groups who provided fresh water. Their destination was the mountain village of Mas de las Matas, in a sheltered, pleasant valley with the river Guadalupe on its outskirts and cypress trees covering its banks.

The troops were billeted in private houses, with the large, former priest's house hosting the machine-gun section. Thankfully, there was no shortage of food and wine, and the cold days of December leading up to Christmas were largely enjoyable. News came on December 24th that Teruel had fallen, a remarkable feat enabled by virtually surrounding the town and the drafting-in of 40,000 to 50,000 troops – in atrocious weather and on icy roads – under the noses of the Nationalists. This great victory was celebrated on the streets of the village. On the following morning, Christmas Day, the British Battalion paraded in the village square, which was a blaze of colour with bunting and a variety of flags – Catalonian, Republican, Russian and Anarchist – and Christmas was joyously celebrated with 'a very fat pig, wine and nuts'.[23]

Harry Pollitt made a surprise Christmas Day visit to the village with letters, food parcels and news from Britain, along with a message of support and encouragement delivered with masterly rhetoric. The Welshmen in the Anti-tanks had access to a little more luxury, with their four big turkeys and five chickens. Men sat at as many trestle tables as could be found, with tin plates, mugs, biscuit tins or anything else usable as a container. The day ended with a chaotic but memorable village dance. The warmth of the hospitality in Mas de las Matas was soon to be cruelly contrasted with the bitter cold of the Aragon countryside, and seasonal peace replaced by the suffering and destruction of the Teruel campaign. Gilbert Taylor related the memorable visit, around about the same time, of Paul Robeson, his wife and Charlotte Haldane. The camp paraded before them and Robeson gave an hour-long concert to a packed hall with Brigaders shouting out requests. In his speech Robeson, 'his gigantic fist lifted above his head in the red front salute', promised to use his voice for Spain when he returned to Britain.[24]

On New Year's Eve, scores of trucks rumbled into the village to take the men

Members of the No 1 Major Atlee Company. Morris Davies (left) is pictured holding the flag, with Tom Glyn Evans (right) and, to his left is Edwin Greening. (© Imperial War Museum)

to the Teruel front. In below-freezing temperatures they sat on steel floors as the trucks crunched their way up steep mountain roads, sliding dangerously on bends until they reached the top of a mountain range. Another march then brought the troops nearer the Nationalists, who had deployed reinforcements with the aim of retaking Teruel. The British position was on a high cliff, north west of Teruel, which protected any enemy approach along the valley. The new arrivals relieved a Spanish Battalion who had been positioned in trenches in the frozen soil on the slopes of the Sierra Palomera. Taking up positions in the icy winds and a few feet of snow, the brigaders set up machine-guns and tried to make the trenches as safe, deep and comfortable as possible.

Alun Menai Williams' memory of Teruel was of a blizzard, with a bitter wind blowing through a railway tunnel used as a clearing station and a shelter from the shells and bullets.[25] It was so cold, his hands were sticking to metal, and frostbite would prove to be a major factor in the battle. In contrast to their pre-Christmas interlude at Mas de las Matas, the scattered positions of the companies on the front line, and the difficulty of getting food to the men brought a shortage of food and clothing and he had no shoes, just rope sandals. At night men sought shelter in barns, ruins and holes in the mountainside. However, lighting fires turned frozen ground to slush, and icicles started to drop from roofs. There was one advantage of such cold weather – it seemed to keep the lice passive!

The Welshmen of the Anti-tank Battery fared no better as they followed the Battalion. Trucks slid off the road, men dashed into snow-filled ditches to avoid enemy aircraft, and there was a lot of hanging around in barns waiting for orders. Temperatures were -20°, and the first hot meal for three days was sardines and bread. New Year was spent lying in open trucks covered with snow, provisions and fellow, freezing comrades. Fred Thomas described how George Baker from Gelli had improvised a canopy of sorts for two and a small candle, both of which just about lasted until New Years' Day, 1938.[26]

Franco responded to the Republican gains with a counter-offensive, delayed until December 29th by the atrocious weather, then launched by a huge two-hour artillery bombardment supported with an aerial assault. On January 14th, the British Battalion took up its cliff-top position – defending Teruel from attack from the north – on the Santa Barbara hill, overlooking the long valley of the Rio Alfambra. The No. 2 machine-gun company was on the edge of the cliff, using the strongly-enforced placements abandoned by the Nationalists. On the other side of the valley were the Canadian Mackenzie-Papineau Battalion (the 'Mac Paps'), with the Thaelmann Battalion further north at El Muleton. The Anti-tank Battery had one gun on the top of the cliff near the machine-guns, one in Teruel itself, and another nearer the Thaelmanns. James Neugass provided a chilling picture of the condition of the British as they walked along the road

The site of the Battalion's position on the hill at Santa Barbara, with the town of Teruel in the background. (© Author)

towards their trench positions. 'The torn blankets over heads and shoulders and tied like skirts around the waist, the shoes wrapped with rags, the rifles on their shoulders gave them the appearance of a battalion of women beggars. Ranks of stretcher bearers with eight-foot spear-like poles added to the Biblical quality of the scene'.[27] Jim Brewer vividly recalled continual dampness amid three feet of snow, mitigated only by being able to take cognac in the morning with the coffee and toast, which saw him contracting a fever, being hospitalised and narrowly avoiding pneumonia.[28] Yet he was back in line to witness a massive artillery assault on Brigade positions on January 17th, resulting in heavy losses for the Mac Paps and Thaelmanns.

Fred Thomas was watching from high on the mountain, a few kilometres from Teruel. One anti-tank gun had been hauled to this height, an unenviable feat. He witnessed the biggest artillery barrage and longest, most intense air-raid he had yet seen in Spain. Their position also felt the effects of the concentrated bombing, with the ground shaking continuously. It was considerably worse on the mountain crest which bore the brunt of the bombing. Although the British guns repelled a Nationalist infantry advance, the Thaelmanns were

Frank Zamora of Abercrave died here on January 20th, 1938, as his company moved from the top of the hill down into the valley. (© Author)

forced from their mountain position the following day, while three British companies were ordered to move down into the valley and cross the river to protect the flank of the Mac Paps. This was a dangerous move, exposing the British to Nationalist shelling.

It was in this manoeuvre, on January 20th, that Francisco Zamora from Abercrave – a Spanish speaker who was acting as an interpreter – was killed.

Frank, as he was usually known, was born and brought up in the mining village of Abercrave and was a member of the Onllwyn Spanish Aid Committee. Some of Abercrave's small Spanish community worked at the Onllwyn No. 1 colliery, were highly regarded as skilled craftsmen and were active politically within the Communist Party. The Spanish families had brought the war closer to the community, and Frank was the third and last of Abercrave's Spanish community to die there, following Roman Rodriguez and Victorio Esteban.

That night the British dug in, checked their weapons and ammunition, and waited for the inevitable. It came, as the sun rose on the icy landscape, with a fierce bombardment from shells and machine-guns followed by bombing from an Italian squadron flying at 1,500 feet. It must have appeared to be the annihilation of the Major Attlee Company, as 21 members of the Battalion were killed, along with 13 from No. 1 Company. When the bombardment finally ended, hundreds of Nationalist troops swept down the valley expecting little resistance, only to be mown down by the British machine-guns they'd neglected to take into consideration, and the Mac Paps. Soon the valley was silent and deserted, save for bodies littering the ground. Amazingly the position was held, and the Nationalist forces retreated, but at the terrible cost to the Battalion of a third of its men. A few days after the action a memorial service was held, although bodies could not be recovered for this tribute to the fallen, and Bill Alexander fixed a board with the names of those who died – Frank Zamora and 20 others – on Santa Barbara overlooking the valley.

It was not long before the British were called into action again, deployed to the village of Segura de los Baños, about 70 kilometres north of Teruel. Bob Clark remembered it as a romantic location surrounded by thick pinewoods and populated with Spanish cavalry sporting red satin-lined cloaks, riding boots and stirrups. The purpose of this surprise action was to take some pressure off the Republican army defending Teruel and, on February 16th, the Lincolns and the Mac Paps moved against the main target, the village of Vivel de Rio Martin.

Under the cover of darkness the British went into position on the Lincolns' flank, on the brow of a long ridge running down the valley into the village. Bombardment from Nationalist artillery and planes was inaccurate but when Bill Alexander led a push towards the village, it met stiff resistance and a counter-attack by the Nationalists. No. 1 Company, led by Tom Glyn Evans of Kenfig Hill, managed to get to the outskirts of the village, but did not have the resources to advance further. Tom was a highly respected soldier. At the Battle of Jarama he had been second-in-command to Alec Cummings, and also for a while commander of No.1 Company. Jim Brewer, who served under him, regarded Tom as – militarily – the outstanding Welshman in Spain, a soldier who knew the discipline of war.[29] Although the objective had not been met, the Nationalists had to deal with an attack that had surprised them and diverted some resources from Teruel. Superior weaponry and air-power were decisive in spite of the bravery, commended once more, of the Brigaders.

However, Teruel was soon to fall to the Nationalists, and the Battalion went into reserve at Puebla de Valverde. Teruel was an awful combination of severe winter weather, appalling street fighting, atrocious flying conditions and heavy casualties on both sides, with Anthony Beevor estimating that the Nationalists lost 40,000 men, and the Republicans losing 60,000. Worse still, a large number of the wounded suffered from exposure and frostbite at an altitude of 1,200 metres and in temperatures as low as -18°C. Beevor argues that the Republic had set out to capture a city of no strategic value which it could never have hoped to hold. The ineptitude of the plan and incompetence of commanders had, again, led to catastrophic losses in lives and equipment.[30]

The Aragon retreat

Any respite after Teruel was short-lived. Franco took advantage of Republican weakness after the long, hard winter battles to launch a massive offensive. Contrary to expectations of a move against the Madrid and Guadalajara front, he chose to attack the experienced formations on the Aragon front, allegedly with information provided by fifth column Republican officers. He wanted a decisive victory leading to a thrust to the Mediterranean Sea, cutting the Republic into two and isolating Catalonia. For this offensive General Davila assembled 27 divisions comprising 150,000 men with 700 guns and hundreds of tanks. His airpower included 600 aircraft from the German Condor Legion, the Italian *Aviazione Legionaria* and the Spanish *Brigada Aerea*, with their

In freezing temperatures a Republican tank battles through the snow at Teruel. (© Wikimedia Commons)

Heinkels, Dorniers and, for the first time, Junkers 87, also known as Stuka dive bombers. With that aerial firepower it is little wonder that Nationalist infantry casualties were the lowest of any battle in the whole of the war. On March 9th, the Nationalist offensive was let loose on a 60-kilometre front, causing much confusion and panic in Republican ranks and the beginning of a retreat which came to a halt across the river Ebro.

In response, the 15th International Brigade was ordered back to Belchite, which still bore the ugly marks of the previous fighting. The town was almost deserted, with the dead buried under piles of rubble. The British Battalion moved beyond the town into olive groves and fields, but came under heavy fire from artillery and strafing from planes. With no Republican troops between them and the Nationalists, retreat was the only option. Unable to hold their position in the town, the Brigade was forced to take cover in ditches, gulleys and buildings. The last Republican forces to leave Belchite were 90 British soldiers with their Medical Corps. The aim was to delay the Nationalists at every turn, with a strategically-placed battalion covering the Brigade's withdrawal. However, an initially orderly retreat was soon to descend into chaos and confusion with men dispersed in many directions and losing contact with their companies.

Edwin Greening, carrying Tom Howell Jones' rifle and Morris Davies' ammunition, made it through the Nationalist encirclement to the village of Corbera.[31] Men were dispersed throughout the area and hiding out in barns and other places of shelter. In one, Greening unexpectedly came across Welshmen Baden Skinner and John Oliver. He then found himself in a group of four, led by Morris Davies, who were dodging artillery, tanks and air attack and taking refuge wherever they could. The fall of the town of Gandesa, which the Welshmen could see burning, forced them to make for the sanctuary of the river Ebro and rejoin the rest of the Battalion. They finally made it to the Ebro at Cherta, making the last part of the journey along a disused railway line which was still vulnerable to strafing by Nationalist planes. A boat across the river took them to the safety of Catalonia, and a reunion with the Battalion. This loss of contact with the Battalion, typical of the chaos of the retreat, was used unfairly by Lance Rogers to accuse Greening of desertion and led to a number of unsavoury conversations on their return.[32]

Something similar was happening to Alun Menai Williams as the retreat became a rout. He described a time of panic, running and hiding, not knowing where they were or in which direction to run. He found himself with stragglers from the Lincoln Battalion making for Corbera, when a skirmish with Nationalists produced even more casualties. They dodged tanks and infantry and headed, like the others, towards the Ebro.[33] This was also to be the last action for the Anti-tank Battery, since only one gun survived

Nationalist artillery and strafing. Alexander mentioned the Herculean efforts of Jim Brewer in rescuing two guns, which were loaded up on to the trucks.[34] However, he was to see one of them blown up by a low-flying plane. Brewer managed to rescue the remaining gun, even after some of his men disappeared into a farm hoping to catch a chicken for dinner and did not return.[35] Continuing with the gun, he ran into a Republican armoured car with its machine gun trained on him. He said he kept 'the old miners' adage of 'a cool head and a sharp mandril'. Identities having been clarified, Brewer was given a tow and rode majestically on the gun into safe territory. The gun, though, was surrendered to the Republican army and sent to the central front, so Brewer attached himself to a Polish machine-gun team.

The following weeks saw a series of phased withdrawals until the Battalion crossed the river Ebro at Cherta on April 3rd. On March 10th, they had taken up a position defending the road to Lecera, south of Belchite, but were constantly pushed back along the road towards Hijar and Alcaniz. A number of positions were established, only to be abandoned when they could no longer resist and there was a danger of being surrounded. Some soldiers became detached from their units, and it became almost impossible to keep together as a viable group. They were joined by troops from other units who had lost their way. There was little respite until they reached Caspe, by which time they could no longer be called a viable battalion.

Gilbert Taylor, manager of the Collet's bookshop in Castle Arcade, Cardiff – the meeting point for volunteers from south Wales – disappeared around this time. Apparently his misuse of Spanish Aid funds came to the notice of Harry Pollitt who gave him the choice of going to Spain or being exposed. There from November 1937 to March 1938, he wrote a remarkable 230 pages of correspondence in letters and cards, most to his wife Sylvia, about such things as the importance of chocolate and cigarettes for boosting morale, his wall newspapers, his illnesses, the work of commissars and his political activities and other Welsh volunteers.[36] His name is on a list of casualties on the Belchite-Caspe front during March 1938 (although Tom Picton and George Baker also appear erroneously) and another dated September 5th of British personnel missing and presumed killed.[37] In addition, a letter from Colonel Antonio Gordon Garcia, written in Spanish, contains a certificate confirming that Taylor had disappeared between March 10th and 17th, 1938 during sustained fighting in the Caspe-Belchite sector. He is deemed by some to have both an inglorious past and a fate which is in some doubt.[38] He had written from Benicassim, where he was hospitalised with flu, early in March shortly before joining the Battalion, and was not seen after March 1938. One letter from the archived collection was written by Alec Cummings, who explained that Taylor's unit was engaged in very severe action and that he was wounded, although it is not clear whether he was captured or left on the battle field.

Taylor was fiercely political and, as an assistant commissar in Spain, quite critical of what he regarded as the negligence, backwardness and stagnation of the political work there. His extensive collection of letters indicate that, despite the ambiguity surrounding his actions and his previous financial ineptitude, Taylor, plagued by illness and latterly tempted to apply for transfer to the medical services and the Albacete auto park, wanted to face all challenges, including service at the front. He wrote that he hated everything to do with being a soldier but recognised the necessity of meeting force with force to protect culture, peace and progress.

On March 17th, Caspe fell to three Nationalist divisions which had surrounded the town. Confusion reigned among the 150 or so remaining British, as they struggled in a rearguard action whose ranks were broken by hand-to-hand fighting. Harry Dobson was one of a group, including Battalion Commander Sam Wild, which was captured by an enemy patrol. Rust describes how they took the opportunity to escape when the Nationalist soldiers, searching through their captives' pockets for something to steal, dropped their guard.[39] Apparently Dobson used a tin of bully beef to assault one of Franco's soldiers and make his escape. Individuals and groups, cut off from the Battalion and with no food or water and little ammunition, struggled to get away and keep out of sight of the enemy. Some were captured, some shot and some managed to make for the next stop – the town of Batea.

Gilbert Taylor, formerly the manager of Collet's bookshop in Cardiff and a prolific letter-writer, wrote 230 pages of correspondence from Spain. (© John Mehta)

At Batea they could gather, wait for stragglers to re-join the Battalion, and rest. It was a time for reorganisation and re-arming, as well as songs around the fire, football matches and morale-raising talks by the political commissar. Yet everything was overshadowed by continuing uncertainty and the potential division of the Republic into two separate territories. Despite that, the men felt deeply for the Spanish people and were angry that non-intervention had denied them the weapons to defend themselves. They were determined to fight to the end against fascism. It was also a crucial time for the Republican army. New recruits from training camps were joined by the return of the previously wounded, to bolstering the Battalion's strength to 650 troops. It was here that Billy Griffiths joined the Battalion, and one of his first experiences was the ambush at Calaceite.

Meanwhile, the Nationalists continued their push against the Republican lines, driving ever more incisively their wedge towards Tortosa, and beyond it the Meditteranean. On March 30th, the British positions came under a huge attack, and the Battalion moved towards Gandesa to support the Communist 11th Division – the Listers. In the confusion, it was not known that the Listers had retreated and that the Battalion was now exposed to the full force of the Nationalists in this sector.

Morien Morgan from Ynysybwl was in No. 2 Machine Gun Company and an eyewitness to the episode which cost 150 men killed and almost as many captured.[40] Companies 1 and 2 were marching near Calaceite in two single lines, with No. 1 taking the lead. When shots were heard from the front group, it turned out that in the poor early morning light they'd turned around a bend, straight into a group of Nationalist armoured cars and tanks. Their forward scouts had missed them, and Morgan claimed they had similar uniforms and were mistaken initially for International Brigade troops returning from the front. Then the tanks opened fire, other Nationalist Italian troops appeared from the woods, and all hell broke loose.

These small Fiat tanks were often mocked by the Russians as patrol cars and their drivers as riot police, but on this day they did their job. The first company were now surrounded, and the second took cover in nearby vineyards. Emrys Jones had dropped down on the right side of the road, a steep slope which stopped the tanks training their guns on the men. A small group managed to take position on a ridge, but were shelled and strafed with one plane making persistent runs.[41] The machine-gunners at the rear made a stand and damaged some tanks, but the outcome was disastrous. Reports of the action by Battalion Commissar Bob Cooney and Commander George Fletcher describe how the tanks passed between two columns of the Battalion before any retaliatory action could be taken.

Among those captured during, or soon after, the action were numerous Welsh volunteers including Jack Jones of Clydach Vale, Tom Adlam of Pentre,

The bend in the road at Calaceite was the scene of a disastrous engagement for the Battalion which led to the death of one Welshman and the capture of many more. (© Author)

David Barrett of Blackwood, Ivor Davies of Neath, Len John and J. Widess of Cardiff, Thomas Jones of Penygraig, Tom Picton of Treherbert, Morien Morgan of Ynysybwl, Ken Bevan of Gorseinon and Robert Watts of Swansea. It also appears that one Welshman died in the action, as 24-year-old Dan Murphy of Cardiff is recorded as going missing, presumed dead, at this time.[42] Other than an address in Ely, Cardiff, not much is known about him except that he was a sailor with no military experience.

There was nothing left now but to retreat. Morien Morgan recounted how another Welshman, Morgan Havard, was badly wounded by bullets to his right arm, shoulder and knee, and was left by the side of a road. For safety's sake, Havard was initially placed in a culvert before being carried away during the retreat. Carrying the stretcher would become impossible at night on the precipitous and hilly terrain as the men, about 20 in all, slid down the ravines. 'So the matter was put to Morgan Havard, explaining to him what the problem was. Without hesitation he said: "All you go on; leave me by the roadside on the stretcher, in the shade of a tree if possible, with cigarettes." He would stay there, wounded though he was. Then we just carried on marching.' Havard was found by the Nationalists, taken to hospital and later imprisoned. His leg was operated on, but he lost his arm. His daughter said that he rarely spoke of his experiences there to his family, nor mentioned his harsh treatment or the anguish and pain of losing his right arm. However, he did say that he could never again face eating sweetcorn or baked beans, as they were the staple diet at the prisoner of war camp.[43]

Most of the captured Welshmen were taken first to the Italian controlled town of Alcaniz, and then to the military academy at Zaragoza. The atrocious sanitary conditions and attempts to break the Brigaders' morale were nothing compared to what they were to endure next at the former monastery in San Pedro near Burgos, where some were imprisoned for up to a year in a brutal, overcrowded and inhumane existence.[44] Ironically, over the main doorway of their new prison was a horseman trampling down Moors. Tom Jones, who arrived there after a stay in hospital, was amazed to find it housed 600 prisoners,

Morgan Havard – front, second from the right – with a group of prisoners after his arrest. (© Julie Norton, Morgan's daughter)

and not just soldiers, but republican-sympathisers such as doctors, Basque priests, lawyers and others. It was not long before a Communist Party committee was set up, as were groups to maintain community and morale in the face of intimidation by the guards and attempts to break their spirit. Classes were set up on various topics, games of chess took place with pieces fashioned out of soap, and there was singing and reading.

However, in a public meeting after returning home, Leonard John related how some prisoners had been beaten and bruised beyond recognition, half-starved but later fattened up before exchange for enemy prisoners.[45] Morien Morgan describes the extreme cold and how, deprived of overcoats and valuables, he was dressed in a shirt, trousers and Spanish slippers. Lice got everywhere, washing facilities were practically non-existent, the lack of proper food affected the men's stomachs and skin, and the guards took great pleasure in beating the prisoners on a regular basis, such as when the Brigaders were beaten to their knees and forced to worship at Mass.

The South Wales Miners Federation twice sent £5 to each of the 20 or so captured Welshmen. The money was pooled to provide exercise books, pencils and tobacco bought in the nearby village by a friendly guard.[46] Jack Jones wrote of the dearth of books and the unremitting diet of beans, bread and sardines.[47] Ironically he had written home only a couple of weeks before his capture to say how well they were eating, despite the shortage of butter and milk and other things which the Spanish people were willing to sacrifice so that the war could be won. Tom Jones remembered sharing one tap and one toilet with 200 other prisoners. He described a medical room with beds for ten people, but that no one who entered it ever came out alive.

Before release some prisoners were transferred to an Italian-run camp at Palencia, south west of Burgos, from where they would be exchanged for Republican-held Italian prisoners. Their treatment at Palencia was not as severe as San Pedro. Tommy Adlam said the closest shave he had there was when an Italian officer pointed a revolver at his head but, apart from a kick on the leg, he did not suffer any abuse, yet a Welsh comrade was beaten with a stick because he whispered and did not maintain the proper attitude on parade. He recounted that they had to attend Catholic services and one priest used to call them "my brothers" and then added: "I would like to bash you up against the walls".[48]

It was the singing that left an impression on Morgan Havard, with old favourites sung with amended words to promote the Brigades or lampoon the fascists. He remembered the day when, inflamed by the Republican advance across the Ebro, the guards used sticks and rifle butts to attack groups of men who were using their carefully created amusements or just talking together.[49] The prisoners were eventually released in batches later in the year, and at the beginning of 1939. Tommy Jones of Penygraig suggested that those who were 'most politically advanced' were kept back for that very reason.[50]

Following the catastrophe at Calaceite, where prominent leaders such as Wally Tapsell had been killed, the Battalion was now in disarray so the order was given to disperse and small groups attempted to find their way out of the danger over the hills towards Gandesa and the river Ebro. Billy Griffiths was further back around the bend at Calaceite and with considerable calm set up a machine-gun which soon ran out of ammunition. [51] He then managed to catch up with a group which included Sid James and Jack Roberts, both of Rhondda, who managed to rescue a Maxim machine-gun and regroup in the village. From there the group of seven took the bottom road out of the town with Griffiths and James dragging the heavy machine-gun. At Gandesa there was a perilous job, of helping to cover the retreat of the men in front-line positions, to be done. The group then made their way to Corbera, and on to Mora de Ebro where they joined other retreating troops waiting to cross the river by the bridge.

The situation there was chaotic, with refugees, soldiers, officers and car and lorry drivers trying to position themselves to cross the bridge. Once across, Sid

The Maxim machine gun – developed by Hiram Maxim in 1884 and used by the British Battalion during the Civil War – was the first fully automatic machine gun but was considered old, heavy and bulky by the late 1930s. (© Alan Warren)

Tom Jones – middle, second row – with other Republican prisoners at the San Pedro Concentration Camp. (© Keith Jones)

James made for a hospital with his badly blistered and cut feet while Billy Griffiths was told by some Americans: "There is no Brigade, no army, it is all over".[52] Now completely lost in Tortosa and thinking the war was over, Griffiths joined a group making for Valencia, but was arrested (presumably as a suspected deserter) on the journey. He successfully made a case that he was trying to return to his unit, and was eventually reunited with them. Griffiths' narrative is strange and confusing and his arrest might seem incongruous in the light of his later involvement in dealing with disciplinary issues.

Harry Dobson was with a group that got lost and wandered into the Nationalist lines. On one occasion they were arrested, but managed to slip away in the darkness; on another when challenged they came up with the reply "*Italiano*"; and on a third hid in the home of a Republican sympathiser who gave them food and information about the enemy's position. Eventually the group made it to the Ebro, which they swam across with the help of logs provided for weaker swimmers. Morien Morgan, after the chaos of Calaceite, continued with his group, marching by night and resting by day. However, he collapsed with a bad bout of tonsillitis and lost contact with the group. Having recovered he started to trek east without food, apart from a crust of bread, for about a week. He began to hallucinate, but then wandered into an encampment which turned out to be a Spanish fascist unit, and was arrested and interrogated. When they found his university diary and what they thought was a silver shaving kit in his pocket, they were convinced that he

Tom Glyn Evans of Bridgend was one of the outstanding and highly respected Welsh comrades in Spain. (© Deputy Director RGASPI, Moscow)

was rich and an important officer. After further questioning by senior officers he was taken back to his comrades at the San Pedro prison camp.[53]

In Calaceite, survivors were rallied by Malcolm Dunbar, now the Brigade's Chief of Staff, and were joined by a group of Mac Paps. After a tortuous route over hills, down into valleys, through gulleys and gorges, they found a position on high ground overlooking the Gandesa-Tortosa road. This was a perfect defensive location to delay the advancing Nationalist troops, and give the retreating Republican army more time to get men and equipment across the river Ebro. The group had now grown to 200 strong: British, Canadian, Spanish, American and Germans from the Thaelmann Battalion. Apart from a small Spanish-crewed tank their weapons were mainly rifles, grenades and one machine-gun.

Yet throughout the day, this poorly armed group of exhausted men managed to delay Franco's pursuing columns of infantry, lorries and armoured cars. At dusk Dunbar ordered an end to the defence of the road and the men withdrew towards Tortosa. Rust was keen to point out that all the men were heroes, but mentions especially a Welshman, Lieutenant Tom Evans of Bridgend, who stood out while leading the group overlooking the road and directing the rifle fire against the tanks.

They left their position around midnight, catching up with the main force marching to Cherta, where they crossed the Ebro over the bridge which carried the railway line to Barcelona. Long lines of men and equipment, and some refugees with a few possessions, trailed over the bridge. Gregory recounted that they must have been among the last of the Republican troops to take that route, since they had not travelled far before they heard the Republican engineers blowing the bridge.

It looked like the end of the Republic. Poor leadership and the massive military superiority of the Nationalist forces were blamed for the near-destruction of the Republican army. The British Battalion had been decimated, and Franco's forces reached Vinaròs on the Mediterranean coast, splitting the Republic into two. Bitter recriminations surfaced after the Brigades were withdrawn and were still potent 30 years later. Edwin Greening recorded that when Sam Wild was asked to say a few words at a miners' gala in Cardiff, Tom Glyn Evans was heard to say of Wild: "Some bloody hero. At Caspe he and HQ of the Battalion buggered off and left everybody to find their own way out".[54]

Notes

1.   Antony Beevor, *The Battle for Spain*, op. cit., pp.332-3.
2.   See Bill Alexander, *British Volunteers for Liberty*, op. cit., p.143ff.
3.   *Brigade Handbook*, p.206.
4.   Bob Condon, *Aberdare Leader*, August 7th, 1937. Condon seems to have enjoyed riding on a *burro* (ass) and describes how soldiers and peasants worked together as brothers. He realised how primitive the methods were in the use of the 'reaping hook' and comments on the fact that most of the peasants were illiterate.
5.   Jim Brewer, Imperial War Museum, interview, Reel 7.
6.   *Colliers Crusade*.
7.   Walter Gregory, *The Shallow Grave*, op. cit., p.77.
8.   Richard Felstead, *No Other Way: Jack Russia and the Spanish Civil War*, op. cit., p.99.
9.   Frank Ryan (Ed.), *The Book of the XV Brigade*, op. cit., p.255.
10. Vincent Brome, *The International Brigades*, London, Heinemann, 1965, p.22.
11. Hugh Thomas, *The Spanish Civil War*, op. cit., p.726.
12. Bill Alexander, *British Volunteers for Liberty*, op. cit., p.150.
13. Frank Ryan (Ed.), *The Book of the XV Brigade*, op. cit., pp.273-4.
14. Edwin Greening, *From Aberdare to Albacete*, op. cit., pp.70-1. For more details see also, Imperial War Museum interview.
15. Frank Ryan (Ed.), *The Book of the XV Brigade*, op. cit., p.281.
16. Ibid., pp.261-6.
17. Alun Menai Williams, *From the Rhondda to the Ebro*, op. cit., pp.168-9.
18. Antony Beevor, *The Battle for Spain*, op. cit., p.334.
19. Bob Clark, *No Boots to my Feet*, Stoke, Students Bookshops Ltd., 1984, p.33.
20. Imperial War Museum, interview, Reel 6.
21. *Our Fight*, December 10th, 1937.
22. Bob Clark, *No Boots to my Feet*, op. cit., pp.32ff.
23. Bill Alexander, *British Volunteers for Liberty*, op. cit., p.161.
24. Letter to Sylvia, December 1937. Gilbert Taylor Letters Collection, Glamorgan Archives, Cardiff.
25. Alun Menai Williams, *From the Rhondda to the Ebro*, op. cit., p.168.
26. Fred Thomas, *To Tilt at Windmills: Memoir of the Spanish Civil War*, op. cit., p.63.
27. James Neugass, *War is Beautiful*, New York, The New Press, 2008, p.147.
28. Imperial War Museum, interview, Reel 6.
29. Ibid.
30. Antony Beevor, *The Battle for Spain*, op. cit., p.359.
31. Edwin Greening, *From Aberdare to Albacete*, op. cit., pp.72-5, and Imperial War Museum, interviews, Reels 3 & 4.
32. Ibid., p.104.
33. Alun Menai Williams, *From the Rhondda to the Ebro*, op. cit., p.176.
34. Bill Alexander, *British Volunteers for Liberty*, op. cit., p.171.

35. Imperial War Museum, interview, Reel 6. Also letter in Marx Memorial Library, Box A-12.
36. Gilbert Taylor Letters Collection, Glamorgan Archives, Cardiff.
37. RGASPI 545/6/39. See also John D. Mehta, 'Forgotten Names, Remembered Faces – The Bookshop Manager', in Anindya Raychaudhuri (Ed.), *The Spanish Civil War: Exhuming a Buried Past*, Cardiff, University of Wales Press, 2013.
38. Robert Stradling, *Wales and the Spanish Civil War*, op. cit., p.152, believes Taylor took measures to avoid being at the front and feigned illness. He uses muster calls on the Ebro and evidence from a private collection to suggest that Taylor went missing during the time of consolidation beyond the Ebro and that he may well have been executed. There is no firm evidence to substantiate the latter. The *Welwyn Times* of July 7th, 1938 was informed that Taylor was 'missing' and surmised that he 'was wounded and left on the field'.
39. William Rust, *Britons in Spain*, op. cit., p.47.
40. Morien Morgan, Imperial War Museum, interview, Reel 2.
41. Letter to George Hill, Marx Memorial Library, Box 50.
42. RGASPI 545/6/176 and 545/2/127.
43. Julie Norton (daughter of Morgan Havard) – private email.
44. For a fuller description see *They Fought in Franco's Jails*, CPGB, 1939, South Wales Miners' Library, D.M. Thomas Box 3. Also Tom Jones' unpublished memoirs (Marx Memorial Library).
45. *Aberdare Leader*, November 26th, 1938.
46. *Colliers Crusade* and Imperial War Museum interview, Reel 3. Also 'Living Conditions at San Pedro de Cardena Concentration Camp' in unpublished manuscript, 1939.
47. Letter to his parents and sister, August 14th, 1938 – *Miners Against Fascism*, p.289.
48. *Rhondda Leader*, November 5th, 1938.
49. *Morning Star*, 1969.
50. In a letter from Morien Morgan to Arthur Horner, September 30th, 1939, Richard Burton Archives, Swansea University.
51. Billy Griffiths, unpublished memoirs, South Wales Miners' Library, Swansea University. (pages not numbered)
52. Ibid.
53. Imperial War Museum, interview, Reel 2.
54. Edwin Greening, *From Aberdare to Albacete*, op. cit., pp.105-6.

7

A Crossing Too Far

The Battle of the Ebro

The banks of the river Ebro offer a variety of environments – fruit trees and rice fields, rocky gorges, semi-desert and lush vegetation – set against a backdrop of stunning mountain peaks. Further along the banks from where people now take river cruises and others fish, the blood of the volunteers of

Welsh volunteers at Darmos, April 1938. Standing (left to right): Rowland Williams, Tom Howell Jones, Jack Roberts, Arthur Williams, John Oliver, Tom Glyn Evans, Emrys Jones, Archie Cook, Goff Price, Sid James, Edwin Greening. Kneeling (left to right): Evan Jones, Billy Griffiths, Emlyn Lloyd, Morris Davies. (© Richard Burton Archives)

Edwin Greening of Aberdare had joined the Battalion in the autumn of 1937. (© Deputy Director RGASPI, Moscow)

the International Brigades flowed in what became known as the last throw of the dice for the Republican army. It was at Asco, a small town nestled in beautiful countryside, that the British Battalion made its crossing during the Ebro offensive of July 1938. Peeping through the trees and bushes and pushing up into the skyline are the crags and crevices, rocks and peaks that made up the relentless terrain that was the scene of the fighting which followed the river crossing.

In the spring of 1938, what was left of the Republican army after the retreat from Aragon began to re-assemble on the north banks of the Ebro. Surviving Brigaders had crossed by boat or simply swam – assembling near the village of Darmos – knowing that many of their comrades hadn't been so fortunate having been taken prisoner or shot dead by the advancing fascist forces. The superior numbers, weapons and tactics of the Nationalists had left a depleted and disheartened brigade and battalion, yet Franco did not press home his advantage. He instead turned to an offensive against Valencia, preferring a long drawn-out war of attrition and the complete destruction of his enemies. This gave the Welsh volunteers a welcome period of rest and recuperation, accompanied by training, reorganisation and the rebuilding of morale through fiestas, singsongs, discussions, reading, football matches and competitions between units and battalions. Men enjoyed hot showers in the travelling shower van, and basked in the warmth of the Spanish sun.

Marca

Among those at Darmos was Edwin Greening. He described how, on May 28th, 1938, the British were transported by lorry, down the Ebro valley, south to

A volunteer sitting next to his chabola – *a rough shelter – which was home to many on the front line during the Civil War. (© Tamiment Library, New York)*

Marca. 'There among the vines and under the nut trees, we the British Battalion of the 15th International Brigade, lived, slept and trained for war.'[1] Some built brush huts and the air was fresh and the food plentiful. The camp was nicknamed 'Chabola Valley' after the Spanish word, *chabola*, for the brush huts.

Greening had been chosen by Captain Sam Wild to be an infantry observer with the No. 1 Major Attlee Company and, in June 1938, was sent to a training school in nearby Marca. The school was held in the village cinema (he describes it 'as big as the Park Cinema, Aberdare'). A large room was stocked with books sent to the Brigades by well-wishers and used by the political officers. The course included reconnaissance trips in the blistering heat along the river Ebro, mapping the terrain and identifying enemy fortifications on the other side of the river. He regularly patrolled on the bank of the river, and often had slanging matches with Nationalists on the other side as they tried to demoralise the British by suggesting that defeat was fast approaching.

This was a time of low morale for the Brigaders. Many of their friends and comrades had not returned across the Ebro, and there were emotional reunions with those who did. The volunteers seized the opportunity by getting to know the local people, enjoying their company and beginning to develop good relationships with their hosts. New volunteers began to appear while fresh Spanish and Catalan conscripts were brought in, some as young as 16. These became known as 'La Quinta del Biberón', 'The Baby Bottle Conscripts'.

Dr Angela Jackson relates how, as well as rest and recuperation, there was time to think about the horrors of the war and the longing to be home.[2] Desertion remained a problem in some battalions, and cases of insubordination and drunkenness increased. Lack of appropriate and basic equipment, including clothes and shoes, was an issue and bouts of dysentery caused further discomfort. There were also concerns about medical care for the wounded, in particular out-of-date ambulances. Medical care for the planned offensive included hospitals based in farmhouses and business premises, the unlikeliest being a large cave near La Bisbal de Falset and a railway tunnel at Pradell station.

The cave hospital was equipped with 80 beds, a store of medical supplies and an operating theatre, with improvised partition walls. Lighting was generated by a car engine and local people brought fruit and vegetables. Those who died

The cave hospital near La Bisbel de Falset, to where injured men were taken for treatment and surgery during the Battle of the Ebro. (© Author)

there were buried in a communal grave in the village cemetery. It was to this cave hospital that Harry Dobson was brought, and here that he died. His picture is displayed in a panel on the wall of the cave. During the war the Republican medical services developed a system of Battalion Aid Posts, a series of forward hospitals with mobile surgical teams and a variety of rearguard hospitals. The aim was to reduce the time-lag between the sustaining of a wound and receiving the appropriate treatment.

The tunnel at Pradell is the longest on the Spanish railway network. One train would be kept under cover in the tunnel as a hospital train, and another used to transport the wounded to hospital in Reus. Those who needed surgery would be dealt with in the operating room on the hospital train, while up to 200 men could be evacuated on the other.

Local people were often requested to give extra help to the wounded, or dig ditches to bury the dead when the village cemeteries were full.[3] Most of the volunteers who died in battle were buried in communal graves.

Welsh volunteer nurse Margaret Powell aboard a hospital train. They were used to transport wounded soldiers to larger towns and cities for medical treatment, but sometimes men would undergo urgent procedures on the train itself. (© Imperial War Museum)

The field where the volunteers not only played football but had machine gun-dismantling competitions, and the rock pools where men enjoyed bathing and relaxed in waters warmed by the hot sun are both still visible 60 years later. Angela Jackson writes about the fiestas enjoyed during the spring and early summer of 1938.[4] There were many football matches, boxing contests and meals in which meat stew, sausages, bread and jam were washed down with copious amounts of *vino rojo*. Memorable celebrations were held on May 1st when visitors from Barcelona arrived and Jackson cites memories of when '*La Pasionaria*' herself visited. Among other visiting officials and politicians, Harry Pollitt was a regular and loyal supporter of the Welsh volunteers in the International Brigades. Concerned about the Battalion's losses, he arrived on a surprise visit with letters from home. Liverpool Labour Councillor J.L. Jones turned up with a

The signage of this former Intendencia *(Brigade storehouse) in Marca remains visible 80 years after the end of the Civil War. (© Author)*

letter from the Liverpool Trades and Labour Council regretting the 'cowardly attitude of the capitalist government here in England'.[5] While newspapers and Nationalist supporters in Britain were making uncomplimentary comments about the competence of the Republican army, volunteers on the banks of the Ebro were honing their skills and building up their resolve as well as their political discipline.

The British Battalion was in slightly better shape than other 15th Brigade Battalions gathered on the banks of the Ebro. The brigade – 500 men divided into five companies with the Spanish now outnumbering the British – was now led by the experienced Spanish Major Valledor, and the Battalion by the widely respected Sam Wild. Numbers had increased, with the addition of new, good quality volunteers, including Ivor Gale of Abertillery, Sid James of Treherbert, Brinley Jenkins and Archie Ledbury of Swansea, Bryn Jones of Tredegar, Evan Price of Coelbren, James Strangward of Onllwyn and William Rogers of Wrexham. The new recruits were quick to volunteer to dig trenches along the Ebro and provided patrols along a ten mile stretch of the river bank. Training began to intensify and take on different methods, such as running across riverbeds and up and down ravines, in preparation to confound both the sceptics at home and the enemy across the Ebro.

The daring Ebro offensive was intended to divide the Nationalist army, restore the land link between Catalonia and the rest of Republican Spain and draw off forces threatening an advance on Valencia in the south. Anthony Beevor describes the plan as 'wildly optimistic' and illustrating a failure to learn from previous mistakes. Any initial surprise was sure to be reversed by rapid redeployment, before air and artillery superiority crushed the move with a catastrophic loss of aircraft and equipment. It was, in short, a 'monumental gamble against very unfavourable odds'.[6] It certainly did extend the war, and drained the resources of the Nationalists, but also sounded the death knell of the Republic.

John Morgan Roberts of Tonypandy, a new recruit in early 1938. (© Richard Burton Archives, Swansea Univ.)

Crossing the Ebro

During July 23rd and 24th, 1938, the 15th Brigade and its equipment were brought closer to the river bank. The intention was for the Republican army, under the command of Lieutenant Colonel Juan Modesto, to cross along a 50-mile front from Mequinenza to the Ebro delta, with the main assault on the curve between Fayon and Cherta. This complicated, detailed manoeuvre, planned in four phases and involving about 80,000 men was the largest campaign of the war. The Republicans, though, were deficient in artillery, having only about 1500 field guns.

Billy Griffiths had come to Spain to bolster the Communist Party within the British Battalion, working on party strength and discipline. Although without rank, he worked at battalion and brigade level as commissar and party secretary and was given special praise as one of the best comrades in Alonso Elliot's final report on the Battalion.[7] Although the Republican Government outlawed party organisations in the army, Griffiths saw his work as building a party which could function in action, both strengthening the command and maintaining

Welsh volunteers photographed before the Battle of the Ebro: (standing, left to right) Alfred Morris of Mardy, Tom Glyn Evans of Bridgend and Morris Davies of Treharris. (© Richard Burton Archives, Swansea Univ.)

the discipline and morale of the rank and file.[8] He established small committees in each company, and contacts at section and platoon level. An early Brigade meeting he attended threw up the potential conflict between military efficiency and party function. The view that each was equally important was not endorsed by all the volunteers. Some have suspected a darker side to him. Stradling has suggested that, while no one worked harder to restore the battalion's discipline and morale, he acted like an informer in reporting men to the secret police, had betrayed confidences and that his actions had led to the incarceration of many volunteers in the brutally inhumane Castelldefels prison.[9]

Griffiths described how training now took on a new character, with preparations to cross the river – in silence – at night, and long route marches by night, and said the morale of the Battalion had been transformed. The military training was accompanied by morale boosting events, such as the concert held the night before the crossing. However, sleep eluded him during the night: 'All night long the traffic roared along the road above. This was a big offensive, along a 100 kilometre front...I looked at the sleeping forms around me, huddled in their blankets, and wondered how many would see the following night'.[10]

The crossing began in the early hours of July 25th, 1938, using boats hidden in bushes and trees along the banks of the river, after specialists from the X1V Commando Corps had swum across beforehand to locate key Nationalist positions. The night-time crossing, on a moonless night, relied on speed and surprise as they launched their wooden boats and inflatables and set up the *pasarelas,* footbridges on cork floats. With the sentries silenced by the commandos, over 100 boats with up to eight men in each were rowed across the swiftly flowing river Ebro.

Billy Griffiths of Tonypandy was tasked with strengthening the Communist Party within the Battalion. (© Tamiment Library, New York)

Thousands of men from other brigades crossed, but the Canadian Mac Paps were the first of the 15th Brigade across, near Ascó. The British and the Lincoln Brigade followed, singing revolutionary songs, but Nationalist bombers had been quickly deployed and were swooping menacingly on the advancing Republicans. While the 15th Brigade had crossed the river with some success, their comrades in the 14th Brigade further south near the delta were suffering heavy casualties. For Edwin Greening, the crossing point for the British Battalion – from Vinebre on the east side towards Ascó on the west – was familiar from his observation duties and he and his fellow observers were able to lead the first group down to the water. At the bank they clambered into long boats which were also pulled from the other side, with a sling on the boat stopping it drifting down the river. Fred Thomas described the roar of tanks, guns and lorries crossing the pontoon bridges and then the chaos and congestion as a bridge collapsed. 'The narrow track was packed solid with vehicles – trucks carrying urgently needed ammunition and material, others pulling or towing big guns, many more crowded with men, some light tanks, everything necessary to the success of the assault and, equally needed, ambulances to bring back the already many wounded'.[11]

Over 100 boats were used to ferry soldiers across the river Ebro for the final offensive. (© Tamiment Library, New York)

Corbera

The British made at first for Corbera, 15 kilometres away, which they reached by late afternoon with little initial resistance, making contact with the 13th Brigade whose task was to enter the town. However, they were held up by fire from Moors on nearby hills, and it took an all-night battle to remove them, enabling the 13th Brigade to take the town. It remained in Republican hands until September 4th when their lines were broken, forcing a retreat. Billy Griffiths, used as a scout and runner by Battalion Commander Sam Wild, seemed to be constantly on the move and often under fire. On one occasion he came across a mule loaded with rifles; on another he shared a tin of tuna with Harry Dobson, crouched under a terrace wall.

The town of Corbera was completely destroyed during the war. The lower part has been rebuilt but the upper part, known as *Poble Vell* (Old Town), left as a reminder of the destruction. An information sign describes the old town as symbolising the tragedy of war and remaining as a silent witness to the violence and brutality of air attacks and artillery fire on the civil population. It is a steep climb, and the only building standing is the church of *Sant Pere*, partially

The town of Corbera d'Ebre was destroyed during the Civil War, with the ruins left as a memorial of the conflict. (© Author)

destroyed with visible damage from shells and bullets. It stands dramatically on the skyline, preserved but not restored, with a cover enabling activities to take place inside. From it, one can enjoy stunning views of the rugged mountains of *La Sierra de Caballs* and *La Sierra de Pàndols*, where most of the 115 days of Ebro battles took place. Sculptures, art and poetry creations are scattered among the shells of buildings with their exposed beams and piles of rubble.

Puig de l'Áliga - Hill 481

The Republicans were still on the offensive, despite the element of surprise wearing off and Franco rushing up air and artillery reinforcements. Intelligence may have forewarned Franco, and it is possible that he chose to let the Republicans extend themselves before retaliating. However, it would take the Nationalists a few months to recapture the ground they had lost. For

Known as 'Hill 481', the Brigade's courageous assault lasted for five days and resulted in the death and wounding of many of the Welsh volunteers.

the British volunteers, the fighting now centred on the hills around Gandesa, an important communications centre with roads and railways criss-crossing the area. The key hill protecting Gandesa from recapture by the Republicans was Hill 481, called the 'Pimple' by Brigaders. Almost impregnable, it offered a distinct advantage to whichever side held it.

Strong fortifications – bunkers, trenches, barbed wire and booby traps – supplemented the powerful natural defences provided by almost sheer slopes. There was very little cover, no support from tanks or artillery, and they were fired on not only from the top of the hill but also from Gandesa itself. Facing an endless barrage of fire in the intense heat, and with little food, water or sleep the Brigaders soon became exhausted. The assault on the hill was a thankless task and meant clambering up and down ridges in full view of the trenches and machine gun posts to which the veteran Nationalist commander of the sector, General Fernando Barrón y Ortiz, had rushed reinforcements to protect, while locals erected barricades to cut off routes into the town.

The British No 1 Company attacked the hill early on the July 27th, 1938, under orders to show audacity, speed and determination but was beaten back by a hail of fire from guns, grenades rolled down the hillside and artillery and the volunteers were mown down in a suicidal death trap. For five days three companies of the 15th Brigade kept up their efforts to take the hill, but were often pinned down and trapped for hours by incessant fire. Casualties were high, and a number of commanders of No. 2 Company were killed or wounded. Billy Griffiths was with Harry Dobson on Hill 481 when his comrade suffered the wound which led to his death. Dobson was one of the most respected of the Welsh volunteers, a coal miner from Rhondda, trade union activist, communist and a fierce campaigner against fascism who'd been jailed for his activities. On release his first response was: "How do I get to Spain?" Recognised as having a shrewd perception of the problems facing the working class, he spent a year as a student in the International Lenin School in Moscow. He was a distinguished veteran of Brunete – where he was wounded while helping two comrades – Belchite and Teruel, and acted as commissar. English Brigader Tony Gilbert cited him as one of the three comrades who impressed him most, calling him the 'stuff that Saints are made of'.[12] Battalion Commissar Bob Cooney poignantly wrote: 'Not the least of fascism's crimes is that it does to death the finest sons of the people – the men who have the greatest right to live'.[13] Harry's name is immortalised with other prominent brigaders on the monument high on the Sierra de Pàndols, and he was the only Welsh volunteer applauded with an obituary in the *Volunteer for Liberty*.[14] There, his many qualities are celebrated including his modesty, quiet yet pungent humour and, above all, his coolness, astuteness and bravery. The meal of tinned tuna shared with Billy Griffiths was his last.

The following day Dobson and Morris Davies of Treharris attacked a ridge on Hill 481. Both were wounded by machine gun fire but, since Davies' wound seemed more serious, Harry insisted that he be stretchered away first. Griffiths tells how Dobson lay for hours, his life blood literally ebbing away. Alun Menai Williams was also on the hill when the two men were shot. He tells how Harry, having been shot in the upper abdomen, dropped with a slight moan, and how Morris Davies was hit in the stomach. Williams thought that Harry had been killed outright, so tended to the wounded Davies by padding his wound and tying his legs to his stomach, before being taken away by the only stretcher party in that forward position.[15] Davies survived but took no further part in the war. After lying in agony for hours, Harry was taken to the cave hospital where Dr Reginald Saxton removed his spleen and gave him two blood transfusions, then a new process, in a desperate attempt to save his life. Despite Saxton's best efforts with salines and adrenaline, the wound was too serious for him to recover. Harry Dobson's condition deteriorated and with former-MP Leah Manning holding his hand, he died. Ironically, they'd recognised one another from an election in south Wales. Manning wrote to

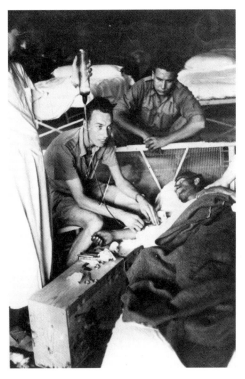

A poignant image of Henry 'Harry' Dobson being treated by Dr. Reginald Saxton in the cave hospital at La Bisbel de Falset. Dobson died of his wounds. (© Imperial War Museum)

a colleague that Dobson had repeated to her: "Comrade, they will never keep back the progressive cause whatever they do". Manning wrote that he 'died a very peaceful death'.[16] Harry Dobson, a hero of the International Brigades, had distinguished himself as a 'brave anti-fascist fighter, cool in danger, a capable and true communist'.[17] He was buried in a *fossa commune, a* mass grave close to the cave hospital.

Juan Modesto had fought in the battles of Belchite, Brunete and Teruel and, in August 1938, was promoted to Colonel, becoming head of the Army of the Ebro. On July 30th, he gave the orders for a fateful final attack on the town of Gandesa. This was going to be on a grand scale, with two columns encircling the town from north to south.[18] They would be supported by two companies of tanks, two of armoured cars and four groups of artillery. On paper this amounted to 72 artillery pieces, 22 tanks and 23 armoured cars, but all were subject to the wear and tear on sometimes unrepairable equipment. In addition, with most planes concentrated in the Levant to protect Valencia, there was limited air support.

The condition of the Republican troops after days of intense fighting was poor. Many were barefoot, and their uniforms in tatters. They often went whole days without water to drink, it was impossible to wash and they were riddled with lice. The final assault on Hill 481 was made on August 1st amidst a pounding from artillery and a barrage of bullets. Some advanced to within 20 metres of the Nationalist positions, but could get no further. By August 3rd, the Republican offensive had stalled completely. Trapped in their positions, they suffered huge casualties – 30,000 dead, 20,000 wounded and 20,000 captured – and it was clear that the attempt had failed. The International Brigades had lost all but 25% of their men. Billy Griffiths described Hill 481 as the altar on which all the men's ideals and passions drove them to such courage and sacrifice; but the scrub of a hill remains as a permanent monument to the treachery of non-intervention.[19]

𝕮ambrian 𝕮ombine 𝖂orkmen's 𝕵oint 𝕮ommittee.

You are invited to attend the

UNVEILING OF A PLAQUE

to the Memory of the late Henry Dobson

(Captain International Brigade in Spain, killed at the Ebro River
Battle on July 31, 1938),

to take place at the Tonypandy Library, on Saturday, Nov. 19, 1938.

The Unveiling will be performed at 5.30 p.m. by Arthur Horner, Esq.
(President S.W.M.F.)

Supported by Representatives of the Lodges and local Artistes.

Chairman · Councillor Jack Davies.

On behalf of the Committee,
L. ELSTON.   W. H. MARTIN.
SIDNEY MITCHELL, Sec.

THOMAS BROS., TONYPANDY

Henry 'Harry' Dobson's death was commemorated in his native Tonypandy. (© Richard Burton Archives, Swansea Univ.)

It was on July 28th or 29th (two different dates are given in the Moscow records) that Brazell Thomas of Llanelli was killed on Hill 481 and his friend Evan Jones, also from Llanelli, wounded. Both had arrived in Spain on the same day, February 25th, 1938, and both were 25 years old. Brazell Thomas had worked at the Burry Tinplate Works and was active politically as a union committee member, a supporter of sports welfare, a past member of the Labour League of Youth and secretary of the Llanelli branch of the Communist Party. His loyalty to his class principles was lauded later by an industrial colleague as 'living and dying for his principles' and in Thomas' case it was 'better death than dishonour.'

A company commissar, his Moscow record describes him as a politically sound and reliable comrade. Alun Menai Williams was there when he died: 'On a ridge of solid rock, we were bombarded for days and nights without shelter from the hot shrapnel and thousands of chunks of flying rocks, and when we were trying to pull Brazell Thomas of Llanelli to safety he was hit a second time and died. I left him where he lay to aid his friend Evan Roberts [*actually Evan Jones*], also from Llanelli, who was badly wounded with a smashed arm. I managed to drag him to some sort of safety. Evan survived; his injured arm was amputated'.[20]

'Hill 481' also claimed the life of Llanelli volunteer Brazell Thomas, who was fighting alongside his friend Evan Jones. (© Tamiment Library, New York)

On the front of the commemoration service pamphlet for Brazell Thomas, held in Llanelli, were the words: 'Democracy must win or humanity will perish' and 'What greater love hath any one, who dies that others may live'.[21] In his last letter to his mother, Thomas wrote: 'There are thousands of the cream of our class who are continually paying the supreme penalty in the struggle for a world fit for everybody to live in. But for you, I am one in particular, your son. You must not grieve. You must be proud that you had a son who was a martyr to the cause of the working class, a cause which must conquer or else the fate of all humanity be destroyed.' His family wrote back in response to the letter they received about Brazell's death: 'Whilst it has left a gap in our home, we feel proud that his death shall be a monument in the fight for democracy in which he believed'.[22]

On July 31st, another Welshman, James Scott of Swansea, also perished in the Civil War. Scott had jumped ship, the *Greatend*,[23] at Valencia to join the Battalion and served in the machine gun company. Although Russian files suggest he went missing in March 1938, Ivan York has located a death certificate for a James Escot, dated July 31st, 1938, in a registry at El Perelló, near the Ebro delta. He had died at 'Hospital Clinic No.3', and was buried in a mass grave in the El Perelló town cemetery. The correct identification of the fallen volunteer has been further confused by the death of James Watt of Swansea, a 35-year-old labourer, who was reported wounded at the Ebro on the same day, and died at Gandesa, but the available evidence suggests that the fallen volunteer was James Scott (Escot).[24]

Evan Jones lost an arm in the fighting to capture 'Hill 481'. (© Deputy Director RGASPI, Moscow)

After 13 days of fighting, on August 6th, the remnant of the British Battalion was moved into reserve. Of the 558 soldiers who had crossed the

Ebro on that first day, only 150 remained. The writing was now on the wall for all to see and the probability of defeat, and even the loss of the International Brigades, was apparent. For the first time there was discussion about saving key men who would be of more value at home. Although some rest was possible behind the front line – with a chance to bathe in the Ebro and wash off the dirt and blood – it was severely hampered by the Nationalists' unrelenting bombing of the Republicans' reserve positions. There was even the promise that some British volunteers would be given leave to return home, but this came to nothing when two days later, on August 11th, the Nationalists started a drive in the mountains to the south of the Sierra de Pàndols.

Happier days before the Civil War. Friends Evan Jones (left) and Brazell Thomas (centre) cycling in Llanelli. (© Peter Qualters)

Hill 666

On what is known as Hill 666, on a seemingly endless ridge with steep sides, a Republican flag blows proudly in the wind alongside a memorial plaque with the inscription: 'People of Spain, you will remember the free men who fought beside you, enduring and dying with you, the strangers whose breath was your breath'. The terrain on the sides is heavily wooded, while nearer the top, little short of 1,000 metres up, boulders and rocks jut out from bushes and shrubs. It is clear how terribly exposed a position this was, with almost no possibility of protection. This is what the 15th International Brigade was called upon to defend. Lacking transport, they marched from Gandesa and took over the Lincolns' position. They were pounded by artillery, attacked by infantry and bombarded day and night from the air. Digging trenches was often out of the question since most of the position was hard rock, and there was little or no cover from enemy fire. Surrounded by splintered rock, shells and shrapnel the casualties were heavy. Billy Griffiths described how they clung to the rock like

The death certificate of 'James Escot' who died on July 31ˢᵗ, 1938, and was buried at El Perello near the Ebro. This is, most probably, James Escott of Swansea. (© Ivan York)

ants. Defensive positions were fashioned in the unforgiving terrain and loose stones piled up into a parapet on the crest of the hill, but these were destroyed on an almost daily basis and rebuilt. At this time, Griffiths began to notice that the new recruits were becoming younger and younger. 'Lesser and I met one young lad climbing the 'death path'. He couldn't have been more than 14. He was so small, his bayonet stood well above his head'.[25]

James Strangward of Onllwyn died on August 17th. Born in Leominster, he had worked in Wales as miner since 1927 and was a founder of the Onllwyn Spanish Aid Committee, a keen trade unionist and student of Marxism.[26] Strangward served in the artillery in Spain, and wrote home about cigarettes, the trenches and the Communist Party. He was wounded on July 28th, probably on Hill 481, but three days before his death, in a letter to his brother, had written that he had 'come through all right' and was 'back having a rest from the line at present'.[27] His memorial service pamphlet extols qualities of enthusiasm, sportsmanship, stubborn courage and selflessness. His last words when he left Onllwyn were: "There is no victory without sacrifice".[28]

An intensive attack on the Republican positions on Thursday August 25th, a warm, beautiful clear day, in which bombs, artillery, mortars and machine gun fire raged continuously, was recounted by Edwin Greening. He recalled being pinned down in stony crevices in a continuous state of anxiety. There was little soil left, and dust and falling stones were everywhere as waves of hundreds of Italian bombers kept up a relentless onslaught on the vulnerable positions, with a regular sequence of mortars doing the most damage. The men were now exhausted, hungry, filthy and surrounded in the burning heat

On this ridge – known as 'Hill 666' – the men, with little cover, were subject to heavy bombardment day and night. (© Author)

by the stench of corpses, urine and excreta. Paths were filled with wounded men struggling back down the hill or being carried on stretchers. 'It was a real slaughterhouse'.[29]

Recalling his saddest moment in the Civil War, Greening wrote how he had taken to a crevice during a pause in the bombing, and was reading a copy of the *Aberdare Leader* sent from home. Then he heard what had happened to Tom Howell Jones, a former miner also from Aberdare. 'Towards what proved to be the end of the bombardment there were frenzied shouts for the medical orderly. Somebody shouted, "Tom Jones has been hit, Greening" … Tom lay with his three comrades, all hideously mutilated by a direct hit of perhaps six mortar bombs'.[30] Jones lay unconscious with a gaping wound at the back of his neck and died within a few minutes, with his head resting on Edwin's knee. Edwin retreated to his crevice but, in a temporary lull, scrambled with others across the rocks to bury the dead men. 'Alun Menai Williams, Lance Rogers and I got Tom's blanket and found a crevice six feet long, a yard wide and a yard deep. We lowered Tom in, and Lance and I went hurriedly

In Proud Memory of

James Strangward

Member of the Onllwyn, Coibren and Maesmarchog
Spanish Aid Committee; Onllwyn Lodge S.W.M.F.;
Onllwyn Branch Communist Party of Great Britain, and
a Student of the Onllwyn Class N.C.L.C.

Who died fighting in the British Battalion of the
International Brigade in Spain.

The memorial pamphlet of James Strangward of Onllwyn reveals a man of principle, who was willing to sacrifice his life for the anti-fascist cause. He died a few weeks after being wounded at the Ebro. (© Richard Burton Archives, Swansea Univ.)

around collecting the stones for Alun to cover his last resting place. When we had finished our tragic task we three said in the growing dusk: "Goodbye Tom. We'll never forget you". I added: Even if fifty years pass.' The tributes to him in the *Aberdare Leader* and at a memorial service, related in Greening's book, portray a popular, calm, intelligent man with a keen philosophical mind, a lover of poetry and Marxist scholar who championed democracy and freedom. Tom had been chairman of the Tower Lodge of the SWMF, and was acutely sensitive to social and economic problems. Although he hated war, he also hated all that was wrong, wicked and cruel and wanted to oppose fascism and fight for democracy. In a letter home to his mam, Cariad, he wrote: 'How is your health, how is your spirit? Never let it flag'.[31] Jones lay in a grave of almond trees overlooking Gandesa, and the Welshmen who came to pay their last tributes at nightfall were Lance Rogers of Merthyr, Jack Foulkes and Alun Menai Williams of Rhondda, Godfrey Price and Alec Cummings of Cardiff and Bill Rogers of Wrexham.

Those whose gathered for the memorial service at The Palladium, Aberdare, on Sunday November 20th, 1938 heard how, from his youth, Tom Howell Jones was a great believer in all things pertaining to socialism, democracy and progress. As a collier he had educated himself during his leisure hours, had a fine library and read widely and deeply. He had laboured unceasingly for unity within the Labour and trade union movement. 'With the culture of an intellectual and the soul of a poet' he remains the typical working-class hero.[32]

Hill 356

There was at last a chance for a short break for the Welsh volunteers, when foreign leave was introduced, initially for long-serving volunteers or those needed at home. Billy Griffiths was savaged by Sid James for refusing him leave: "You don't want to go home yourself and you are determined to stop everyone else." Soon, however, the Republican lines were being threatened by the superior air power of the Nationalists and a deluge of shells. Chris Henry estimated that the Nationalists had more than 350 artillery pieces at the front plus extra equipment and supplies, while Republican artillery was becoming less serviceable and ammunition was low.[33]

Tom Howell Jones, killed on 'Hill 666', was described as having the 'culture of an intellectual and the soul of a poet'. (© Richard Burton Archives, Swansea Univ.)

The Nationalist offensive began on September 3rd, focussed on a narrow front, which made the Sierra de Caballs range key to the defence of Republican Spain in Catalonia. Colonel Modesto's troops fought hard to avert breakthroughs in several places and, on September 7th, the British Brigaders were deployed, with every available vehicle, to a site near Ascó (often called 'Sandesco' by the volunteers). Against all the odds and ferocious bombardment, the British Battalion managed to recapture the Nationalist position on Hill 356 and held it for a week.

Billy Griffiths was in a cave housing the Brigade HQ when the bombing started. The cave, about 80 feet deep and 20 feet wide, can still be found on the mountain, and somehow housed the nerve-centre of the Brigade in a number of partitioned rooms. Its entrance was built up with stones and sandbags, and the noise from shelling was frequently deafening. When communications broke down, which was often, it was necessary to go out and follow the lines which tumbled out of the cave until the break had been located. Griffiths was eating a tin of crabmeat when a number of shells exploded in the cave, creating havoc by wounding chief of staff, Captain Malcolm Dunbar and many others.

William Rust relates the record of the events from September 6th to the 11th compiled by Captain Smrka of the Brigade staff. 'Counted more than 100 fascist planes in the air. Front has been boiling since dawn…the enemy starts a new attack following an intense artillery preparation. The Brigade is doing an excellent job…the flying activity again intensifies, but our troops are used to aviation by now. But they keep coming, 21-24 bombing planes at a time, about ten times a day. Savoia 81, Junkers 52, Heinkel III, each squad capable

During the fighting on the Sierra de Caballs this cave housed the Brigade's Headquarters. (© Author)

of dropping 50,000 kilo of explosives".[34] Once the situation had been stabilised, the Battalion was, once again, withdrawn into the reserve.

Sid James of Treherbert had been recruited by Billy Griffiths and, as it was illegal to recruit volunteers for Spain, he had let Billy know he was going via a telegram stating: 'the birds were flying that day'. On September 8th, during the heaviest day of the bombardment in the Sierra de Caballs, James was badly wounded in the stomach. Only a few days earlier he had been recommended for promotion by Sam Wild, who'd commented that James was 'capable of handling men, especially bad elements'. It seems a shell or bullet had set off the ammunition in his cartridge pouch and inflicted the wound, and James died in the ambulance taking him to a hospital.[35] James and Johnny Foulkes, also from Treherbert, had fought side-by-side, but lay in different hospitals after being wounded. When Johnny returned home in December 1938, it was with the news that Sid James had died, and the story of how he had been awarded a gold watch for bravery after arresting five fascists in Barcelona and marching them to prison.[36]

In letters home to his sister, brother and brother-in-law, Sid James talked about not fighting in vain and the whole world waking up to the rights of the workers. 'If the people in England and Wales only knew half we have gone through…there would a revolution at home'. He asked about the 'ranch', a smallholding he owned, on which he kept chickens, ducks and greyhounds. As the brigade was getting ready to cross the Ebro he wrote to his mother and brother that, in spite of the Valencia to Madrid road being cut, they would win if they could get arms. He promised, when he returned home, to 'stir up the halfwits in our Labour movement' and in a postscript wrote that he could not say where he was because of spies. His last words home were: 'We will soon be in action. You will be reading about our success before you receive this'.[37] His Moscow character reference understandably described him as 'very good'.

The Sierra de Caballs claimed the life of Sid James of Treherbert, when bullets in his cartridge pouch exploded. (© Tamiment Library, New York)

By now there were rumours that the International Brigades were to be withdrawn, since Prime Minister Negrin hoped that Franco might, in exchange, withdraw the Nationalists' foreign allies. On September 21st, assured by his military leaders that the depleted and exhausted Brigades were now of marginal value, Negrin informed the League of Nations of this intention.

The Last Action

Yet there was to be one last action. Late at night on September 21st, the 15th International Brigade was taken in trucks to replace the 13th Dombrowskis, who had been holding out desperately – incurring heavy losses – in trenches midway between Gandesa and Ascó. Among them, in a special unit of heavy machine guns at the disposal of the 15th Army Corps, was Tom Jones. Tom's family came from Lancashire, but settled in the Welsh-speaking coal mining village of Rhosllannerchrugog, near Wrexham. He worked for 14 years as a miner and joined the Labour Party and then the Communist Party before joining the International Brigade with the elite Anti-tank Battery in 1937. Now he was part of the last action as, after three days of deepening their trenches in preparation, they were subjected to a massive attack of strafing, bombing and shelling.

The Nationalists eventually broke through and into the trenches whose defenders had run out of ammunition. Tom's company were completely surrounded and 'fought like mad men'.[38] Despite surrendering, they were mown down with machine guns. Tom took a bullet in the thumb while a piece of grenade shrapnel caused severe bleeding from his arm, which he staunched with a dead comrade's shirt. Before being captured and taken to the military headquarters in Zaragoza he managed to bury some documents. From there he was taken to a prisoner of war hospital in Bilbao where the treatment was cruel and neglectful, with wounded men lying in lice-ridden beds and being mocked by Franco's military doctors.

He was then taken to a prison in Zaragoza packed with men and women who were often cruelly beaten. A military tribunal in Zaragoza demanded his execution, yet the sentence was commuted and he was transferred to Burgos. His Brigade record had read 'Killed (missing presumed dead) Ebro, September 17th, 1938'. The Republican government told his parents that he was dead, and issued a death certificate. He was not released until March 1940.[39]

Early in the morning of September 23rd, Nationalist artillery began an enormous barrage, shelling at a rate of one every second with 250 bombers and fighters dominating the sky. This last battle was to last only 24 hours, but was one of the hardest and fiercest of the war, in part because trenches had been dug too shallowly and on the wrong side of the hill

The Major Attlee Company came off worst in an overwhelming five-hour artillery barrage. William Rust noted in the Battalion Diary: 'What a day it was. Such artillery bombardments as I have never seen before. They literally churned up our positions. Under the cover of the artillery the fascists advanced with infantry and tanks...somehow or other we managed to hold on till dark when we went out to get our wounded. It took us four hours to evacuate our wounded'.[40]

Edwin Greening described the confusion and chaos in his book.[41] Having advanced about 400 yards, he and three others were caught in a massive bombardment which cut them off from the rest of the troops. They dodged shells, hid in holes and avoided tanks and fascist guards. Exhausted and with no food and with just a couple of hours sleep, they walked for miles, over two days, before finding a stretch of the Ebro shallow enough to cross. Greening put all his valuables – watch, pen, notebook – in his beret and top pocket and with the others walked into the warm slow-running waters. On the other side they were picked up by a Republican patrol and taken to a *hacienda* where there were others – Americans, Poles and Germans – in the same situation.

Eventually, they linked up again with the Battalion. One of the last Welshmen to die, although not with the British Battalion, was Baden Skinner, formerly of Tredegar. Having moved from Wales to Canada, 'Taffy' Skinner volunteered with the Mac Paps and died at Corbera on September 23rd, 1938, their last day in the front line.[42]

It is estimated that 23 of the British Battalion were killed and about 150 wounded in these final few days. It is believed that Alec Cummings of Tonypandy, Willie Durston of Aberaman, and Alwyn Skinner of Neath were killed, although it cannot be confirmed, and 19 other Welshmen were wounded. Greening describes an unfortunate encounter between Sam Wild and the families of Durston and Skinner at the dinner in Whitechapel Co-operative Hall following the arrival home of the British volunteers. When Durston's mother and Skinner's sister asked about their missing relatives, Sam Wild was alleged to have snarled: "Skinner and Esteban deserted to the fascists. You'd better ask the Franco government about them", and to Mrs Durston: "I know nothing about your son. He is posted missing, believed killed".[43]

Alec Cummings is another anomaly. Presumed killed at the Ebro in September 1938, the 27 pages of his Moscow files paint a complex and contradictory picture. Rhondda-born, he had been a Welsh Guardsman, WEA lecturer in Liverpool and a Communist Party activist in Cardiff before arriving at Albacete in February 1937. Almost immediately he was in action at Jarama as a section leader and commended for bravery as a company leader at Villanueva de la Cañada. He also served as a battalion adjutant, political commissar and head of personnel. In a note dated January 7th, 1938, at Albacete, Cummings was described as organised, a very good anti-fascist and was recommended for bravery by the Battalion Commander. In another dated February 1st, he is called 'a steady and reliable soldier with a sense of responsibility, keen to learn and a good soldier'.[44]

Yet early on in the Jarama campaign he is reported to have 'begged' to be transferred to the ambulance section as a driver, and the claims that he became 'demoralised and unsteady' are borne out by a series of uncomplimentary remarks in a number of files. It appears likely that being wounded in the shoulder and lung at Villanueva had scarred him psychologically as well. As early as February 1937 he was regarded as sectarian and 'high-hattish', nervous at the front and having lost the respect of the men. One note describes him as '*un pequeño burgues, fatuo y burocrata'* (a petty bourgeois, windbag and bureaucrat). In his memoirs, Billy Griffiths described the 'most reprehensible conduct' of an officer, presumed to be Alec Cummings (described as 'Captain X') who had been wounded at Brunete and was a broken man. After approaching Griffiths, pleading exhaustion and illness to avoid the front, and threatening to desert if forced into action, 'Captain X' was court-martialed by, among others, Griffiths and Harry Dobson. Their recommendation, that Cummings be shot so as not to affect morale, was ignored by the panel.

Yet as late as September 10th, 1938, he was included in a list of cadres useful to the British Communist Party.[45] The same complaints recurred. Sam Wild in late 1938 reckoned his contribution to the political agenda was 'nil', setting a poor, resentful example and spending a lot of time in the rearguard. Another report said he was unable to stand criticism, cried like a baby when wounded and was afraid to return to the front. One note was headed 'Alec Cummings – coward, careerist'. He was accused, at the Ebro, of setting up his position too far behind the trench lines, and in his files reported as 'missing, killed or captured' following the Ebro battle. Billy Griffiths states in his memoirs that Cummings was killed on the last day in the line – September 22nd, 1938 (although the Moscow Archive states it was the following day) – 'I have no doubt that to his family and friends Captain X was a great loss, but I must say hardly that to the movement'.[46]

What really happened in the last couple of weeks in September 1938 is a mystery. Robert Stradling, citing local information, argues: 'Perhaps he was indeed killed or captured by the enemy. Perhaps he had deserted before being captured and killed. But it seems equally likely that someone in authority on his own side took the law into his own hands'.[47]

Alwyn Skinner was a member of the Neath Communist Party and an active anti-fascist. He had been dismissed from his job as railway clerk for political activities, and had opposed a Mosleyite march through Swansea. In Spain he undertook clerical duties, produced a Brigade wall newspaper, was company quarter-master but was often ill and in hospital and did not see action until October 1937. His Moscow record is vague and contradictory. Rumoured to have changed sides, he is listed several times in the Moscow Archives as a deserter and as 'believed missing'. Comments made about him are not complimentary – 'very bad element…disruptive tendencies…thoroughly useless and rotten lot'. He had survived the sinking of the *Ciudad de Barcelona*, but does not seem to have seen much action.

However, his numerous letters and postcards to family and friends paint a complex picture.[48] Certainly he coped badly with the exigencies of war and was often hospitalised, with instances of losing three stone rapidly, inability to sleep and extreme weakness, although doctors could find no abnormality.

He wrote about the pleasantness of the hospital environment: 'I had looked forward to being at this delightful hospital over the festive season, a far more congenial place than the lines'. He also often wrote of his need for leave and desire to see his family, yet also voiced his commitment to the front line and how he would be happy to see his comrades again and do that for which he left home and country. In a strongly worded letter he condemned William Thomas of Aberavon: 'He left the Battalion during the recent big battle by anti-communist means – without permission. It is true that things were very hard, the shelling intense and the bombing terrific, but that does not justify one leaving his post'. It seems he was in action at Teruel, and was given work with the commissariat. His name appears on a list of deserters dated March 17th, 1938.[49] He did not return from Spain and his fate is unknown.

William Durston, of Aberaman and Wembley arrived in Spain in late 1937, and was regarded as a useful and conscientious clerk in Tarazona, but was prevented by silicosis from physically demanding work. He sought repatriation on medical grounds before the Ebro battle and the Moscow Archives note that in June 1938 he was accused of being a dubious element who boasted of being a member of the Brigade's secret service.[50] He appeared on a later list, of men who deserted or were in jail and in October 1938, although with a question mark by his name, of those still in Spain. Edwin Greening reported seeing him when attacking Hill 481, and that he was never seen again.[51]

Not every volunteer for such a stressful and horrific theatre of war will be a hero. Some had no idea what was to be expected of them, but the commitment and sacrifice of the majority is indisputable. The cruel taste of defeat is somewhat sweetened by the raw courage and determined bravery of men who knew the rightness of their cause in a battle, but were crushed by a superior military machine.

Notes

1. Edwin Greening, *From Aberdare to Albacete*, op. cit., p.78.
2. Angela Jackson, *At The Margins of Mayhem*, Pontypool, Warren and Pell, 2008. Also Angela Jackson, *Prelude to the Last Battle*, Marca, Cossetania Edicions, 2008.
3. Angela Jackson, *At the Margins of Mayhem*, pp.117ff
4. Ibid., pp.83ff.
5. William Rust, *Britons in Spain*, op. cit., p.169.
6. Antony Beevor, *The Battle for Spain*, op. cit., p.390.
7. RGASPI 545/6/22. Alonso Elliott worked at the headquarters of the political commissars in Madrid. He wrote a report, produced in French in the Moscow Archives, about the British volunteers.

8. Billy Griffiths, memoirs.
9. Robert Stradling, *Wales and the Spanish Civil War*, op. cit., p.138.
10. Billy Griffiths, memoirs.
11. Fred Thomas, *To Tilt at Windmills: Memoir of the Spanish Civil War*, op. cit., p.114.
12. Imperial War Museum, interview, Reel 10.
13. Marx Memorial Library, Box A-12.
14. *Volunteer for Liberty* Vol. 2, No.32, September 1938. In Alonso Elliott's report, Dobson is mentioned alongside Fox and Cornford in a list of *'magnifique cadres'*.
15. Alun Menai Williams, *From the Rhondda to the Ebro*, op. cit., p.168.
16. Letter to 'Gwen', Marx Memorial Library, Box A-12. In her autobiography, Leah Manning describes how a young Spanish surgeon asked her to sit by Harry's bedside and then write to his mother to tell her that he had great courage. She was impressed by the loving care that the Spanish medics showed to the Brigaders who had travelled and volunteered to fight fascism.
17. RGASPI 545/6/125.
18. For a fuller description of the battle, see Chris Henry, *The Ebro*, Oxford, Osprey Publishing,1999.
19. Billy Griffiths, memoirs.
20. Alun Menai Williams, *From the Rhondda to the Ebro*, op. cit., p.169.
21. 'To Commemorate Brazell Thomas', Richard Burton Archives, Swansea University.
22. William Rust, *Britons in Spain*, op. cit., pp.136-7.
23. The *Greatend*, a cargo ship of 1,424 tons, was built by Thornycroft at the Woolston yard, Southampton. In 1937 it was owned by the Newbigin Steam Shipping Company of Newcastle. It is on a *Hansard* list of British ships that had been damaged by air bombardment after the outbreak of the Spanish Civil War and was, in fact, bombed at Valencia on May 28th, 1938, then refloated, repaired and put back in service as *Castillo Noreña*.
24. Ivan York, IBMT Newsletter, Issue 41/1-2016 and RGASPI 545/6/197. The suggestion that the James Scott of Swansea is referred to here is likely despite the fact that there is another volunteer with a similar name – Cyril James Scott of London – who, in the Moscow Archives, is reported wounded at the Ebro on July 30th and mentioned, by Captain Sam Wild, to Cyril Scott's relatives, as possibly being in a small Spanish hospital. Cyril James Scott, however, has a repatriation report dated December 2nd, 1938, and he is also reported to have been hospitalised for five weeks.
25. Billy, Griffiths, memoirs.
26. Pamphlet published for the unveiling and dedication service of the memorial stone, July 19th, 1996.
27. Letter to his brother Ivor in *Miners Against Fascism*, p.288.
28. Memorial pamphlet, Richard Burton Archives, Swansea University.
29. *Colliers Crusade.*
30. Edwin Greening, *From Aberdare to Albacete*, op. cit., p.83. Also Imperial War Museum, interview, Reel 5.
31. Hywel Francis, *Miners Against Fascism*, op. cit., p.27.

32. Hywel Francis, doctoral thesis, Appendix 8:13, p.60. A poignant letter with striking Biblical phraseology in the *Aberdare Leader* from a 'friend' reflects the high regard held towards Tom Howell Jones: 'We salute you! You have fought the good fight. You have run the straight race. You have given your life – so that we may have it more abundantly…we shall pick up the flag of liberty where you let it fall, and we shall struggle unceasingly to accomplish the work you set out to do….we live and must fight the holy war of the deliverance of the human race'.
33. Ibid., pp.64ff.
34. William Rust, *Britons in Spain*, op. cit., pp.184-5.
35. RGASPI 545/6/153.
36. Reported in the *Rhondda Leader*, December 17th, 1938.
37. Letters kindly provided by David Williams.
38. *A Very Brief Outline of My Experiences in Spain during the Civil War*, unpublished manuscript, 1940. Marx Memorial Library.
39. Jane Pugh, *A Most Expensive Prisoner*, op. cit., pp.66ff., for rest of story.
40. William Rust, *Britons in Spain*, op. cit., p.186.
41. Edwin Greening, *From Aberdare to Albacete*, op. cit., pp.86ff.
42. RGASPI 545/2/127
43. Edwin Greening, *From Aberdare to Albacete*, op. cit., p.110.
44. RGASPI 545/6/121.
45. RGASPI 545/6/95.
46. Billy Griffiths, memoirs.
47. Robert Stradling, *Wales and the Spanish Civil War*, op. cit., p.149. That such an action was not unlikely is demonstrated also by Stradling regarding the fate of Irishman Maurice Ryan. Having fired on his own men, Ryan is believed to have been taken on a *paseo* by Sam Wild after a drumhead court martial. Also see Robert Stradling, *The Irish and the Spanish Civil War*, Manchester, Manchester University Press, 1999, p.191. In Alonso Elliott's report of the British Battalion he is unclear about Cumming's fate and wishes that the stories about him could be verified.
48. Richard Burton Archives, Swansea University.
49. RGASPI 545/2/126.
50. RGASPI 545/6/126.
51. Imperial War Museum, interview, Reel 7.

Epilogue

Withdrawal and Return

Juan Negrin's decision to repatriate foreign volunteers was a gesture of compromise towards a peace negotiation when it was clear the Republic could not win the Civil War. There was no shouting or cheering when, in late September 1938, Captain Sam Wild hastily convened a meeting of the Brigade at Marca and told them that they were going to leave Spain. Bob Peters spoke for many with similar emotions: 'we felt we were quitting them and leaving them to their fate'.[1] Edwin Greening was both glad and sad – glad that the unequal struggle was over, but sad that the Republic was being left to deal with fascism on its own.[2] After the singing of *'There's a valley in Spain called Jarama'* and the *'Internationale'* and a warning not to write home about the evacuation, the men returned to their quarters – many now vacant following heavy losses – to sleep.

Tensions were often high during the long bureaucratic wait in Ripoll at the foot of the Pyrenees. Billy Griffiths collapsed with a fever and spent five weeks in hospital. On being discharged he had no idea where he was and his journey back to Ripoll was fraught. Ironically he was reported as missing during this time. On his return he was asked to be secretary of a commission to enquire into the conduct of Communist Party members, and to ensure that only those beyond reproach would leave Spain as members of the prestigious Spanish Communist Party, as a volunteer returning home with a Spanish membership card would be trusted and given a position of responsibility. Each man, irrespective of rank, was to be investigated so as to 'purge the party of disreputable elements'.[3] The outcomes, evident in the volunteers' Moscow files, often had composite comments which might praise a man's military achievement but also include some aspect of 'anti-party' attitude or behaviour.

Desertion is a contentious issue in the reports. The Moscow Archives lists almost 300 British volunteers as deserters, and a further 400 variously as provocateurs, under suspicion, incorrigible, demoralised, weak and useless. Certainly many men had left their posts under merciless bombardment by highly trained Spanish, German and Italian Nationalist forces with the latest armaments. Others left because they were refused leave, genuinely believing that this had been promised after six months of service. Disillusionment, disagreement with the leadership, disappointment with the privileges given to leaders in a communist army, or opposition to the 'Stalinisation' of the Battalion were more prevalent than cowardice. Many others may have shared the experience of W.J. Thomas of Aberavon, who was imprisoned for desertion. He was wounded at Jarama and suffered shell shock at Brunete. His family made innumerable appeals for his return after learning of his condition, which included septic poisoning, bladder and kidney disease and inflammation of the liver.

Trotskyism and desertion were often rolled up into the same disciplinary accusation. Some volunteers accused of 'desertion' had been separated from their company and lost contact with HQ in combat. This was common, particularly during the Aragon retreat, so comments such as 'reported missing' do not necessarily denote desertion. Edwin Greening highlighted the atmosphere of suspicion and recrimination pervading the Battalion at Ripoll. Lance Rogers and Jim Brewer questioned Greening's 'absences' in April and September, whereupon Greening inquired about their absences at about the same time.[4] Battalion officers had also come under attack for their actions following the chaos at Caspe and Batea.

The Welshmen were at the farewell parade in Barcelona, where the British Battalion marched behind the Presidential Guard. Jim Brewer was chosen to march at the front, carrying the Battalion banner with its battle honours, as crowds cheered, fighter planes circled overhead to protect the occasion, and women broke cordons to kiss the flag, and sometimes the men. Harry Stratton was not so comfortable since, like many others, he was still infested with lice. He was also aware of the grim life of the people of Barcelona, with long queues at the shops and continuing air raids.[5] The city's most important avenue, the Avinguda Diagonal, was strewn with roses as the volunteers lined upon it were addressed by President Azaña and Prime Minister Negrin, and heard the emotional and now iconic speech from *La Pasionaria,* which included the words: "Mothers! Women! When the years pass by and the wounds of war are staunched; when the memory of the sad and bloody days dissipates in a present of liberty, of peace and of wellbeing...speak to your children. Tell them of these men of the International Brigades."[6]

Thousands welcomed them with similar enthusiasm at Victoria Station in London on December 7th, 1938. Edward Heath, a pro-Republican Oxford University student who became a Conservative Prime Minister, was there. So was Clement Attlee, with other Labour dignitaries, family members, trade union organisations and other supporters. The atmosphere was electric with loud cheering, and the singing of *'There's a Valley in Spain called Jarama'* as the volunteers, many unshaven, tired and wounded, marched to a meal at the Whitechapel Co-operative Hall. Edwin Greening described the chaos after the meal as relatives found their way into the dining hall, some in tears and wanting to know about their missing loved ones.[7] It was the beginning of some fraught relationships and confusion, as accusations of desertion and other incidents hovered in the background.

Most Brigaders were well received in their communities, as were those who later returned from prisons in Spain. Their villages and towns were often decorated with flags and bunting. The *Rhondda Leader* described welcomes such as the hoisting of flags and the large crowd waiting at the railway station for Archie Cook in Ystrad. A similar welcome awaited Tommy Adlam after imprisonment in San Pedro, with a dramatic reunion with his father, and it was reported that more than 1,000 people turned out to greet Jack Jones of Blaenclydach on his release. Twenty volunteers were given an honorary tour of Rhondda Fawr – the larger of Rhondda's two valleys – with a hot lunch at the Co-operative Hall, Tonypandy, followed by a public meeting at the Judge's Hall, Trealaw. The *Aberdare Leader* described the heroes' welcome given to Edwin Greening and Ron Brown at Aberdare railway station and the Communist Party meeting the following Sunday night at Aberdare Unemployed Centre at which both described their experiences. Also there was Bob Condon, who had arrived home earlier. Paul Robeson sang at the Welsh National Memorial Service at Mountain Ash, which was attended by more than 7,000 people.

Yet not all public events were straightforward. Alun Menai Williams spoke at many successful gatherings, but was heckled and challenged at others about his account of some events such as the bombing of Guernica and Barcelona. Accused of promoting communist propaganda, he crawled into a shell, as he put it, for many years and found his peace with the memories of his comrades in their unmarked graves.[8] Others too, throughout Britain, experienced curiosity, suspicion and little likelihood of employment. Some were broken and demoralised by their experiences. For Lance Rogers it was his 'Gethsemane'. Others were inactive, or became disillusioned as they reflected on what they regarded as Stalin's political manoeuvrings at their expense, in particular following the Molotov-Ribbentrop Pact, the German-Soviet Non-aggression Pact between Germany and the Soviet Union. Both Morien Morgan and Edwin Greening became teachers and experienced opposition from conservative elements in the education establishment. Yet many continued to campaign both for the dependants of Brigaders and those still imprisoned. They addressed public meetings, and some exercised their political zeal in trade union activities, in particular in the South Wales Miners' Federation.[9]

While the exploits of the volunteers in Spain, the deaths of some and the return home of others, were covered in generally favourable and sympathetic terms in their local papers such as the *Rhondda Leader* and *Aberdare Leader,* which published many letters from Will Lloyd and Bob Condon, the *Western Mail* – established in Cardiff in 1869 with a conservative readership drawn from the professional and business classes in south Wales – took an altogether different line. From its first editorial on the war, on July 21st, 1936, when it asked whether the Spanish people who 'suffer from serious temperamental or deeper defects' could ever maintain a democracy, the self-proclaimed 'National Newspaper of Wales' supported the Nationalists and the British Government's non-intervention policy.

In the period before Guernica, the *Western Mail* was a keen advocate of non-intervention and argued for strict neutrality as the safest course to follow, while its sister paper, the *South Wales Echo* regarded British non-intervention as absurd when Germany and Italy, who had signed up to the agreement, had disregarded their obligations. After Guernica, however, the *Western Mail*'s editorial line grew increasingly critical of Franco.

The Newport-based *South Wales Argus*, however, was pro-Republican throughout the Civil War yet tended to present the conflict in terms of international rather than local factors. It has also been suggested that the Welsh-based press revealed a high degree of ignorance about the war, included many inaccuracies – especially in the *South Wales Echo* – offered simplistic and superficial analysis and showed a widespread prejudice against Spanish people.[10] Indeed, some of it bordered on the risible: 'The form of Government which will satisfy the arrogant individualism of the Spaniard has yet to be devised'.[11]

As far as the religious press was concerned, unlike the London-based Catholic publications *The Tablet* and the *Catholic Herald* which unsurprisingly supported the Nationalists, *Seren Cymru* – the weekly publication of the Welsh Baptists – was an unlikely supporter of the Republican cause. Reflecting the political philosophy of the non-conformist chapels, with their history of democratic organisation and social and political engagement – indeed, many of the Welsh volunteers came from staunch chapel-going homes – *Seren Cymru* often defended the Spanish government's more excessive actions, and laid the blame for the uprising at the feet of the oppressive landowners.[12]

Legacy

What then was the legacy of the Welsh volunteers? Certainly the Comintern regarded the brigades as a highly disciplined force which played a huge part in resisting fascist aggression. Their contribution was arguably decisive in some battles for the survival of the Republic. They were seen as the embodiment of international proletarian solidarity and future revolutionary warriors, as well as potential Soviet agents.[13] Early Communist Party writers such as William Rust portrayed the Brigades as withdrawing in a 'blaze of glory' having earned themselves the proud title of the 'Shock Battalion' of the 15th Brigade. At Victoria Station, he saw them as soldiers of the 'real Britain' still mobilised in the cause of democracy and peace, knowing that comrades who would not return had not died in vain.[14]

Of approximately 2,500 British volunteers, more than 500 died, and about 1,200 were wounded. The *Daily Worker* (December 10th, 1938) related their pledges to continue the fight for world democracy – it was only the battleground that had changed. For Rust and others like him, the Brigaders' sacrifice 'stands as an eternal rebuke to those in power in Western bourgeois democracies whose preference for collaborating with fascism in the 1930s rather than confronting it made inevitable the horrors of the Second World War'.[15] Much was made of saving the honour of Britain amid the shame of non-intervention. Bill Alexander, writing much later, argued that the volunteers understood that fascism led to war, and the three years of resistance in Spain gave time for people everywhere to learn lessons and prepare for their own struggle against fascism. He stated that the lessons to be learned are that fascism must be exposed, fought as soon as it appears, and can only be defeated by struggle. His view was that despite the loss and suffering of so many of the finest working people, those sacrifices were an essential part of 'the wider struggle for democracy and peace and against fascism and war'.[16]

Revisionists have tried to blame the Civil War on the political extremism, public disorder and social unrest of the Republic, in particular the uprising in 1934, and to play down the advantage that German and Italian foreign intervention gave the Nationalist cause.[17] At the same time the Brigades have been represented as pawns manipulated by Stalin's geopolitical strategies, in particular his attempt to buy time for the Soviet Union. Even if this were true, what cannot be diminished, as Paul Preston argues, is the 'idealism and heroism of those who sacrificed their comfort, their security and often their lives in the anti-fascist struggle'.[18] Nor should the boost the presence of the Brigades gave to the morale of the people of Spain be underestimated.

It is true that, while tending to find their place together in No 1 Company, the Welsh did not develop as strong a national identity as the Irish volunteers. Yet Will Paynter was keen that there should be no separation by nationalities, only close cohesion and better relationship with Spanish comrades.[19] The Brigade newspaper *The Volunteer for Liberty,* said little about the Welsh, nor did they feature much in the volunteer accounts in *The Book of the XV Brigade* edited by Irishman Frank Ryan. Yet Welshmen served as company commanders and political commissars, and attended officers' training schools. Certainly their largely militant coalfield background, mining experience and singing ability left their mark. Fred Copeman recalled how the singing of Welsh miners raised the spirits of the multi-national group on the way to Brunete and Miles Tomalin's limerick about the confusion caused by similar Welsh names always raised a smile: [20]

> *'There was a young fellow named Price.*
> *And another fellow named Price.*
> *And a fellow named Roberts.*
> *And another fellow named Roberts.*
> *And another young fellow named Price.'*

Hywel Francis points out that the special regard, even reverence, for Welsh International Brigaders was illustrated both by numerous memorial meetings and the welcomes organised for those who returned. He states: 'They were in the same tradition as the Chartists at Newport and were to be celebrated in spite of their respective defeats, because they were all men before their time'.[21] Yet, while the Welsh Dean of Chichester declared that the Brigaders had given their lives for something of eternal value and that God would not forget such sacrifices, Pope Pius XII sent a telegram to Franco giving thanks to God for the long-desired Catholic victory in Spain. Peman's 'smoke of incense and the smoke of cannons' remained to adulterate the Spanish climate. Alun Menai Williams felt he had been part of a 'truly international force of volunteers spurred on to action by the heartfelt cries of *No Pasarán!* of a beleaguered nation and its people'.[22] They fought for an ideal, but lost out to superior force. In 2009, Carles Casajuana, Spanish Ambassador to the UK, told the group of veterans receiving Spanish citizenship: "Your efforts were not in vain. Your ideals are part of the foundations of our democracy in Spain today."[23] There is no more fitting tribute to the Welshmen of the International Brigade than the words of *La Pasionaria* on their departure in 1938:

"You are history. You are legend. You are the heroic example of democracy's solidarity and universality…we shall not forget you; and, when the olive tree of peace is in flower, entwined with the victory laurels of the Republic of Spain – come back."

Notes

1. Greg Lewis, *A Bullet Saved My Life*, op. cit., p.47.
2. Edwin Greening, *From Aberdare to Albacete*, op. cit., pp.93-4.
3. Billy Griffiths, unpublished memoirs. A letter sent by André Marty to Harry Pollitt on December 7th, 1938, explains that the 'characterisations' of the Brigaders were made to enable them to be given responsibilities based on their work in Spain. (RGASPI 545/6/87). He criticises the British Government for the delay in agreeing to receive the 500 volunteers.
4. Edwin Greening, *From Aberdare to Albacete*, op. cit., p.103.
5. Harry Stratton, *To Anti-Fascism by Taxi*, op. cit., p.51.
6. http://www.english.illinois.edu/maps/scw/farewell.htm .
7. Edwin Greening, *From Aberdare to Albacete*, op. cit., pp.110-11.
8. Alun Menai Williams, *From the Rhondda to the Ebro*, op. cit., pp.179-80.
9. For more information about the returning volunteers see Francis, *Miners Against Fascism*, pp.248-259.
10. P. Lewis, *The Anglo-Welsh Press' Response to the Spanish Civil War*. Unpublished MA thesis, 1990.
11. *Western Mail*, January 3rd, 1939.
12. Tom Buchanan, *Britain and the Spanish Civil War*, op. cit., pp.169-88. Also Robert Stradling, *Wales and the Spanish Civil War*, op. cit., pp.18-19.
13. For Comintern politics see, R. Dan Richardson: *Comintern Army*, op. cit., pp.90-118.
14. William Rust, *Britons in Spain*, op. cit., pp.186-8.
15. *Morning Star*, February 18th, 2004.
16. Bill Alexander, *British Volunteers for Liberty*, op. cit., p.259.
17. For a fuller discussion see 'Killing the Dream' in Jump, Jim (Ed.), *Looking Back at the Spanish Civil War*, op. cit., pp.45-64.
18. Paul Preston, *The Spanish Civil War*, op. cit., p.174.
19. General letter to comrades on leaving, in *Volunteer for Liberty* Vol.20, October 1937.
20. Fred Copeman, *Reason in Revolt*, op. cit., p.123.
21. Hywel Francis, *Miners Against Fascism*, op. cit., p.258.
22. Alun Menai Williams, *From the Rhondda to the Ebro*, op. cit., p.180.
23. Baxell, Jackson and Jump, *Antifascistas*, London, Lawrence & Wishart, 2010, p.103.

Appendix

The Welsh Volunteers

The following lists those men and women who served on the Republican side in Spain for whom I found a recognisable footprint. They were either born in Wales, or had strong Welsh connections. No doubt there are many others about whom nothing now is known, and I have found the names of some who fall into that category. Those who died in the conflict have a longer description in the main text, where information is available.

The sources are various and include files in the Moscow Archives, Richard Burton Archives at Swansea University, South Wales Miners' Library, Abraham Lincoln Brigade Archives, National Archives MI5 files, 'Sidbrint' project

Tom Jones' International Brigade record card. (© Moscow Archives)

Extracts from the International Brigade file of Lance Rogers. (© Moscow Archives)

University of Barcelona, International Brigade Memorial Trust records in the Marx Memorial Library, and articles in the *Western Mail, South Wales Echo, South Wales Evening Post, Rhondda Leader, Aberdare Leader* and *Neath Guardian* newspapers.

Information has also been derived from the interviews given by, and research of, Hywel Francis, Robert Stradling, Jim Carmody, William Rust, Anthony Richards, Kevin Buyers, Graham Stevenson, Terry Norman, Ivan York, John Mehta, Antonio R. Celada, Manuel Gonzales de la Aleja, Daniel Pastor Garcia and the families of volunteers.

Written by a number of different individuals in mainly English, French, Spanish, German and Russian, the documents in the Moscow Archives need to be carefully contextualised. They consist of biographies, interviews, comments and observations written on different occasions by political commissars and battalion officers. Many are 'repatriation' documents which are essentially investigations made in the autumn of 1938 into the volunteers' combat records, political views and contributions, and other matters relevant to the future interests of the Comintern. I have indicated where some comments are derived from the Moscow Archives with the letters 'MA'. Often the comments in these files are contradictory and formulaic, and reflect what some have regarded as the 'Stalinisation' of the Brigades. They do not always acknowledge possible positive changes in behaviour over a period of time. For example, some men who deserted and were arrested and imprisoned, returned to the battlefield with a different resolve; others became demoralised and indifferent as the war dragged on. Many accusations of desertion are more accurately explained by separation from a company in combat. Since it was the intention to report both on a volunteer's military and political merit, the files can seem ambiguous and ambivalent. It is also important to appreciate the different forms of service: for example, volunteers might be performing one or more of a variety of roles including frontline soldiers, stretcher-bearers, ambulance drivers, secretaries, administrators, censors and so on. There were those who André Marty called the 'conscious or unconscious agents of Franco' who were accused of provoking desertion and likened the action of the Republican Government in dealing with them to the way miners dealt with blacklegs.

I include the comments 'warts and all' so that readers may appreciate the political nature of the conflict and experience the attitudes and perceptions of those making judgements on the returning men, albeit made in a 'battle context' and not for public consumption but for future political usefulness. The latest categorisation, sent to the secretariat of the Communist Part of Great Britain, was signed by André Marty on December 12th, 1938. A distinction was made between communist and non-communist volunteers, and the latter were assessed with standards a little lower than the former. Judgements were made recognising the severe circumstances of months of fighting, which had made great demands of the men's political, moral and physical resources.

The categories were:

Cadres: comrades who have displayed outstanding qualities militarily and politically and who can play a leading part in the Communist Party in the future.

Good: those who have shown themselves in military and political spheres to be good anti-fascists without serious weaknesses. These can be used immediately as cadres in local committees.

Fair: comrades who have made positive contributions but with weaknesses in some spheres which have been harmful to their work in Spain. They could be good Communist Party members.

Weak: those with important defects in the political or moral spheres which made them completely useless to the anti-fascist cause. They could, nevertheless, be helped to do some useful work in the Communist Party.

Bad: those who have shown themselves to be largely useless or harmful to the anti-fascist cause. Their serious defects include drunkenness, cowardice, indiscipline, disruption and Trotskyite tendencies. They should be excluded from the Communist Party.

The dates below are, where the information is available, those when volunteers left for, or arrived in, Spain, or joined the Battalion, and when repatriated or returned home. Please note that dates held by different organisations sometimes vary.

A. The Welsh Volunteers Killed in the Civil War

1. William Coles: Cardiff, labourer, 22.12.36 – 02.37, killed at Jarama.
2. Alec Cummings: Cardiff, lecturer/ Welsh Guards, 04.02.37 – 22.09.38, killed/missing.
3. Harold Davies: Neath, hospital cook, 23.01.37 – 14.02.37, killed at Jarama.
4. William J. Davies: Tonypandy, miner, 10.12.36 – 19.07.37, killed at Brunete.
5. Harry Dobson: Blaenclydach, miner, 02.06.37 – 03.08.38, died at the Ebro.
6. William Durston: Aberaman, diecaster, 05.11.37 – 25.08.38, probably died at the Ebro.
7. Victoriano Esteban: Abercrave, miner, 20.09.37 – unknown, killed.
8. George Fretwell: Penygroes, labourer, 10.01.37 – 12.02.37, died at Jarama.
9. Sidney Hamm: Cardiff, student, 28.04.37 – 06.07.37, killed at Brunete.
10. Jack Harries: Llanelli, miner, 11.02.37 – 02.04.37, killed at Jarama.
11. Richard Horridge: Swansea, 8.06.37 – 07.37, killed at Brunete.
12. Sidney James: Treherbert, miner, 28.02.38 – 08.09.38, killed on the Sierra de Caballs.
13. David Joseph Jones; Penygraig, miner, 18.12.36 – 13.02.37, killed at Jarama.
14. Ramadeesis: Cardiff, no information – Jim Brewer describes him as 'Indian from Cardiff'.
15. Thomas Howell Jones: Aberdare, miner, 07.37 – 26.08.38, killed at the Ebro.

16. Sydney Lloyd Jones: 04.10.36 – 16.10.36, killed at Chapineria.
17. Arthur Morris: Cardigan/Canada, miner, 11.02.37 – 27.02.37, killed at Jarama.
18. Sam Morris: Ammanford, miner, 10.12.36 – 17.07.37, killed at Brunete.
19. William Morris: Llanelli, copper worker, 13.05.37 – 07.37, killed at Brunete.
20. Dan Murphy: Cardiff, 20.12.37 – 03.04.38, missing/killed at Calaceite.
21. Frank Owen: Mardy, miner, 16.05.37 – 07.07.37, killed at Brunete.
22. Tom Picton: Treherbert, miner, 2.04.37 – 04.38, killed in Bilbao prison.
23. Roman Rodriguez: Dowlais, steelworker, 29.04.37 – 06.07.37, killed at Brunete.
24. James Scott: Swansea, merchant seaman, 13.11.37 – 31.07.38, killed at the Ebro.
25. Alwyn Skinner: Neath, railway clerk, 05.06.37 – 22.09.38, missing/killed.
26. Baden Skinner: Tredegar/Canada, 07.37 – 23.09.38, killed at Corbera.
27. James Strangward: Onllwyn, miner, 24.03.38 – 17.08.38, killed.
28. Gilbert Taylor: Cardiff, printer, 15.11.37 – 17.03.38, killed in Calaceite/Belchite.
29. Jack Taylor: Cardiff/London, 12.36 – 12.02.37, died at Jarama.
30. Brazell Thomas: Llanelli, 28.02.38 – 28.07.38, killed at the Ebro.
31. Robert Traill: Radyr, killed at Brunete, 07.37.
32. James Watts: Swansea, labourer, 25.03.38 – 08.38, killed at Gandesa.
33. Fred White: Nant-y-moel, pit stoker, 07.01.37 – 07.07.37, killed at Brunete.
34. John (Jack) E. Williams: Ammanford, carpenter, 10.12.36 – 07.37, killed at Brunete.
35. Frank Zamora: Abercrave, labourer, 20.09.37 – 20.01.38, killed at Teruel.

B. The Welsh Volunteers Who Survived the Civil War

1.   Thomas Adlam: Pentre (Rhondda), miner, 28.4.37 – 25.10.38.
Persuaded to volunteer by Will Lloyd, Adlam was taken prisoner at the end of March 1938 at Calaceite, along with a number of other Welsh volunteers' when confronted by Italian tanks. Held at San Pedro Concentration Camp, Adlam was amongst the first group of volunteers to be released and arrived home to a rousing reception. However, his Moscow record describes him in quite negative terms as being demoralised, weak, cowardly, unreliable and having deserted from the front. (MA)

2.   George Baker: Gelli (Rhondda), miner, 05.1.37 – 17.09.38.
As an active and valued communist in the fight for improvement in the mining industry, Baker was regarded as 'a full time activist' and was involved in a variety of union and community issues. A quartermaster with the Anti-tank Battery in Spain, he is described as having done his work in an exemplary manner, and was reported as exceptionally cool under fire, hardworking and trustworthy, a loyal communist and a reliable comrade. Baker was wounded in the shoulder on February 2nd, 1937, leading to paralysis of the arm. (MA)

3.   David Barrett: Blackwood, labourer, 07.02.38 – 09.38.
A member of Tredegar branch of the CPGB, and in the GMW union, Barrett was taken prisoner at Calaceite along with a number of other Welsh volunteers when confronted by Italian tanks and is on the official prisoner list at San Pedro Concentration Camp.

4.   Ken Bevan: Gorseinon, fitter, 07.02.38 – 25.10.38.
His record in Spain praises him as a good armourer and machine-gunner. (MA) He is recorded both on a "missing" list and as having been taken prisoner in Gandesa in April 1938. His name does not appear on the San Pedro list.

5.   William Bevan: Penygraig (Rhondda), miner, 17.04.37 – 02.07.37.
Repatriated as a result of fatigue and exhaustion on July 2nd, 1937. (MA)

6.   Henry Boddy: Cardiff/London, seaman, 21.12.36 – 03.05.37.
Boddy sailed for Dunkirk in December 1936. His name appears on a deserters' list in July 1937. (MA)

7.   Jim Brewer: Rhymney, miner, 13.5.37 – 07.12.38.
Always very politically aware, Brewer was a hunger marcher and a student of politics at Coleg Harlech and Ruskin College. In Spain he served in the Anti-tank unit and was regarded as a good comrade who did his work well, was hard working and a good example to other men. After Brunete he suffered from the consequences of the shelling and became nervous and war weary. (MA) Regarded as a 'good communist', Brewer was the standard bearer for the volunteers' final march through Barcelona.

8.   Les Brickell: Tredegar, miner, 05.8.37 – 20.02.39.
Commended for bravery at Hill 481 when, under bombing and machine gun fire, he threw hand grenades at a fascist machine gun on the summit, and also praised for his exceptional bravery as a runner. However, Brickell was also

regarded with suspicion and reported as weak and undisciplined, i.e. he was docked three days pay in May 1938. (MA) Wounded in August 1938, Brickell rejoined the Battalion in September 1938 and was one of those captured at one of the last battles, Corbera d'Ebre, on September 23rd, 1938, and imprisoned at San Pedro Concentration Camp until February 5th, 1939.

9.   Ronald Brown: Aberaman, lorry driver and miner, 30.5.37 – 03.12.38.

Named as an official survivor when the *Cuidad de Barcelona* was torpedoed, Brown is described as a very good worker as ambulance driver and mechanic, sincere, earnest and capable. It was suggested he should be given further political development towards leadership. He worked in difficult and arduous conditions with 'high morale and a quick intelligence'. (MA)

10.   Arthur Bush: Port Talbot, sailor, 15.1.37 – 03.05.37.

Served as a runner and ammunition loader at Jarama, and was briefly in prison in Valencia in March 1937. Bush returned to Cardiff from Barcelona as a stowaway on the *Clintonia* on May 26th, 1938. (MA)

11.   Bob Condon: Aberaman, miner, 15.12.36 – 09.04.38.

An early recruit of Will Lloyd, Condon wrote letters home about the high morale of the Brigaders and the citizens of Madrid. During the fighting at Jarama he suffered shell-shock and bruising of the head and from then suffered from a nervous condition. In May 1937 he asked to be transferred to a transport unit and on July 24th, on the Brunete front, he suffered a shrapnel head wound. His Moscow records portray a normally disciplined comrade who is recommended for more political training. (MA)

12.   Archie Cook: Ystrad (Rhondda), miner and Territorial Army soldier, 29.04.37 – 17.12.38.

An activist on hunger marches, Cook was regarded as a good comrade in Spain who, as a member of the Anti-tank Battery, did his work in an excellent manner and was a good example: disciplined, steady and brave in all circumstances. After attending the officers' training school he was promoted to sergeant. At the Ebro he was commended for efficiency in carrying out orders and being the first in the attack. In August 1938 he suffered multiple shrapnel wounds and was hospitalised for 10 weeks. (MA)

13.   James Cope: Cardiff, soldier, 01.37 – 07.37.

Known as 'Tanky' to his comrades, Cope had deserted from the Royal Tank Corps to go to Spain. Arrested for involvement in stealing paintings from a church in Barcelona during May 1937, his release was secured by Sam Lesser, one of the last survivors of the war. Wounded and returned or deserted in June 1937. (MA)

14. Robert Cox: Tredegar, miner, 11.02.37 – 19.08.37.

Inspired by Aneurin Bevan to stand against fascist violence, Cox became a member of a 'workers freedom group'. One of the older volunteers at 38, he served at Jarama and Brunete, before being repatriated with fatigue.

15. Owen Darcy: Dowlais/Vancouver, 19.08.37 – ?

Held the rank of sergeant and was described as a 'good anti-fascist'. Wounded on March 10th, 1938, Darcy's record states that there is nothing unfavourable about him. (MA)

16. Reginald David: Ton Pentre/Canada, industrial first-aid attendant, 21.08.37 – 21.09.38.

A committed activist, taking part in strikes and lock-outs, in Spain he worked as a corporal with the 'Mac Paps' medical unit and was at the front in Teruel, Aragon and the Ebro. David distinguished himself for bravery and discipline, with Major Smith of the Mac Paps noting: 'The finest and most reliable first aid man I have ever seen.' (MA)

17. Ben Davies: Cwmbran, labourer, 07.01.37 – 18.04.38.

Served for seven years in the South Wales Borderers as rifleman and signaller and was an active trade unionist and hunger marcher before becoming a quarryman. In Spain, Davies was firstly deployed as a telephonist and runner at the Battalion's headquarters – where he was wounded three times – and was hospitalised for a month at Elda hospital, Alicante, after suffering a wound in the biceps of the right arm at Jarama. He attended officer training school and was described as quiet, reserved and disciplined but also 'drinks rather a lot'. (MA)

18. Daniel D. Davies: Pentre (Rhondda), driver/mechanic, 28.04.37 – 07.12.38.

A Coleg Harlech contemporary of Jim Brewer, and described in a letter written by Tom Picton as having worked in the public baths in Treherbert, Davies was a highly commended sergeant, described as a steady leader and good party man, disciplined, brave and respected. Deployed as a chauffeur, Davies was wounded at the Ebro on July 30th, 1938, and hospitalised at Mataro. (MA)

19.   David R. Davies: Crumlin, electrician, 17.02.37 – 25.10.37.
A number of episodes of bravery are recorded about him in his files, before being recommended immediate repatriation on health grounds in September 1937. (MA)

20.   Ivor Davies: Neath, miner, 01.37 - 26.10.38.
Taken prisoner at Calaceite along with a number of other Welsh volunteers when confronted by Italian tanks, Davies described in the *South Wales Evening Post* how he was taken to San Pedro and thrown into a dirty room where five men died in the first week through lack of food and fresh air. He was taken to another prison, Palencia, under the control of the Italians, where he was treated more humanely.

21.   Morris Davies: Treharris, miner, 17.04.37 – 07.12.38.
A union activist who later joined the army and served in India, Davies was a company commander (March 1938 to July 1938) and lieutenant in Spain where he excelled in all military and political duties. He was wounded near Gandesa in July 1938. Most comments were positive: always showing initiative and self-reliance; good conduct under fire and good example to the men both morally and politically. He was also described as 'full of courage and a fine soldier' (October 1937) and a 'good cadre'. Although sometimes demoralised, he remained disciplined, steady and brave. (MA)

22.   Thomas E. Davies: Penygraig (Rhondda), miner, 29.04.37 – 13.07.37.
Volunteered for Spain aged 45, with a disability pension of 8 shillings a week. On arrival he was taken to the Jarama front, but was repatriated for family reasons in early July 1937.

23.   Thomas R. Davies: Bedlinog, miner, 07.01.37 – 07.07.37 (returned to Spain 13.10.37).
Wounded at Jarama on February 15th, 1937, it seems Davies returned from Spain without permission to see his ill mother. Before he returned he addressed a number of public meetings. Davies worked as an electrician at Tarazona and was reported by Battalion headquarters, in January 1938, as not being in Spain and having deserted after being given 3,000 pesetas and sent to purchase supplies. In another file he is described as being repatriated because of illness.(MA)

24.   William J. Davies: Pantffynnon, Miner, 10.12.36 - ?
Better known locally as *Wil Castell Nedd* (Wil Neath) Davies earned a living also from winning sprint races at fairs and carnivals and from playing rugby

(despite it being an amateur game). He volunteered after receiving a letter from Sam Morris of Ammanford. After his return Davies' health suffered and he never played rugby again, although he remained politically active.

25.   Euripides Dimitriou: Cardiff, seaman, 28.02.38 – 18.12.38.
A British subject from Cyprus, and with an alias (James Peters), Dimitriou was regarded as having consistently disciplined behaviour and being good, politically. He was recorded as missing at Gandesa on April 3rd, 1937, and was wounded on August 1st, 1938. (MA)

26.   Edward Walker Edwards: Machynlleth, seaman, 14.1.37 – at least 09.38.
Born in Wales but lived in Cheshire and then California, from where he volunteered, Edwards served as secretary of the Battalion and was promoted to sergeant and then lieutenant. Noted as a good soldier under fire and commended at the Ebro for working day and night during intense bombardment, he performed duties in exemplary fashion. A conscientious worker and tower of strength to the Battalion, he was seen, however, as needing to improve political awareness and strength, and with a tendency to drink too much. (MA)

27.   Evan Ellis: Caerphilly/London, pharmacist's assistant, 10.01.37 – 19.09.38.
A good propagandist in the Communist Party and very active in the shop assistants union, Ellis was reported in Spain to have been a very disciplined and moral comrade. He was wounded in the stomach at Brunete. (MA)

28.   Alfred Evans: Neath.
Local family information indicates he stowed away on a ship, but was discovered and taken ashore at Las Palmas, where he was imprisoned by the Nationalists and eventually sent back to Britain.

29.   J. Evans: Ferndale (Rhondda), 24.07.37.
MI5 files indicate that he was still in Spain in September 1938.

30.   J.J. Evans: Llanelli, 19.12.38.
MI5 files indicate Evans was repatriated on December 19th, 1938. Family members recall accounts of Evans walking over the Pyrenees to Spain.

31. Peter Evans: Dowlais (Merthyr), 07.04.37 – 27.07.37.
The available evidence suggests that Evans was treated for wounds in Madrid before being repatriated for health reasons on July 27th, 1937.

32. Tom Glyn Evans: Bridgend, miner, 10.01.37 - 01.08.38.
Regarded by his comrades as outstanding, Evans had served for three years in the South Wales Borderers before working for three years in the dairy industry while studying mining. Despite discouragement from his family, he left for Spain where he was highly respected as a good, brave soldier, able officer and excellent comrade. Evans attended officer training and was appointed No. 1 company leader in August 1937. In his repatriation report he is described as 'a good soldier and able officer'. He had all the required qualities of discipline and bravery and was regarded as an excellent comrade. As a result of illness he was hospitalised at Benicassim and Valls.

33. William Faraday: Goodwick (Pembrokeshire).
It is not clear when Faraday arrived in Spain. In a newspaper report he describes being wounded by a bullet in the left forehead and being unconscious for a long time. He is also reported to have survived in the trenches for several days on cats and dogs. He was invalided from Alicante on HM Destroyer *Garland*, in April 1937.

34. W.J. Foulkes: Treorchy (Rhondda), ex-miner, 22.12.36 – 07.12.38.
Reported as deserting from both Jarama and Brunete and, because of his nervous disposition given a job as a cook in the rear, Foulkes was praised for his anti-fascism and cheerfulness but regarded as erratic and irresponsible and punished for drunkenness. One of his Rhondda colleagues called him a 'real numbskull' and Jack Jones (England) once found the popular 'proverbial jester' in Barcelona docks and took him back to the front. He suffered shrapnel wounds in the chest at Gandesa. (MA)

35. Reuben Gainsborough: Carmarthen/London, 20.12.37 – 01.12.38.
Listed as one of the Jewish volunteers and with the name 'Ginsburg', Gainsborough had developed previous communication experience in the British army. On repatriation he was reported as not being a Communist Party man and should be watched. Indeed, there was criticism of his anti-communist attitude, unreliability and egotism, but he was regarded as brave at the front, while described in one report as a 'rotten type'. Wounded on the Sierra Pàndols on August 17th, 1938. (MA)

36. Ivor Gale: Abertillery, 10.05.38 – 31.05.38.

His short stay is explained by the fact that on arrival at Figueras he complained that he was unable to eat the food provided and wanted to return home. Consequently, the Medical Commission declared him unfit and sent him back home. (MA)

37. Maurice (Moses) Goldberg: Merthyr/London, 10.12.36 – 16.11.37.

Born in Merthyr, Goldberg was a member of No 2 machine gun company and captured at Jarama. He was held as a prisoner of war, sentenced to death at a Spanish trial, but this was commuted. Goldberg was imprisoned until after the war. (Info by courtesy of Martin Sugarman, https://www.jewishvirtuallibrary. org/jsource/History/spanjews.pdf)

38. Edwin Greening: Aberaman, miner, 09.37 – 07.12.38.

An activist and agitator against war, poverty and unemployment in his community, in Spain Greening was regarded as being efficient and having considerable ability with a wide knowledge of political affairs. The Battalion leaders were not, however, always impressed. They regarded him as a grumbler, individualistic and critical, nervous and erratic. In addition, in his files he was accused of deserting (although the dates do not bear this out) from Corbera in the Battle of the Ebro. (MA)

39. Emrys Griffiths: Pontypridd/London, doorman, 20.12.37 – 14.10.38.

Griffiths headed for Spain with four years' experience in the British Army, but was soon suspected of holding Trotskyist views and regarded as a bad element in the company for showing insolence towards the section commander. On one occasion Griffiths was reported as trying to steal a blanket from a Spanish comrade. He was arrested on May 27th, 1938, and charged with attempted desertion. (MA)

40. William J. Griffiths: Tonypandy (Rhondda), miner, 02.03.38 – 07.12.38.

Sent to Spain to build up Communist Party strength and discipline, Griffiths worked at battalion and brigade level as commissar and party secretary and was regarded as a brave and industrious worker, a good cadre, energetic, politically developed and a good organiser. He was also respected by the volunteers for swiftly responding to their problems. (MA) Having formed a battalion committee, he was involved in issues of repatriation and judgments of volunteers' actions. Never physically strong, he spent five weeks in hospital in Reus with a fever.

41.   Timothy Harrington: Dowlais (Merthyr), miner, 29.02.37 – 09.09.37.

A World War I veteran who had been gassed in France and posted to Mesopotamia (modern day Iraq) – where he contracted malaria – Harrington became an activist and hunger marcher. He was once asked by Labour politician Stafford Cripps to be photographed at the front of a hunger march wearing his World War I medals. Harrington had tried to reach Spain independently and, in February 1937, he left a note for his family simply saying 'gone to Spain'. During the Civil War he was described as a bit of a grumbler and, suffering from chronic bronchitis, was recommended for repatriation in August 1937.

42.   Carl Hausmann: Conwy/San Francisco, arrival date unknown.

Born in Wales, Hausmann's family emigrated to the US where, for four years, he is described as a 'unionised' miner, before setting sail for Spain on August 11th, 1937, aboard the *Queen Mary*. He was wounded at Teruel, captured at Belchite in March 1938, imprisoned in San Pedro, and exchanged at the end of October 1938 with the first 100 British prisoners. Described in Spain as a good comrade, Hausmann returned to the US on December 5th, 1938, aboard the *President Roosevelt*.

43.   Morgan Havard: Craig-Cefn-Parc (Rhondda), welder, 17.04.37 – 05.02.39.

Havard served with the Anti-tank Unit and was wounded in the arm and leg at Calaceite when confronted by Italian tanks on a bend in the road. At his suggestion, his retreating comrades who were carrying him on a stretcher left him at the roadside. Once captured, Havard was taken to San Pedro Concentration Camp where he lost an arm to gangrene, but told his family that he had been grateful for the care of a German doctor whom he believed was responsible for saving his leg.

44.   David Hooper: Gelli/Kilburn, fitter, 10.12.36 – 23.05.37.

An RAF deserter, in Spain Hooper was regarded as not suitable for the front. Described as disruptive and malingering, he tried to get repatriated and was reported deserting from Jarama – on the first day – and also from Brunete claiming to have suffered shell-shock. He is reported to have suffered a superficial hip wound in August 1937 and was described in one document as a 'very low demoralised type'. (MA)

45.   William Hopkins: Carmarthen or Aberdare, miner, 29.04.37 – 18.07.38.

Viewed as causing considerable trouble as an agitator and imprisoned, on September 14th, 1937, in Valencia with two other Welsh comrades for desertion, Hopkins managed to escape from the monastery building in Puig on July 10th, 1938. Back in Wales he campaigned for the release of his comrades, pleading that they had been misunderstood and had committed no crime. (MA)

46.   Glyn (John Daniel) Howells: Pontycymmer/Wembley, miner/ bottle sorter, 13.10.37 – 7.12.38.

A member of the Transport and General Workers Union (T&GWU) since 1935 and the Young Communist League (YCL) since 1931, John Daniel was the brother of David John Howells. One comment in Moscow files complains about his heavy drinking, while another dated July 23rd, 1938, contains a note about his being disciplined for a rowdy incident and subject to a tribunal. (MA)

47.   David John Howells: Trealaw (Rhondda), colliery wagon repairer, 05.05.37- 12.08.37.

The brother of John Daniel, David John was repatriated for reasons of ill health in August 1937. (MA)

48.   John Hughes: Marian Glas (Anglesey), 12.04.37- ?

Having worked as a journalist, radio commentator and ambulance driver, Hughes volunteered with the Welsh Ambulance Unit in Spain motivated by humanitarian concerns. He helped raise money for two ambulances to go out to Spain before leading the Welsh Ambulance Unit, in Valencia and Madrid. He also sent broadcasts on the progress of the war from Madrid, in English and Welsh.

49.   Charles Humphreys: Caernarfon, mechanic, 20.03.38 – 14.08.38.

A trained motor mechanic with Ford, who had also served seven years with the Royal Tank Corps, Humphreys was regarded as a good soldier requiring further political development. Billy Griffiths mentions him fighting in a gun unit overlooking the Ebro, almost blind due to his broken glasses. Humphreys was wounded at the Battle of the Ebro on July 7th, 1938. (MA)

50.   Thomas J. Hurley: Treharris/Cardiff, miner, 11.03.37 - ?

Regarded as a good comrade, Hurley was wounded on September 26th, 1937, and hospitalised at Mataro. (MA)

51. Tony Hyndman: Cardiff, secretary and journalist, 01.01.37 – 08.37.

A former soldier with the Coldstream Guards, Hyndman had a relationship with the poet Stephen Spender before setting off for Spain with Giles Romilly. It seems he was separated from comrades in the shock and horror at Jarama and jailed for desertion. Hyndman was given a repatriation note, along with John Lepper, for continuous vomiting and a stomach ulcer and, not wishing to return to the front, later escaped to Valencia with Lepper for a possible rendezvous with Spender. For him Spain was a 'scar on his mind and heart'.

52. William F. Jacobsen: Newport/London, 4.01.37 – 10.38.

Jacobsen was treated for wounds in Benicassim and repatriated.

53. Percy James: Crymych/Vancouver, engineer, 06.37 - 10.38.

Born in Crymych, Pembrokeshire, James emigrated to Canada in 1927 and initially fought with the Lincolns at Brunete before joining the Mac Paps and being captured and imprisoned around April 1938. He worked at the Royal Ordnance factory in Pembrey during and after World War II, and was quite deaf after severely damaging his ear.

54. Brinley Jenkins: Swansea, 04.38 – 07.12.38.

Jenkins served as a stretcher-bearer and was described as 'young and entirely unpolitical', yet a brave, steady and sincere comrade. He was wounded in July 1938 on the Ebro and hospitalised in No. 1 military hospital at Figueras. It was suggested that he should be assisted in his political development to be an organiser. (MA)

55. Harold Rhys Jenkins: Barry, seaman, 29.04.37 – 15.10.37.

Jenkins served with the transport section in Madrid but, on September 14th, 1937, was recommended for immediate repatriation as a result of heavy drinking. (MA)

56. Joseph Jenkins: Pontardawe, salesman, 24.02.37 – 21.09.37.

A letter dated September 15th, 1937, written from Brigade Headquarters to the Perpignan committee requests for assistance for Jenkins to be returned to London via Paris, and his medical records indicate extreme mental tension and anxiety and symptoms of concussion. (MA)

57.   Leonard John: Cardiff/Canada, clerk, 11.03.38 – 25.10.38.
Born in Canada but resident in Cardiff since March 1937, John was captured at Calaceite in March 1938 and is on the official San Pedro prisoner list.

58.   James Johnson: Tonypandy (Rhondda), 02.05.37 - ?
Listed with no information in the Russian archives, MI5 files indicate Johnson sailed for Dunkirk in May 1937.

59.   Bedlington Jones: Tredegar, miner/bricklayer, 28.04.37 – 05.05.38.
One of the older volunteers at 38, Jones served at Jarama and Brunete. He was regarded as a good soldier, party sympathiser, and a socialist and anti-fascist who was a steady and disciplined comrade. (MA)

60.   Bryn/Bob Jones: Tredegar/Swansea, miner/commercial traveller, 01.06.38 - ?
A member of one of the 'workers freedom groups' inspired by Aneurin Bevan to prevent and obstruct the growth of local fascist activity, Jones was wounded at the Ebro on July 25th, 1938.

61.   David Arthur Jones: Ammanford, driver, 30.01.37 – 26.03.37.
Jones was wounded in the hand after being caught in enemy fire on February 15th, 1937, while carrying ammunition up to the line with Jack Harris of Llanelli. He wrote from hospital in Murcia asking to return home for treatment and stating concern for his wife and child. He was repatriated in March 1937.

62.   David Meirion Jones: Mardy (Rhondda), miner, 13.05.37 – 14.10.38.
Jones suffered from stomach trouble and was hospitalised in Badalona, Mataro and Olot, where he spent a lot of time reading and was noted for the quality of his political discussions. Some reports indicate that he was having a problem with drunkenness and displaying very bad behaviour. Jones was described in one file as someone who should not have been sent to Spain. (MA)

63.   David Howell Jones: Maesteg, miner and activist, 30.01.37 – 12.08.37.
A hunger marcher in 1936, Jones was described by the chief constable of Glamorgan as 'a dangerous revolutionary'. Wounded in Spain, there is a record of his hospitalisation at Elche on April 22nd, 1937, and he was repatriated for health reasons in August 1937.

64.   Emrys Jones: Tonypandy (Rhondda), miner, 21.02.38 – 18.12.38.
Having escaped unhurt from the ambush at Calaceite, Jones was wounded in the right leg in an attack on Hill 481 during the Ebro offensive and was hospitalised, in Mataro and Villafranca del Penedés, for most of August and September. Although not taking an active part in political work, he was regarded as fiercely anti-fascist and a good soldier, never shrinking danger; disciplined, reliable and brave. (MA)

65.   Evan Jones: Llanelli, tinplate worker, 27.02.38 – 18.12.38.
Born in Newcastle Emlyn, Jones worked with his friend, Brazell Thomas, at the Richard Thomas & Co tinplate works, Llanelli. He was politically active and had taken part in the 1936 hunger march. As a member of the No. 4 company he had stormed Hill 481 at Ebro and was later recommended for a bravery award. Badly wounded at the Ebro, he spent almost four months in three Spanish hospitals during which his arm was amputated.

66.   Griffiths Jones: Dowlais (Merthyr), miner, 29.04.37 – 25.10.38.
Very active in unemployment demonstrations, Jones was reported missing in Aragon in March 1938 and then 'practically certainly' deserted from the Aragon front at the end of August. Records indicate that he deserted with two other colleagues and was imprisoned at Valencia and then at a monastery building in Puig. (MA)

67.   John   (Jack)   Jones: Blaenclydach   (Rhondda),   colliery checkweigher, 13.03.38 – 5.02.39.
A trade union activist and founder member of the South Wales Communist Party, Jones took part in hunger marches and recruited volunteers for Spain. One of the oldest Brigaders at 41, he was captured at Calaceite, imprisoned and released in early 1939, when the *Rhondda Leader* described his return home to a welcome from 'a thousand people'. Letters from prison to his sister and parents illustrate his hope of being released in the second group of repatriated volunteers and asks for cigarettes, and socks! His letters describe how the people were giving their all in the war despite serious shortages, and that much more could be done by the British trade unions and political parties.

68.   Morris Jones: Kenfig.
No further information discovered.

69.   Owen Jones: Wrexham/London, milkman, 14.02.38 – 18.12/38.
Living in London when he volunteered, Jones had been a member of the
Edmonton branch of the T&GWU since April 13th, 1935, and had joined the
YCL in the same year. He was repatriated on December 18th, 1938.

70.   Richard Jones: Merthyr Vale/Canada, miner, repatriated 07.02.39
Captured at Calaceite in March 1938 and imprisoned at San Pedro, Jones
was one of many north Walians who had travelled south to find work before
migrating to Canada where he volunteered.

**71.   Thomas (Tommy) Jones: Penygraig (Rhondda), miner, 16.05.37 –
25.10.38.**
Reported to have deserted from Brunete after the Anti-tank Battery was wiped
out, and arrested by civilian police in Cartagena, Jones was imprisoned from
July 30th to November 12th, 1937. (MA) However, he worked hard to redeem
himself and rejoined the Battalion in December 1937. Later he was captured
at Calaceite and imprisoned in San Pedro Concentration Camp, Burgos. He
was repatriated with the first prisoner release.

**72.   Thomas Jones: Rhosllanerchrugog (Wrexham), miner, 16.04.37 –
29.04.40.**
Born in Lancashire before moving to Wales as a boy, Jones was a member
of the Anti-tank Battery and mistakenly reported killed. Badly injured in
the right arm at the Ebro he was taken prisoner and interned in San Pedro
Concentration Camp, and released in March 1940 after a government deal.
His record in Spain indicates that he had potential, and did some very good
work with a fairly good understanding of the Brigade's political work. (MA)

73.   Urias Jones: Tumble (Carmarthenshire), miner, 01.37 -06.37.
A former soldier with the Welsh Regiment who fought with the POUM and
PSUC militia.

74.   Joseph Jorro: Cardiff/Slough, driver, 05.01.38 – 05.38.
Jorro, who lived at Hunter Street in the Cardiff district of Butetown, volunteered
for Spain as a 23-year-old but was – in a list published in September 1938 –
regarded as having deserted and believed to have migrated to England. (MA)

75.   Archie D. Ledbury: Swansea, miner, 29.03.38 – 07.12.38.
A sapper in the Battalion, Ledbury was reported missing – believed killed – at
the Ebro on July 31st, 1938, but returned to the Battalion in August and then

was wounded shortly afterwards on August 21ˢᵗ. He was listed as being with the Battalion in October 1938 and was repatriated via France. He was assessed as being weak politically and 'not too bad but lacks enthusiasm' (MA).

76.   Matthew Levin: Caerphilly, miner, 23.08.37 – 28.04.38.
Following his hospitalisation in Benicassim, Levin was believed to have deserted on August 23ʳᵈ, 1937, and returned home on board the *Essex Judge* (MA), an Essex Shipping line vessel which in June 1938 sunk at Alicante after a Nationalist air attack.

77.   Archie Lewis: Rhondda.
No further information discovered.

78.   David Rolfe Llewellyn: Blaengarw, miner, 13.05.37 – 09.09.37.
A trade union activist and organiser as well as a 1936 hunger march leader, in Spain Llewellyn worked as a chauffeur in the autopark at Albacete. A member of the Communist Party from 1925, he was one of the Welshmen appointed a political commissar.

79.   Emlyn Lloyd: Llanelli, radio shop manager/Old Castle Tin Works, 02.06 – 07.12.38.
An active trade unionist who demonstrated against the means test, Lloyd was a survivor when the *Cuidad de Barcelona* was struck by a torpedo. He was hospitalised at Brunete with a damaged ankle and rheumatism in his legs, then wounded in the right thigh at Corbera on August 18ᵗʰ, 1938, after which he spent time in hospital in Mataro. Recorded as militarily unsatisfactory. (MA)

80.   Evan Lloyd: Bedlinog, 13.05.37 – 18.12.38.
A member of the Anti-tank Battery, Lloyd returned to Spain after – his record suggests – he deserted on April 8ᵗʰ, 1938, along with Archie Yemm of Pontypridd. His desertion was triggered when ammunition for the battery failed to appear, because he could no longer resist and was very homesick. Lloyd was wounded in the hand and shoulder on the Sierra Pàndols on July 26ᵗʰ, 1938 and hospitalised. (MA)

81.   Harold Lloyd: Cwmtillery, miner/boot repairer, 05.05.37 – 16.09.38.
An anti-unemployment activist with his brother, Clarence, Lloyd was once charged with unlawful assembly and disturbing the peace in Abertillery. In Spain he was regarded as indecisive and not really interested in anything,

yet his record also indicates that he was good politically, steady, reliable and honest. His health was not good, however, and after advice from the Medical Commission he worked with the Press Service. (MA)

82.   William Lloyd: Aberaman, ex-miner/labourer, 15.12.36 – 09.09.37.
A miner at Cwmaman pit at 14 years of age, Lloyd was raised in a staunch communist family who lived in a house called 'Red Square': "I was practically born in the Communist Party" he recalled. Lloyd was an anti-fascist activist and, after being victimised at Gadlys Pit, moved to London where he took part in the Battle of Cable Street. He was an early arrival in Spain and deployed as a battalion runner at Jarama. Following a request made in March 1937, he was sent back to Britain to raise funds and recruit for the Battalion.

83.   Charles Magner: Cardiff/Swansea, seaman, 13.11.37 – 19.12.38.
Magner jumped ship on his way to Valencia in order to join the Brigades, yet was regarded as a politically confused volunteer who 'drank too much'. After being wounded at Caspe on March 16th, 1938, he is reported as being 'accidentally wounded' by a grenade on July 22nd and wounded again in Sierra Pandols on August 17th. (MA)

84.   Hector Manning: Dinas (Rhondda), miner, 28.04.37 – 18.12.38.
Recruited by Will Lloyd, in Spain Manning was recorded as displaying bad conduct and 'mixing with bad elements'. He was wounded in the foot at Brunete and at Belchite, and in the wrist at Gandesa (Hill 481) when he was hospitalised for three months. He was also reported to have deserted twice – using the train and the bus to get to Valencia – and was imprisoned in Calaceite, but when the Italian tanks attacked he escaped and rejoined the Battalion in July 1938. (MA)

85.   F. Mari: 12.37.
MI5 files indicate that Mari was fighting with government forces in Spain but no further information has been discovered.

86.   Tom McNulty: Cardiff/London, seaman and electrician.
A torpedo operator in World War I, McNulty was an anti-fascist activist and propagandist whose links with Cardiff were through his friendship with Dan Murphy and due to being arrested and imprisoned in Cardiff, among other places. In Spain, his record was poor due to his heavy drinking and anti-leadership attitude which saw him serve a 60-day jail sentence in Tarazona and recommended for expulsion from the Communist Party. He was believed to have gone missing on July 9th, 1938. (MA)

87. Frank Middleton: Trealaw (Rhondda), miner, 13.05.37 – 18.12.38.
A volunteer at the age of 47, Middleton served as a stretcher-bearer and in the stores at Brunete and the Ebro. He was suspected of deserting from Brunete but claimed to be ill. Later on May 27th, 1938, he was arrested for attempted desertion and imprisoned in Campo Lukács, Albacete. Middleton's records note that he was accused of rallying others against the leadership and the Communist Party, was regarded as Trotskyist and, as a result of his ineffectiveness, he should be repatriated. (MA)

88. George Milbourn: Dyserth/Wallasey, seaman, 21.12.36 – 15.01.37.
Milbourn worked as a navigation officer on a 3,000-ton ship and was 27 years of age when he volunteered stating that he wanted to go to Spain to use his skills.

89. Morien Morgan: Ynysybwl, student, 11.03.38 – 05.02.39.
Morgan was studying languages at Cardiff University when he became involved in political debate. He was appalled by the lack of response to Mussolini in Abyssinia and Hitler's rearmament of Germany, so volunteered for Spain. A rifleman in No. 2 Company, he was engaged in battle at Calaceite and escaped with a group of comrades. However, ill and hallucinating, he became separated from them, and walked into a Nationalist camp by mistake and was captured, to spend the next six months in San Pedro concentration camp. On his repatriation Morgan taught French in Pontypridd.

90. Alfred Morris: Mardy (Rhondda), bricklayer, 22.05.37 – 18.12.38.
Morris served as a section and company leader from October to November 1937, before being promoted to sergeant and then lieutenant. He was wounded on two occasions, once in his left biceps and once in his left forearm, and hospitalised for 43 days. He was regarded as having a poor attitude to orders and was relieved of his company command for indiscipline. Yet he 'did excellent work in most of the major battles'. (MA)

91. William Morrissey: Cardiff, unemployed seaman, 13.05.37 – 12.38.
Of Irish descent, Morrissey was involved in anti-unemployment activism, hunger marches and anti-fascist activities. In Spain he worked mainly in censorship and propaganda and was described as a very good comrade, reliable, serious, steady, disciplined who worked conscientiously and consistently. Morrissey was regarded as always thoughtful and acting in the best interests of the Communist Party. (MA)

92.   Patrick Murphy: Cardiff, seaman, 01.12.36 – 14.04.38.

An early volunteer, Murphy was wounded in action at the Cordoba front before being brought back to Madrid. He had a good record in the frontline and was commended for bravery at Jarama as armourer for the Maxims, but a bad influence behind the lines who drank 'very heavily'. He was wounded again at Brunete and twice arrested in December 1937, for drunkenness and missing a parade. In early 1938 he deserted to Valencia but was brought back to work as a bricklayer in the *Intendencia* (stores). He was also accused of helping others to desert. (MA)

93.   John Murray: Nantyfyllon, miner, 30.01.37 – 09.04.38.

Regarded as a warm-hearted, emotional Welshman devoted to his family and who kept a diary, Murray's conduct at Jarama was recorded as fairly good. He was wounded at Brunete and hospitalised where there was a drunken episode. He was also reported as causing disruption when drinking too much and questioning orders. (MA)

94.   William Nash: Nantyglo, miner, 30.02.37 – 09.03.37.

Nash served in South Africa in World War I and volunteered for the International Brigade – aged 58 – early in 1937. However, he was taken seriously ill at the front and soon returned home for health reasons and on account of his age. On his return he spoke of the excellent morale of the government troops and the plentiful supply of food at that time.

95.   Matthew (Gwilym) Nicholls: Cardiff, railwayman, 13.05.37 – 22.02.39.

Nicholls fought at Brunete but is reported to have deserted after three days. He was arrested in Valencia in July 1937 and imprisoned in the International Brigade detention centres at Camp Lukács and Villa Maruja. In one report he is imprisoned in Montjuic Castle, Barcelona in May 1938 and does not seem to have been released until early 1939. The Moscow Archives suggest that he was regarded as rather weak and not courageous enough for the front.(MA)

96.   Michael O'Donoghue: Merthyr Vale, miner, 12.03.36 – 08.37.

O'Donoghue was a former soldier who had joined the British Army under age and served in India and Ireland. As a miner he was a militant activist – especially against the 'scab' union blacklegs – and a hunger marcher. He saw action at Jarama and Brunete and witnessed the deaths of Jack Harries and Ramon Rodriguez. Having stowed away on a ship at Valencia, he jumped overboard at Gibraltar, was arrested, released and finally landed in Edinburgh.

97.   John Oliver: Blackwood/London, miner, 29.01.38 – 07.12.38.
The unemployed miner was working in London and virtually 'dragged', after a few pints, to Paris by his Yorkshire mate. Although he was described as 'pleased to give any help' he was recorded in Spain as not being useful for the front.(MA)

98.   D.W. Owen: Dowlais (Merthyr), miner, 13.05.37 – 01.08.38.
MI5 files reported him missing in August 1938, after action with the artillery. (MA)

99.   Charles Palmer: Llandudno/Surrey, painter, 02.04.37 – 12.37.
Palmer served as a soldier, cook and armourer in Spain. He was wounded twice, in the knee and elbow, while stretcher-bearing and in combat and spent two months in hospital. However, reports suggested that, although a sincere anti-fascist, he was lacking in political understanding, was critical, and he 'grumbled at every opportunity'. He eventually requested repatriation because of the ill-health of his wife. (MA)

100.   Cyril Parfitt: Maesteg, miner, 27.01.37 – 25.10.38.
Parfitt believed that Franco was right to stem communism but fought for the Spanish 'workers and Government'. The Moscow Archive reports of him in Spain are very negative and portray him as a heavy drinker, unreliable, inactive and 'in prison most of the time'. (MA). He is on the official San Pedro prisoner list.

101.   Evan Parry: 23.04.37.
MI5 files – the only information discovered to date – report him sailing for Calais in April 1937.

102.   Harold Patterson: Penarth, welder, 12.36 - 28.04.37.
An early arrival in Spain and a member of the machine-gun company at Jarama, Patterson reported sick at Jarama and then disappeared. He either deserted (as reported in his Moscow records) or was captured with other comrades and released in April. He later had newspaper articles published about the Civil War and his battle wounds.

103.   Will Paynter: Cymmer (Rhondda), Communist Party organiser, 24.04.37 – 03.11.37.
Originally a miner who developed a deep interest in Marxism, Paynter progressed into a prominent trade union and Communist Party activist. He was imprisoned as a result of his activities and was one of the leaders of three major hunger marches. Paynter went to Moscow to study at the Lenin School, where the most promising young communist leaders were sent, and worked

for the Comintern in Nazi Germany before being asked to travel to Spain to provide political and emotional support to the Battalion.

104. Evan Peters: Merthyr/London, miner, 28.04.37 – 19.08.37.
Before volunteering, and in common with many other unemployed colliers, Peters had moved from the coalfield to London to find work. Once in Spain he wrote, with others, to the *Merthyr Express* in June 1937 to emphasise that the volunteers were not adventurers but were there to express a real spirit of unity and were there to defend freedom and democracy. In July 1937 the Medical Commission recommended his repatriation, possibly as a result of a heart condition.

105. Robert Peters: Penarth, plasterer, 03.37 – 07.12.38.
Peters was born in Penarth and emigrated to Canada in 1931 where he worked as a farm hand, construction worker and deckhand on the Great Lakes before volunteering, with a friend, for Spain, serving with the Lincolns and Mac Paps. Pinned down in a gulley at Villanueve, he was shot in the back and hospitalised at Benicassim. After recovering, he worked as a motorcycle dispatch rider at Albacete and was later posted to Barcelona. Peters was reported as having good morale and a political soundness. (MA)

106. Philip A. Phillips: Tredegar/Sheffield, miner, 20.02.38 – 12.12.38.
MI5 files record Phillips leaving for France on February 18th, 1938, but little of his service is recorded.

107. George Poustie: Cardiff/Treorchy/Dundee, master stonemason, 02.04.37 – 24.10.38.
A staunch trade unionist, campaigning for improved working conditions and wages, it seems Poustie volunteered while in Treorchy and his name is inscribed on the memorial in Rhondda. He was wounded at Brunete on July 11th, 1937, captured at Calaceite then imprisoned at San Pedro. His Moscow record is ambivalent: a reliable and disciplined soldier up to July 1937 but, after Brunete, accused of desertion to Barcelona, as well as 'anarcho-Trotskyist' and disruptive views. (MA)

108. Edwin Powell: Treorchy (Rhondda), miner, 13.05.37 – 01.07.37.
Powell served with the artillery and was repatriated for health reasons.

109. Margaret Powell: Monmouthshire, nurse and midwife, 24.03.37 – 02.39.

Born at Cwm Farm, Llangenny, Powell lived on a small Welsh hill farm. Having trained as a nurse and, after finishing midwifery training, she was accepted by the Spanish Medical Aid Committee and left for Spain in early 1937. She served as a frontline nurse in Aragon, Teruel and the Ebro and assisted in thousands of operations, often performed in the light from a cigarette lighter. Powell was described as 'sincere, disciplined and hardworking…conscious of her duty as a communist'. (MA) Before her return she was interned in a French concentration camp.

110. Evan Glyn Price: Coelbren (Neath Valley), miner, 08.05.38 – 07.12.38.

Price's departure for Spain was sudden, and without telling his friends. His recollections are recorded in local history publications, which describe him having suffered extreme starvation and eating greased ropes to ease the hunger. Price was reported missing on April 29th, 1938, and his name appears on a deserters' list. (MA) Wounded at the Ebro on July 30th, 1938, Price returned home to work at the Onllwyn No.3 colliery.

111. Godfrey Price: Cardiff, miner, 13.05.37 – 18.12.38.

Born in Chepstow, Price lived in Riverside, Cardiff, and was a coalfield activist, who was imprisoned, with others, at the Bedwas trial. In Spain he was wounded in both thighs at the Ebro on September 23rd, 1938, and wrote to his wife from hospital in Mataró telling her not to worry as no bones were broken. He was reported to have consistent morale and discipline. (MA)

112. Leo Price: Abertridwr (Caerphilly), miner, 15.05.37 – 05.38.

Price was a committed and intelligent coalfield activist. Having written to his sister, in February 1938, that he was in fairly good health, he was wounded in the chest from a rifle at close range at Brunete on July 6th, 1937 and afterwards, in a 'weak and nervous' condition (MA), spent a considerable time in hospital and rehabilitation. On return to the Battalion he was given a non-combatant desk job with many posting visits to Albacete. He was reported, on May 21st, 1938, to have been sent to Barcelona to collect mail but accused of deserting into France with an American comrade.(MA)

113. Reginald Price: Bedlinog (Caerphilly), miner, 10.03.38 – 07.12.38.
From the communist stronghold of Bedlinog, Price was another volunteer enlisted by Billy Griffiths. In Spain he was reported to have been conscientious, disciplined and steady. Price was wounded at the Ebro on July 31st, 1938, and was in the International Brigade hospital at Santa Paloma until September when he was reported missing. (MA)

114. William Price: Pentre (Rhondda), miner, 13.05.37 – 10.11.37.
A letter in his files dated September 30th, 1937, describes his domestic situation which led to his swift return home. His wife, gravely ill with tuberculosis, was not expected to live and his three children also were suffering from the same condition. (MA)

115. Richard Priestley: Tremadoc, mechanic, 24.03.38 - ?
Little is known of Priestley except that he was wounded and repatriated in 1938.

116. William (Wally) Rees: Glanaman (Carmarthenshire), 31.01.37 – 03.02.39.
A brave and disciplined comrade, Rees is recorded as never shirking a dangerous job, displaying good conduct, and devoted to his duty as machine-gunner He was regarded as a keen Communist Party member and a very good comrade. (MA)

117. Thomas Reynolds: Swansea, miner, 21.03.38 – 04.38?
Reynolds originally committed to six months' service but was told that he was to stay until the end of the war. He appealed against this on the grounds of being physically unfit for the front but the appeal was dismissed.

118. Jack Roberts: Senghenydd (Caerphilly), miner, 15.05.37 – 01.38.
A committed coalfield activist and a 'Christian Communist' who became a local hero, popularly known as 'Jack Russia'. His political activism led to numerous arrests and court appearances including a six-month jail sentence. In 1935 he won a seat on the local council as a communist. A company commissar, he was wounded by a bullet in the right shoulder at Quinto in the attack on Purburell Hill and hospitalised in Benicassim. On returning to battle he attended officers' training at Tarazona de la Mancha and is recorded as a 'good anti-fascist with good record in Spain'. (MA)

119. John Charles Roberts: Trealaw (Rhondda), tramway worker/ labourer, 13.05.37 – 18.12.38.

Following a month of the frontline, Roberts then served in administrative and medical work in Barcelona. He was regarded as steady and reliable, diligent and sincere, and recommended for promotion to sergeant. (MA)

120. John Morgan Roberts: Tonypandy (Rhondda), miner, 22.02.38 – 14.12.38.

A trade union activist – who volunteered despite being the main breadwinner in a large family – Roberts was active in strikes and demonstrations and took part in the 1936 hunger march. He is often referred to by other volunteers as 'young Jack Roberts'. He served in the machine-gun company as a runner, and in the kitchens at the Battle of the Ebro. Roberts was regarded as a good, disciplined soldier and good Communist Party member.

121. Robert Penry Roberts: Caernarfon, slate quarry miner, 14.02.38 – 05.02.39.

Roberts was a former British soldier, who had joined the army in 1924. In Spain he worked in the Servicio Sanitario and, after being captured at Belchite in March 1938, was imprisoned in Bilbao, Saragossa, San Pedro and the Italian-run 'pre-release' prison at Palencia. The latter he described as the most humane, where the prisoners were allowed to smoke, swim and have a drink.

122. Thomas Roberts: Bedlinog (Caerphilly), miner, 30.01.37 – 18.12.38.

Roberts was hospitalised in Barcelona with a very bad wound and suffered a leg amputation.

123. Lance Rogers: Cefn Coed (Merthyr), miner, 13.04.37 – 07.12.38.

A lodge secretary who was committed to democracy and anti-fascism, Rogers served with the machine-gun company and his records are contradictory. More of a pacifist than a militarist, some regarded him as a steady and reliable comrade but with a nervous temperament. He returned from Brunete after a nervous breakdown, became demoralised and was arrested in June 1938 while trying to board a ship at Barcelona. Following imprisonment in Castelldefels Rogers was hospitalised before returning to the Battalion.

124. William Rogers: Wrexham/Bristol, plasterer and lorry driver, 30.06.38 – 07.12.38.

A late arrival to Spain, Rogers did not endear himself to the Communist Party and was accused of denying its effectiveness in the Civil War, for being weak and selfish and disliked by comrades. He is also recorded as attempting to desert to the Nationalists during his first action at the front and spending some time in the Brigade prison. (MA) Other records, however, praise his political activity in north Wales and describe him as steady and enthusiastic.

125. Thora Silverthorne: Abertillery, 08.36 – 09.37.

The daughter of a Bargoed miner who joined the Young Communist League at the age of 16, Silverthorne had moved to England where she trained as a nurse at Oxford, and gave medical assistance to the passing hunger marchers. After volunteering for Spain she was one of the first nurses to be sent with the British Medical Unit which pioneered the Brigade's first hospital in Granen commandeered by cleaning up an old farm house. Thora also nursed in Huesca and other fronts, sometimes working up to 20 hours a day, and was admired for her kindness, sense of humour and regarded as 'outstandingly competent' and a 'first class theatre nurse'. (MA)

126. R. Thomas Stickler: Cardiff/London, brass moulder, 29.04.38 – 07.12.38.

Reported to have displayed very good conduct and regarded as steady and brave under fire, Stickler was recommended for promotion to sergeant: 'a very fine comrade' and 'politically intelligent'. (MA)

127. Harry Stratton: Swansea, taxi driver, 04.02.37 – 13.10.37.

A life-long communist activist and trade union member, Stratton worked on the management committee of the *Daily Worker* and its successor the *Morning Star*. While in Spain, he spent months in the trenches, where his sense of humour and sketching ability entertained his comrades and he also served in the medical units based near the Escorial Palace, close to Madrid. Stratton's long-term ill-health and a serious nervous disorder, as well as domestic issues, led to his repatriation.

128. George Taylor: Blackwood/Canada, 10.37 - ?

Born to a mining family in Blackwood, Taylor emigrated to Canada with his family in 1929 where he worked as a book keeper, stenographer, farm labourer and organiser of the Young Communist League. He was an anti-fascist activist in Ottawa and Toronto and volunteered for Spain 'to fight to maintain world peace'. Taylor is described as disciplined, steady and showing great potential for political work. (MA) Interestingly, there is a also character reference for his father in the Moscow Archives.

129. Glyn Thomas: Cwmbach.
Recruited by Will Lloyd, Thomas left for Spain with Bob Condon, but had to return after being declared medically unfit in Paris. In the *Aberdare Leader* he refutes, as absolutely false, suggestions in the *Daily Mail* that recruits were offered substantial financial inducements to fight.

130. Llew Thomas: Bedlinog (Caerphilly), miner, 24.04.37 - ?
MI5 files indicate Thomas sailed to Dieppe in April 1937 and he was last heard of as serving with the artillery.

131. John Thomas: Bedlinog (Caerphilly), 30.01.37 – 08.37.
Thomas is believed to have deserted by ship and returned home in August 1937.

132. Harry Parry Thomas: Carreglefn (Anglesey), 10.01.37 – 24.05.37.
A soldier with the King's Liverpool Regiment in World War I, Thomas fought with the POUM and was wounded and hospitalised at Ermita Salas. His medical records also indicate sciatic nerve pain.

133. William John Thomas: Aberavon, miner, 22.12.36 – ?
Wounded at Jarama, Thomas also suffered from shattered nerves after Brunete. His record suggests he deserted with Griffiths Jones and William Hopkins and was imprisoned in Puig near Valencia. The desertion is mentioned by Alwyn Skinner in the context of intense shelling and horrific bombing, yet a letter from André Marty, head of the brigades, shows no sympathy. However, Thomas was hospitalised for many months and was in poor health with kidney and liver problems when released in early 1939. (MA)

134. Alex Tudor-Hart: Llanelli, doctor, 06.05.37 - ?
Born in Italy, Tudor-Hart initially worked as a general practitioner for the Llanelly Miners' Medical Aid Scheme – his name appears on the memorial pamphlet of Brazell Thomas – before moving to London. He married Edith Suschitzky, a Soviet spy, then left his general practice in Brixton to volunteer for Spain. As a surgeon he worked in a number of hospitals including Murcia, Huete and Mataró, and is photographed in a field operating theatre with Thora Silverthorne. A demanding professional, Tudor-Hart set high standards for himself and others and his methods of dealing with fractures and wounds helped procedures in World War II.

135. Bertram Vranch: Abertillery/Birmingham, miner, 28.04.37 – 12.38.

A coalfield activist who was charged, with others, with unlawful assembly and disturbing the peace in Abertillery, Vranch had studied at the International Lenin School and while in Spain was attached to the political commissariat of the Brigade. Later, on the promotion of George Aitken, he became political commissar of the Battalion yet, when repatriated, he was described as 'good' but politically weak.

136. William Ward: Barry/London, 25.02.38 – 12.38.

Born in Barry, Ward worked as a sea-going radio operator and a tester with a London radio manufacturer. He was a committed anti-fascist activist and served as a corporal in a light machine-gun group in Spain, where he was commended for outstanding work as a military and political commander. During a night attack on Hill 481 – Gandesa – on July 31st, 1938, Ward was wounded on his left side by a hand grenade and is mentioned as refusing to be seen before other wounded comrades. He was the last of seven men to be evacuated.

137. Wyndham Watkins: Abertridwr, labourer, 17.03.37 – 10.38.

Watkins suffered wounds and shell-shock at Brunete, and was hospitalised in Madrid for three weeks before reportedly deserting and spending a long time in jail in Alicante. Remarkably, he is also reported to have been spotted walking down the fashionable Las Ramblas in Barcelona. His Moscow files are not complimentary about his character and heavy drinking. (MA)

138. Robert Watts: Swansea, nurse, 26.10.37 – 12.12.38 (or 05.02.39).

Previously a collier, Watts moved to London where he trained as a medic before seeing service in Egypt with the Royal Army Medical Corps. Wounded in the Battle of Cable Street, he volunteered for Spain and he served – in a number of battalions – as a medic in all battles from Jarama onwards. Wounded at Brunete and captured at Calaceite, Watts was commended for good work at the front and was regarded as having a friendly attitude and good conduct. (MA)

139. J. White: Barry, 02.01.37.

The only available information remains White's MI5 files which indicate he left Dover for Dunkirk in January 1937.

140. John Widess: Cardiff, 19.02.38 – 25.10.38.

Captured in Calaceite, Widess is on the official San Pedro prisoner list.

141. Alun Menai Williams: Penygraig (Rhondda), miner/medic, 16.05.37 – 12.12.38.

After working at the local colliery, Williams moved on to London, joined the army and trained as a medic, seeing service in Egypt with the Royal Army Medical Corps. He took part in the Battle of Cable Street against Moseley's Blackshirts in October 1936, successfully entered Spain after a number of attempts and was a survivor of the torpedoed *Cuidad de Barcelona*. Williams served as a medic in the field with a number of battalions including the British at the Ebro, and was wounded in the leg at Brunete. Regarded as a good comrade with a friendly attitude, his work and conduct were deemed good. (MA)

142. Bert Williams: Abertillery/Birmingham, miner, 13.2.37 – 08.37.

Having studied at the Lenin School in Moscow, Williams volunteered for Spain at 42 years of age where he served as the Battalion Commissar. He described his work as dealing with morale, answering men's questions, sorting out complaints and ensuring that the men understood the reason for the steps they took. Repatriated for 'political and health reasons', Williams' Moscow files describe that his sincerity was appreciated by his comrades. (MA)

143. Edwin Williams: Newport, seaman, 21.02/38 – 07.12.38.

Williams wanted to return home in order to recruit more volunteers but was persuaded to remain for the duration of the war. He disappeared at Calaceite but does not seem to have been captured.

144. Frank Williams: Newport/Canada, chauffeur, 19.02.38 - ?

Born in Canada, Williams' family moved to Newport in Monmouthshire where he studied buying and selling. A member of the National Union of Railwaymen, he was involved in strikes and rioting in 1929, and was once arrested for the unlawful distribution of food to strikers. A change of direction saw Williams spend six months training at Sandhurst before serving in India. In Spain he was promoted to sergeant and, at the Ebro, was commended for bravery in rescuing burning lorries after a bombing raid, and for his energy and initiative as a battalion armourer. His record indicates Williams was an efficient, reliable and conscientious comrade. (MA)

145. Henry Arthur Williams: Penygraig/Birmingham, miner, 28.04.37 – 18.12.38.

An activist in the 1926 strike and hunger marches, his Moscow Archive records describe him as disciplined, brave, good politically, and a popular comrade. Williams was wounded on the Sierra Pandols on August 17th, 1938 and hospitalised in Mataró. (MA)

146. Jack S. Williams: Dowlais (Merthyr), 28.04.37 – 21.09.37.

An unemployment activist and hunger march organiser, initially Williams helped screen volunteers for the Civil War before heading to Spain himself. He served for two months at the Jarama front and, in June 1937, was wounded and hospitalised in Madrid with gastritis. Returning to duty, Williams worked behind the frontline, acting as commissar when moved to the cookhouse to organise a better system of food supply, and his letters home describe the volunteers' pay and conditions of workers and receiving Lewis Jones' book *Cwmardy*. One of his abiding memories was singing the *Internationale* under a barrage of machine-gun bullets.

147. Robert Williams: Anglesey/Liverpool, 01.37 – 12.38.

The only available information is that Williams fought with the POUM.

148. Rowland Williams: Trelewis, miner, 28.03.37 – 07.12.38.

A collier at Deep Navigation Colliery and an activist in the 1926 strike, Williams served as battalion postman. In the attack on Villanueva de Cañada he was wounded in the right hip and carried away in a blanket by Michael O'Donogue. Although regarded as lacking in political understanding, he was excellent in discipline, bravery and showed good conduct. (MA)

149. Archie Yemm: Pontypridd/Letchworth, newspaper seller, 02.08.37 – 26.04.39.

Yemm is recorded as displaying fairly good conduct as a brigade soldier, yet his grumbling, agitating amongst the soldiers and tendency of being easily led astray is noted. A member of the Anti-tank Battery, he deserted with Evan Lloyd in March 1938 – who called Yemm a 'fool' – and his Moscow file states: 'last heard of with the Mac Paps'. He was wounded on the Ebro in July 1938 and his leg was amputated. Taken prisoner in September 1938, Yemm was incarcerated in Duesto Prison, Bilbao and released in April 1939.

BIBLIOGRAPHY

Albrighton, James: *Diary*, IBA Box 50, File L.

Alexander, Bill: *British Volunteers for Liberty*, London, Lawrence & Wishart, 1982.

Baxell, Richard: *British Volunteers in the Spanish Civil War*, Pontypool, Warren and Pell, 2007;

Unlikely Warriors, London, Aurum Press, 2012;

'Myths of the International Brigades', Bulletin of Spanish Studies, Volume XCI, Numbers 1–2, 2014.

Baxell, Jackson and Jump: *Antifascistas*, London, Lawrence & Wishart, 2010.

Beevor, Anthony: *The Battle for Spain*, London, Phoenix, 2006.

Borkenau, Franz: *The Spanish Cockpit*, Michigan, University of Michigan Press, 1937.

Brenan, Gerald: *The Spanish Labyrinth*, Cambridge, Cambridge University Press, 1960.

Brome, Vincent: *The International Brigades*, London, Heinemann, 1965.

Buchanan, Tom: *Britain and the Spanish Civil War*, Cambridge, Cambridge University Press, 1997

Buckley, Henry: *Life and Death of the Spanish Republic*, London, I.B.Tauris, 2014.

Carr, E.H.: *The Comintern and the Spanish Civil War*, London, Macmillan, 1984.

Casanova, Julian: *A Short History of the Spanish Civil War*, London, I.B. Tauris, 2013.

Celada, Antonio R, Gonzales Manuel, Garcia, Daniel Pastor: *Los Internacionales*, Barcelona, Warren and Pell, 2009.

Clark, Bob: *No Boots to my Feet*, Stoke, Students Bookshops Ltd., 1984.

Copeman, Fred: *Reason in Revolt*, London, Blandford Press, 1948.

Cule, Cyril: *The Spanish Civil War: A Personal Viewpoint*, Unpublished manuscript, Richard Burton Archives, Swansea University.

Cunningham, V. (Ed): *Spanish Front Writers on the Civil War*, Oxford, Oxford University Press, 1968.

Darman, Peter: *Heroic Voices of the Spanish Civil War*, London, New Holland Publishers, 2009.

Davies, D.R.: *In Search of Myself*, London, Geoffrey Bles, 1961.

Davies, Hywel: *Fleeing Franco*, Cardiff, University of Wales Press, 2011.

Day, Peter: *Franco's Friends*, London, Biteback Publishing Ltd., 2011.

The Bedbug: Klop Ustinov: Britain's Most Ingenious Spy, London, Biteback Publishing Ltd., 2015.

Eaton, George: *Neath and the Spanish Civil War*, self-published, 1980.

Eby, Cecil D.: *Comrades and Commissars*, Pennsylvania, Pennsylvania State University Press, 2007.

Emsley, Clive, and Weinberger, Barbara: *Policing Western Europe*, Santa Barbara, Praeger, 1991.

Esenwein, George, and Shubert, Adrian: *Spain at War*, Harlow, Longman, 1995.

Felstead, Richard: *No Other Way: Jack Russia and the Spanish Civil War*, Port Talbot, Alun Books, 1981.

Francis, Hywel and Smith, David: *The Fed*, London, Lawrence & Wishart, 1980.

Francis, Hywel: *Miners against Fascism*, London, Lawrence & Wishart, 2012.

Frazer, Ronald: *The Blood of Spain*, New York, Pantheon Books, 1979.

Fyrth, Jim, and Alexander, Sally: *Women's Voices from the Spanish Civil War*, London, Lawrence & Wishart, 2008.

Gardiner, Juliet: *The Thirties: An Intimate History*, London, Harper Press, 2010.

Graham, Frank: *Battle of Jarama*, Newcastle, Self-published, 1987.

Graham, Helen: *The Spanish Civil War: A Very Short Introduction*, Oxford, Oxford University Press, 2005;
The Spanish Republic at War 1936-1939, Cambridge, Cambridge University Press, 2002.

Greening, Edwin: *From Aberdare to Albacete*, Pontypool, Warren and Pell, 2006.

Gregory, Walter: *The Shallow Grave: A Memoir of the Spanish Civil War*, London, Victor Gollancz, 1986.

Gurney, Jason: *Crusade in Spain*, Newton Abbot, Readers Union, 1967.

Havard, Robert: 'Thomas Picton and Sir Thomas Picton: Two Welsh Soldiers in Spain', *Transactions of the Honourable Society of Cymmrodorion* 2000, Vol.7, 2001.

Heaton, P.M.: *Welsh Blockade Runners in the Spanish Civil War*, Risca, The Starling Press, 1985.

Henry, Chris: *The Ebro 1938*, Oxford, Osprey Publishing, 1999.

Hopkins, James: *Into the Heart of the Fire*, Stanford, Stanford University Press, 1998.

Hopkins, K.S. (Ed.): *Rhondda Past and Future*, Rhondda Borough Council, 1973.

Hughes, Ben: *They Shall Not Pass: The British Battalion at Jarama - The Spanish Civil War*, Oxford, Osprey Publishing, 2011.

Ibarruri, Dolores: *They Shall Not Pass*, London, Lawrence & Wishart, 1966

Iturriarte *et al*: *The Bombing of Gernika*, Gernika-Lumo, 2010.

Jackson, Angela: *At the Margins of Mayhem*, Pontypool, Warren and Pell, 2008.
Preludi de L'Ultima Batalla, Valls, Cossetania Edicions, 2008.
Beyond the Battlefield, Pontypool, Warren and Pell, 2005.

Jones, Tom: *A Very Brief Outline of My Experiences in Spain During the Civil War*, unpublished manuscript, 1940.

Jump, Jim (Ed.): *Looking Back at the Spanish Civil War*, London, Lawrence & Wishart, 2010.

Kenwood, Alun, (Ed): *The Spanish Civil War: A Cultural and Historical Reader*, Oxford/ USA, Berg Publishers.

Lee, Laurie: *A Moment of War*, New York, New York Press, 1991.

Lewis, Greg: *A Bullet Saved My Life*, Pontypool, Warren and Pell, 2006.

Lewis, P.: *The Anglo-Welsh press response to the Spanish Civil War*. Unpublished MA thesis, 1990.

Lewis, Wendy, and Davies, Ray: *In the Footsteps of the Spanish Civil War*, IBMT, 2005.

Lloyd, Will: Unpublished memoirs, www.crazydruid.net

Metcalfe, Mark: *Tom Jones – A Fighter for Freedom and Working People*, Unite Education, 2014.

Neugass, James: *War is Beautiful*, New York, The New Press, 2008.

Orwell, George: *Homage to Catalonia*, London, Penguin Books, 1986.

Palfreeman, Linda: *Salud: British Volunteers in the Republican Medical Service During the Spanish Civil War*, Brighton, Sussex Academic Press, 2012.

Paynter, Will: *My Generation*, George Allen and Unwin Ltd., London, 1972.

Pettifer, James (Ed): *Cockburn in Spain*, London, Lawrence & Wishart, 1986.

Preston, Paul: *The Destruction of Guernica*, London, Harper Press, 2012;
   The Spanish Civil War, London, Harper Perennial, 2006.
   Comrades, London, HarperCollins, 2000.
   We Saw Spain Die, London, Constable, 2008

Price, Leo: Unpublished memoirs, Richard Burton Archives, Swansea University.

Pugh, Jane: *A Most Expensive Prisioner*, Llanrwst, Gwasg Carreg Gwalch, 1988.

Raguer, Hilari: *Gunpowder and Incense*, Abingdon, Routledge, 2007.

Rankin, Nicholas: *Telegram from* Guernica, London, Faber and Faber, 2003.

Raychaudhuri, Anindya (Ed): *The Spanish Civil War: Exhuming a Buried Past*, Cardiff, University of Wales Press, 2013.

Richardson, R. Dan: *Comintern Army*, Kentucky, The University Press of Kentucky.

Rust, Bill: *Britons in Spain*, Uckfield, The Naval and Military Press Ltd, 2007.

Ryan, Frank (Ed.): *The Book of the XV Brigade*, Pontypool, Warren & Pell, 1976.

Serrano, Caridad: *Recuerdalo Tu*, Madrigueras, www.brigadasinternacionales.org

Sommerfield, John: *Volunteer in Spain*, New York, Borzoi Books, 1937.

Steer, G.L.: *The Tree of Gernika*, London, Faber and Faber, 2009. (First edition published in 1938)

Stradling, Robert: *Wales and the Spanish Civil War*, Cardiff, University of Wales Press, 2004;
   Cardiff and the Spanish Civil War, Cardiff, Butetown History and Arts Centre, 1966;
   Brother Against Brother, Stroud, Sutton Publishing, 1998.
   The Irish and the Spanish Civil War, Manchester, Manchester University Press, 1999.

Stratton, Harry: *To Anti Fascism by Taxi*, Port Talbot, Alun Books, 1984.

Thomas, Fred: *To Tilt at Windmills: Memoir of the Spanish Civil War*, East Lansin, Michigan State University Press, 1996.

Thomas, Hugh: *The Spanish Civil War*, Harmondsworth, Penguin Books, 1977.

Williams, Alun Menai: *From the Rhondda to the Ebro*, Pontypool, Warren and Pell, 2004.

Wintringham, Tom: *English Captain*, London, Faber and Faber, 2011.

INDEX